THUCYDIDES ON STRATEGY

ATHANASSIOS G. PLATIAS
CONSTANTINOS KOLIOPOULOS

Thucydides on Strategy

*Grand Strategies in the Peloponnesian War
and their Relevance Today*

HURST & COMPANY, LONDON

First published in the United Kingdom in 2010 by
C. Hurst & Co. (Publishers) Ltd.,
41 Great Russell Street, London, WC1B 3PL
© Athanassios G. Platias and Constantinos Koliopoulos, 2010
All rights reserved.
Printed in India

A Cataloguing-in-Publication data record for this book
is available from the British Library.

ISBN: 9781849040228 *hardback*
9781849040112 *paperback*

www.hurstpublishers.com.

Published under the auspices of the Center for International
and European Affairs, University of Piraeus.

"*My history is an everlasting possession,
not a prize composition which is heard and forgotten*"

THUCYDIDES

ABOUT THE AUTHORS

ATHANASSIOS G. PLATIAS is Professor of Strategy at the University of Piraeus, Greece. He received a degree in Public Law and Political Science from the Law Faculty of the University of Athens. He also received an MA and PhD in International Relations from the Department of Government at Cornell University (1986).

He has been a Ford Foundation Fellow at the Center for Science and International Affairs, Harvard University, a Research Fellow at the Peace Studies Program, Cornell University, a MacArthur Fellow in International Peace and Security at the Program for Science, Technology and International Security, MIT, and the Center for International Affairs, Harvard University.

Professor Platias is the author of numerous books and articles and writes in five principal areas: strategy; international relations theory; arms control and nuclear proliferation; foreign and defense policy; international relations and strategy in Thucydides' *History of the Peloponnesian War.*

CONSTANTINOS KOLIOPOULOS is Lecturer of International Politics at Panteion University, Athens. He graduated from the Department of Political Science and International Studies, Panteion University, in 1993. In 1997 he was awarded a PhD in Strategic Studies from Lancaster University.

Since 1998 he has been affiliated with the Institute of International Relations, Panteion University. He has also taught Strategic Studies at several Greek military academies, including the Hellenic National Defence College and the Hellenic Supreme Joint War College.

His publications include books and articles on strategic surprise, guerrilla warfare and the grand strategy of Ancient Sparta.

To my daughter Maria-Alexia
A.G.P.

To my parents
C.K.

CONTENTS

CONTENTS

PREFACE

Which is the best treatise on strategy? The purpose of this book is to demonstrate the contribution of Thucydides to strategic thought. It argues that the basic concepts of strategy originated in Thucydides' *History of the Peloponnesian War*. Consequently, Thucydides' text is a masterpiece of strategic analysis that vies with Sun Tzu's *The Art of War* and Clausewitz' *On War* for the honour of the best treatise on the subject.

We should forewarn the reader that it is not our intention to provide a detailed historical description of the Peloponnesian War. Our preoccupation shall be with strategy and strategic analysis, albeit examined against the background of the Peloponnesian War. In other words, it is our intention to use the text of Thucydides[1] to draw some pertinent conclusions with regard to the strategic choices made by the main players in world politics.

The book aims to show that, although material conditions may change, the logic of conflict between organised entities remains constant throughout the millennia. The issues tackled by Thucydides have recurred through the centuries and remain relevant today. Organised entities, in their quest for security, still create and implement strategies similar to those employed twenty-five centuries ago. There is a thread of irony within this consistency, as even the blunders are replicated through history (e.g. overextension, underestimation of the enemy, etc). Indeed there is no reason to believe that this trend will not persist into the future. Consequently, the writings of Thucydides and the grand strategies contained therein are as relevant today as they were in the past and there is no reason to believe that their relevance shall diminish with time.

Louis Halle did not exaggerate when he claimed that "Thucydides, as he himself anticipated, wrote not only the history of the Peloponnesian War. He wrote the history of the Napoleonic Wars, World War I, World War II, and the Cold War."[2] Despite the recent debate concerning the alleged "discontinuities in international politics",[3] and the "transformation of world politics",[4] it is difficult to disagree with Robert Gilpin when he states that "international relations continue to be a recurring struggle for wealth and power among independent actors in a state of anarchy. The classic history of Thucydides is as meaningful a guide to the behavior of states today as when it was written in the fifth century B.C."[5]

The book assumes no prior knowledge of Thucydides' work or the politics of Ancient Greece. A copy of Thucydides' *History of the Peloponnesian War* would undoubtedly be helpful to the reader but by no means necessary, even though we hope that our work will provide the reader with the incentive to further explore the text of Thucydides.

This book is a joint effort by its authors. By exception, Athanassios Platias retains responsibility for Chapter Three, which is based on some of his earlier work.[6]

We wish to express our gratitude to a number of people that have positively influenced this book. The editors of the journals *Études Helléniques/Hellenic Studies* and *Comparative Strategy* provided both encouragement and outlets for our ideas on Thucydides' contribution to strategic thought.[7] Karl Walling made a thorough review of the book and produced a great number of pertinent suggestions and corrections. Colin Gray, Panayiotis Ifestos and Vassilis Fouskas came up with highly useful points. Of course, it goes without saying that we retain sole responsibility for the views expressed in this book, errors and shortcomings inclusive.

A.G.P. and C.K.
Athens, March 2009

CHRONOLOGY

(ALL DATES ARE B.C.)

490   The Persian King Darius sends an army against Greece, which is defeated by the Athenians at the battle of Marathon.
480   The Persian King Xerxes brings a larger army against Greece; battles of Thermopylae and Salamis.
479   Battle of Plataea: the Greek allies defeat the Persian army.
478   Fortification of Athens.
477   Foundation of the Delian League.
464   Catastrophic earthquake in Sparta.
461–29 The age of Pericles in Athens.
460   Outbreak of First Peloponnesian War.
458   The Athenians build the long walls to protect the road to their seaport at Piraeus.
454   The treasury of the Delian Lague is transferred to Athens.
447–33 Athens builds the Parthenon.
446–5   Athens and Sparta conclude the Thirty Years' Peace.
432   The 'Megarian Decree' is passed in Athens.
431–21 Peloponnesian War, first phase (Archidamian War).
430   The Plague breaks out in Athens.
429   Death of Pericles.
427   Surrender of Mytilene to Athens.
427   Surrender of Plataea to Sparta and Thebes.
427   Civil war in Corcyra.
425   Capture of 120 Spartan soldiers on Sphacteria.
424   Thucydides goes into exile.
421–14 Peace of Nicias.
418   Battle of Mantinea.

CHRONOLOGY (ALL DATES ARE B.C.)

416   Slaughter of the Melians.

415   Athenian invasion of Sicily.

414–04   Peloponnesian War, second phase (Decelean or Ionian War).

413   Destruction of Athenian army and navy outside Syracuse.

412   Revolt of Athenian allies.

411   Thucydides' *History* breaks off.

405   Destruction of the Athenian navy at the Battle of Aegospotami.

404   Surrender of Athens to the Spartans.

1

GRAND STRATEGY

A FRAMEWORK FOR ANALYSIS

Introduction

It is widely acknowledged that renowned classic treatises in their respective fields provide, *inter alia*, a standard of evaluation for all other field-related work and serve as a cornerstone upon which new theories can be developed. As far as the study of strategy is concerned, Michael Handel has claimed that strategists are fortunate to have access to two enduring classic texts: Sun Tzu's *The Art of War* and Clausewitz's *On War*.[1] However, we believe that another classic masterpiece needs to be added to this short list, namely Thucydides' *History of the Peloponnesian War*.[2] The purpose of this analysis, therefore, is to demonstrate Thucydides' contribution to the study of strategy.

Undoubtedly, Thucydides ranks as both a great historian and the forefather of the discipline of international relations. Robert Gilpin has wondered whether contemporary scholars of international relations actually know anything about state behavior that was unknown to Thucydides.[3] What has been ignored is that in Thucydides' text we encounter for the first time in history an outline of a complete theory of grand strategy; a comprehensive theory of how states ensure their security. Thucydides' theory incorporates the economic, diplomatic, military, technological, demographic, psychological and other factors upon which a state's security depends. It is highly interesting that Thucydides did not confine his analysis to traditional strategies that focus on the military dimension. He also took into account grand strategies that emphasise dimensions other than the military one, pointing out that these may well provide states with a path to victory.

1

The main argument of this study is that Thucydides' text is a classic masterpiece of strategy that contains significant strategic insights and a wealth of strategic concepts (see Appendix). Seen in this light, Thucydides *History* has at least equal right with Clausewitz' *On War* to be considered 'the strategist's toolkit'.[4] Needless to say, Thucydides did not use contemporary strategic jargon. One has to delve in the text in order to uncover these insights and concepts. This is where our own contribution lies: to bring to the surface and translate into modern strategic parlance the aforementioned concepts and insights.

One might perhaps doubt that a book written twenty-five centuries ago retains any relevance for today's strategic issues and problems. However, it has been correctly pointed out that *"there is an essential unity to all strategic experience in all periods of history because nothing vital to the nature and function of war and strategy changes."*[5] This is the guiding principle of the present analysis and will hopefully be demonstrated as far as Thucydides' work is concerned.

Before proceeding to the examination of Thucydides' contribution to the study of grand strategy, and strategy in general, we first need to clarify and elaborate upon these concepts. The essence of strategy and grand strategy needs to be understood, and the various characteristics of these two concepts outlined. Consequently, in this chapter we shall first elaborate on the nature of strategy and outline its various levels. We shall then examine grand strategy and certain aspects thereof while also making an attempt to categorise grand strategies, both according to the nature of the means employed and the general approach to be followed in the pursuit of policy objectives. The final issue touched upon in this chapter is that of the planning and evaluation of grand strategy. This analysis will help us comprehend the contribution of Thucydides to the study of strategy (discussed in Chapters Two to Five).

The Nature of Strategy

There have been many definitions of the term 'strategy' throughout the ages. While strategy was initially defined as "all military movements out of the enemy's cannon range or range of vision"[6] or "the art of making war upon the map"[7], nowadays the term has acquired a broader meaning. Two modern definitions of strategy are "the art of distributing and applying military means to fulfil the ends of policy"[8] and "the art of the dialectic of two opposing wills using force to resolve their dispute".[9] These definitions make it clear that strategy is about a state coupling means and ends in the context of international competition, both in peacetime and wartime, and both during potential as well as actual conflict.

Strategy never exists in a vacuum; it implies an opponent, a conflict, a competition, a situation where somebody is trying to achieve a goal against somebody else. Thus, strategy is always formulated against one or more opponents, who, in turn, develop their own strategy and try to counter the former. Each side's moves are intimately connected with those of the opponent. As Clausewitz comments "war is nothing but a duel on a larger scale".[10] This interaction between the strategic designs of both belligerents has been referred to as the 'horizontal dimension' of strategy.[11] The very existence of an opposing will gives strategy a comparatively paradoxical logic of its own, which differs from the traditional definition of logic that governs one's actions when no opponent is present. Thus, while a traveler, as a rule, chooses the shortest route and the best weather conditions for his/her journey, the existence of an opponent will make a military commander attack through a roundabout route instead of launching a head-on assault, attack at night instead of daytime, etc. An even more striking example of the paradoxical logic of strategy is the well-known Latin aphorism *Si vis pacem, para bellum* (If you want peace, prepare for war). Even though in other areas of life similar aphorisms would be clearly absurd (e.g. "if you want to be sober, prepare some drinks"), in the realm of strategy this aphorism is accepted as conventional wisdom.[12]

However, states in general, and military organizations in particular, sometimes 'forget' that they are facing opponents possessing an independent will and employing a strategy of their own. Overlooking this can have dire consequences. For instance, the German Army moved from Moltke's conviction that "no plan of operations extends with certainty beyond the first contact with the enemy's main strength",[13] to the concept of "war by timetable" as promulgated by Schlieffen a century later. In strict adherence to this approach, the German invasion of France in 1914, the capture of Paris and the subsequent transfer of the German troops to the East in order to fight the Russians had been preplanned down to the last detail. However, as the failure of the Schlieffen Plan revealed, strategy can seldom be subjected to such meticulous planning–the opponent, as a rule, is bound to interfere with one's plans.[14] But it is certainly far more pleasant for an army during peace-time to contemplate what it will do to the enemy on D-day than what the enemy will do to it.[15]

Something that accentuates the difficulty of formulating strategy is that in strategy, as in economy, resources are normally scarce, espe-cially as far as the smaller states are concerned.[16] Precisely due to this scarcity of resources, strategy ought to rate the objectives to be pur-sued and prioritise them accordingly.

The Levels of Strategy

Traditionally, 'strategy' has been distinguished from 'tactics'. Tactics has to do with the execution of strategy. The rule of thumb for distin-guishing between the two has been that strategy ends and tactics begin the moment the opposing forces make contact.[17] In other words, while strategy decides *where*, *when* and *with what forces* an action will be conducted, tactics govern *how* this action will be conducted.[18] Conse-quently, the term 'tactics' refers to what takes place on the battlefield, taking into account the extension of the concept of 'battlefield' brought about by the advent of aircraft as well as medium and long-range mis-siles. In general, tactics are used in 'battle' and strategy in 'war'.[19]

The need to distinguish between strategy and tactics shows that strategy operates on various levels; this is the so-called 'vertical dimen-sion' of strategy.[20] Although still relevant, the traditional distinction between strategy and tactics far from exhausts the issue. To get the full picture, one has first to examine the roots of strategy. The governing mind behind strategy is policy. Policy sets the aims that strategy will subsequently be called upon to achieve. As far as strategy is concerned, the process by which the aims are set and the nature of the political leadership that sets them are irrelevant. As a matter of fact, the concept of political leadership varies from country to country, depending on the country's political system. Political leadership may at times even comprise individuals who happen to be outside the official state insti-tutions. For instance, Stalin and Deng ruled their respective countries for considerable periods of time without in fact holding any state office.[21] An individual or a group of individuals may belong to the 'political leadership' irrespective of whether they are actually politi-cians or not. At times, the political leadership of various countries has included hereditary rulers (like the kings of Saudi Arabia and Morocco nowadays), clerics (Richelieu in France, Alberoni in Spain, Makarios in Cyprus) or military men (Napoleon, Pinochet, the Japanese Army leadership during the 1930s and 1940s, and the Turkish Army leadership from the 1960s onwards). In other words, as far as strategy is concerned, political leadership refers to "those who run the country". The leadership may be democratic or authoritarian, legitimate or illegitimate, but it is still this leadership that will set the aims that strategy will then serve.[22]

As illustrated, when the policy objectives are coupled with the various means and care is taken to overcome the opponent's resistance, one enters the realm of strategy. We shall shortly examine the various levels of strategy. Despite their differences, they are all governed by the paradoxical logic of strategy. In addition, none of these levels are free from the difficulty of scarcity of resources that compels strategic planners to assign priorities among the objectives to be pursued. Finally, there is constant interaction with the opponent at every one of these levels; in other words, the horizontal and the vertical dimensions of strategy are constantly intermingled (see Table 1.1). The various levels are not conceived as rigidly separated and contrasted categories, but as successive areas of a continuum,[23] especially since they continuously interact amongst each other.

Table 1.1: Horizontal and Vertical Dimensions of Strategy

State A		Opposing State B
Grand Strategy	↔	Grand Strategy
↕		↕
Military Strategy	↔	Military Strategy
↕		↕
Operational Art	↔	Operational Art
↕		↕
Tactics	↔	Tactics

The highest level of strategy is grand strategy. Grand strategy refers to the use of all available means (military, economic, diplomatic, etc) at a state's disposal, in order to achieve the objectives set by policy in the face of actual or potential conflict.[24]

Grand strategy is formulated by the political leadership, as this is defined above. It is grand strategy that deals with the fundamental issues of war and peace. Grand strategy will decide whether a state will go to war in order to achieve the objectives set by policy. In addition, grand strategy will align the military strategy of the war with the political, diplomatic and economic strategies that form part of the war effort, making sure that they interact harmoniously and that one of these strategies does not have a detrimental impact on another (see also below).

The domain of grand strategy is chiefly the international system. A state's grand strategy is extensively (but, as we will soon see, not solely) influenced by such factors as the structure of the international system, the international balance of power, the international diplomatic scene, and the trends in international economy. In addition, grand strategy covers the whole of sovereign space and population. This is the case both because it makes use of all national means, material and nonmaterial, and because a grand strategy must ensure its domestic legitimacy.

When a grand strategy is applied to a specific war, with a specific opponent within a specific international environment, it becomes a theory of victory. A theory of victory explains how a specific war can be won.[25] Although a theory of victory is by definition related to a specific context, certain theories of victory contain elements of permanent importance. A highly interesting example of such permanent elements can be found in Clausewitz's analysis of how one could achieve total victory against Russia. According to him, this country could not be forcibly conquered, in contrast to the other European countries–neither Napoleon's 600,000 men in 1812 nor Hitler's three million in 1941 proved sufficient for a conquest. Russia can only be destroyed from within, that is by exploiting its internal divisions. Since its government retained its composure and the Russian people remained loyal to the government, Napoleon's campaign could not succeed.[26] Although Clausewitz's analysis did not examine the broader international context, it nevertheless provided the essential elements of a theory of victory against Russia, at least in the pre-nuclear era. In simple words, this theory stated that: "If your aim is total victory over Russia and the international environment allows it, your only chance of success lies in exploiting the internal divisions of that country." This analysis has been historically vindicated. The collapse of Russia in the First World War was caused by internal revolutionary movements that had been to some extent assisted by the Germans.[27] On the contrary, in the Second World War, the rallying of the Soviet people behind their government and the final failure of the German invasion was precisely the result of Hitler's refusal to exploit the internal divisions of the Soviet Union (by playing either on the anti–communist sentiments of the population or on the division between Russians and non-Russians) and his insistence on treating the whole of the conquered Soviet population as 'sub humans' (*Untermenschen*).[28]

Supporting grand strategy are the military, economic, diplomatic and political strategies. The economic, diplomatic and political strategies will be discussed in the next section, where grand strategy will be elaborated upon. The rest of this section will deal with military strategy and the levels below that, namely operational and tactical.[29] Military strategy is the use of all military means at a state's disposal, in order to achieve the objectives set by policy in view of actual or potential conflict.[30] It is military strategy that determines the structure and the mission of a country's armed forces. Irrespective of the various administrative divisions adopted in different countries, a state's armed forces may be divided into land, naval, air and (where in existence) mass destruction forces.[31] The degree of participation of each of these branches in the attempt to achieve the state's policy objectives in peace and war is the object of military strategy.

Military strategies may attempt either to retain or overthrow the status quo. Both of these can be achieved either by the threat or the actual use of force. Depending on this ends-means mix, military strategies may be classified as offensive, defensive, deterrent and compellent (see Table 1.2).[32]

An offensive military strategy aims at overthrowing the existing status quo by the use of force. A 'pure' offensive strategy is characterised by the emphasis it places on a) first strike; b) territorial conquest;

Table 1.2: Military Strategies

Means		Political Objectives	
		Overthrow Status Quo	Retain Status Quo
	Use of Force	Offensive	Defensive
	Threat of Force	Compellent	Deterrent

c) decisive victory over the armed forces of the enemy. An offensive military strategy may have unlimited or limited territorial aims, i.e. either complete conquest of an opponent (e.g. the Iraqi conquest of Kuwait), or seizure of a specific piece of territory (e.g. the Argentine conquest of the Falklands).

A defensive military strategy, on the other hand, attempts to retain the existing status quo by the use of force; in other words, it aims at repelling the enemy's offensive. A 'pure' defensive strategy is character-ised by the emphasis it places on a) absorbing the opponent's first strike; b) denying the territorial objectives of the enemy by holding ter-ritory; c) denying the decisive victory of an adversary by limiting dam-age to one's armed forces. The Soviet Union followed such a strategy during the period 1941–1944, replacing it with an offensive one during the period 1944–1945.[33]

It is to be noted that between offensive and defensive military strate-gies there exists the grey area of anticipatory first strikes. An anticipa-tory attack aims at the destruction of a potential source of threat before the said threat actually materialises. Depending on the maturation time of the perceived threat, anticipatory attacks may be either preventive or pre-emptive.[34] Prevention deals with threats expected to mature after years, while pre-emption deals with threats expected to mature within weeks, days, or even hours. The logic of prevention is that of fighting early and creating a *fait accompli* while this is still possible; that is before the balance of power tips in any decisive way and the strategic opponent becomes strong enough to be threatening (e.g. the Israeli strike against the Iraqi nuclear reactor in 1981).[35] In contrast, pre-emption does not have to do with long-term threats, but revolves around immediate crises: a state strikes against the offensive forces of another, so as to blunt an attack that is assumed to be imminent–in other words, the attack is already viewed as a matter of fact rather than as conjecture about the distant future.[36]

There are important legal and moral distinctions[37] between preven-tion and pre-emption that make pre-emption a borderline case between offense and defense. However, in our study both strategies will be con-sidered as offensive on the grounds of their behavioral manifestation, namely war initiation.

Deterrence is a strategy of using threat to dissuade opponents from attempting to achieve their objectives. A deterrent military strategy attempts to retain the existing status quo by the threat of force. There are three types of deterrent threat: denial, retaliation/retribution, and punishment. The aim is that the opponent does not attack at all, fearing that the resulting cost will be greater than the likely benefit.[38] There are some deterrent military strategies that, although meaningful before an opponent violates the status quo (*ex ante*), may not constitute rational choices *after* an opponent violates the status quo (*ex post*). The most characteristic example is the U.S. threat of nuclear retaliation in case of a Soviet invasion of Western Europe during the Cold War. When the Soviet Union itself acquired the capability of large-scale nuclear strikes on US territory, the American threat of nuclear retaliation did retain its deterrent value, since it signified very serious consequences indeed; however, the rationality of its execution if the Soviet Union did actually invade Western Europe was put into considerable doubt.

Finally, compellence is a strategy of using threat to persuade the opponent to perform some desired action. There are several examples of compellent military strategies, namely strategies where the aim is to overthrow the existing status quo by the threat of force; in other words, to make the opponent submit without war. In most instances military strategies of this kind are synonymous with the offensive ones–the best way to make opponents accept an adverse change of the status quo without war is persuading them that you can bring about this change by the use of force anyway. However, as in the case of deterrent strategies, there have been some military strategies that were suitable for compellence in peacetime, but unsuitable for a victory in war. For instance, Germany launched an ambitious program of naval development, putting emphasis on battleship construction. The aim was to create a naval threat against Great Britain, so that the latter would make concessions to Germany in order to win Berlin over to London's side. During the First World War, however, the German Navy rarely used its expensive battleships and basically resorted to submarine warfare. The conclusion; battleships were suitable for compellence in peacetime, but the submarines were suitable for victory in war.[39]

The success of a deterrent threat is measured by its not having to be used. The success of a compellent action is measured by how closely and quickly the adversary conforms to one's stipulated wishes. In compellence, as Robert Art explains, A is doing something that B cannot tolerate; then, B initiates action against A in order to get him to stop his intolerable actions; at the end, A stops his intolerable actions and B stops his (or both cease simultaneously). In deterrence, A is presently not doing something that B finds intolerable; B tells A that if A changes his behavior and does something intolerable, B will punish him; finally, A continues not to do something that B finds intolerable (see Figure 1).[40]

Figure 1

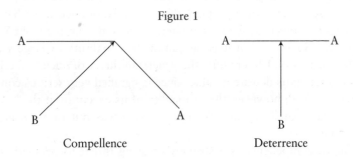

Compellence   Deterrence

The domain of military strategy is far narrower than that of grand strategy. Military strategy covers the whole of the sovereign space, as well as the whole of the actual or potential theatre(s) of operations. Still, broader considerations are not necessarily absent from military strategy. For instance, if armaments are imported from abroad, then it is obvious that arms' procurement, which constitutes an important part of military strategy,[41] can be influenced by the international environment. Military strategy used to be formulated by the commander-in-chief of the armed forces, who more often than not happened to be a hereditary king. The advent of the general staff and defense ministries brought more professionalism to the making of military strategy, which nowadays is viewed as the domain of the political and military leadership of a state's defense ministry.

In the context of war, military strategy determines the role of each branch of the armed forces, as well as the relative priority of the various theatres of operations. Thus, the Schlieffen Plan assigned priority to the Western theatre of operations (France) over the Eastern one (Russia), in the same way that the military strategy of the Western allies in the Second World War gave priority to the European theatre of operations over the Pacific one.

Immediately below the level of military strategy, but above that of tactics, lies the operational level. The concept of the operational level of war[42] has only recently entered the strategic thought of the Western countries, being borrowed from the Soviets, who, in turn, had taken it from the Germans.[43] Whereas military strategy has to do with the 'war' and tactics with the 'battle,' the operational level has to do with the 'campaign'. The operational level is the domain of large military units (conventionally starting from the army corps) of one or more branches of the armed forces, that operate within a certain theatre of the war. Theatres of war vary in size. There are theatres as vast as the Pacific Ocean during the Second World War and as small as the Golan Heights during the Yom Kippur War (1973). Even within a particular theatre, it is possible that some smaller yet completely autonomous theatres may evolve; the Crimean theatre within the broader Russian front in 1942 was such a case.[44] The operational level is basically the domain of the generals.

The scale of operations and the variety of military units are conditions necessary but not sufficient for talking about an independent operational level; the actions of these units must constitute something more than the sum of their tactical parts.[45] In practice, however, these two conditions normally prove sufficient. For instance, while the single pikeman or the small band of pikemen stood no chance against the single cavalryman or the small band of cavalrymen, large units of pikemen could hold their own against similar bodies of charioteers or cavalrymen.

Some analysts believe that, since different operational situations may exist and different operational methods may be used within the same theatre of operations, one should discern both a separate level of 'theatre strategy', located immediately below that of military strategy and covering the activities within a theatre, and an 'operational level', located below the level of theatre strategy and dealing with the various operational methods of action.[46] The Kosovo War (1999) is a striking example of different operational conditions and methods co-existing within the same theatre. On the one hand there was the high-technology air-war, while on the other the irregular operations on the ground reminded one of the wars of the Middle Ages or the Thirty Years' War. Nevertheless, the continuum 'battle-campaign-war' is neat enough and we see no compelling reason why it should be broken by the introduction of another level dealing with the style in which war is waged.

We have already devoted some attention to tactics, the lowest level of strategy.[47] Clausewitz defined tactics as "the use of armed forces in the engagement".[48] The tactical level is characterised by its small scale.

The military units that operate within it can be as small as a rifle squad or a machine gun crew (there are even 'individual tactics', referring to the conduct of the individual soldier), and their actions take place in comparatively limited space. Details of weather and terrain are crucial and the same applies to details of the order of battle.[49] Last, but not least, the tactical level is the area of personal bravery.[50] Tactics are basically the domain of the officers and, where very small units are concerned, the non-commissioned officers (NCOs).

When making a strategic analysis, it is very important to think in terms of the levels of strategy. This is for two reasons: a) a course of action feasible or advisable on a certain level may be impractical or even detrimental on another level; b) since there is constant interaction amongst the various levels, a possible malfunction in one of them may have an adverse impact on the whole strategic structure.

Regarding the second point, both Clausewitz and Moltke have emphatically pointed out that when strategy is wrong, tactical dexterity is not enough to make up for the strategic mistake. The examples of Japan and Germany in the Second World War have often been used to make this point. Although their armed forces (especially Germany's) displayed a high degree of effectiveness at the tactical and operational level, gross blunders at grand strategy level (going to war against vastly superior opponents) condemned these two countries to defeat.[51]

It is still rather early to talk about the political consequences of the recent Iraq War (2003), let alone pass judgment on the soundness of the American grand strategy that led to it.[52] Nevertheless, it does not seem unlikely that the US will not only fail to achieve one of its core political objectives of that war, namely creating a stable and democratic Iraq ruled by a friendly regime and serving as a model of democracy in the Middle East, but will also remain entangled in a deepening morass for a long time. The American armed forces performed excellently indeed in the realms of military strategy, operational art and tactics during the conventional phase of the Iraq War.[53] They have also displayed high-quality performance at these levels during certain stages of the counterinsurgency phase of that war.[54] However, if the dire predictions regarding Iraq's future come true, then this war will prove to be another example where dexterity in the lower levels of strategy could not help a flawed grand strategy achieve the policy objectives of the state.

However, the interaction of the levels works the other way round as well; lower levels may influence the higher ones. As Sir Basil Liddell

Hart stated, a strategy's success depends on whether it is tactically feasible. Thus, Stalin's generals, after pushing back the Germans from the outskirts of Moscow in December 1941, launched a massive counteroffensive in the middle of winter 1941–42, aiming to shatter the German Army, whose vulnerability he had correctly grasped. Despite their enthusiasm though, the Soviet troops and their commanders had not yet reached the necessary level of operational and tactical efficiency. The result was that they suffered casualties disproportionately high compared to the meagre results of their offensive.[55] It took the Red Army less than two years to improve on its operational and tactical skills. Then, by following the same strategy that had failed in the beginning of 1942, the Red Army proved capable of achieving total victory.

We conclude the discussion of the levels of strategy by pointing out that, apart from strategies (grand and military) that are or have not been feasible at lower levels, there are also instances of strategies that are in principle feasible operationally and tactically, but nevertheless fail because of mistakes at those levels. Xerxes' Persian invasion of Greece (480 B.C.) is such a case. Xerxes' grand strategy consisted of taking care to amass immense military power, so as to ensure the achievement of his political objective (conquest of Greece), while at the same time exploiting the divisions among the Greek city-states and winning many of them over to his side. His military strategy placed emphasis on cooperation between army and navy, so as to keep his immense army supplied with wheat from Asia. Everything was going well and Athens was captured. However, the disaster came at the operational level, namely Xerxes' decision to engage in battle at the straits of Salamis (480 B.C.). The narrow front neutralised Persian numerical superiority, and the heavier ships of the Greeks gave the latter victory. The Persians, however, could still have achieved their objectives, since their remaining forces in Greece were substantial. Nevertheless, through a tactical blunder they contrived to lose the battle of Plataea (479 B.C.), where they initially had held the advantage: the main body of their army was moved behind the archers that had been confronting the Spartans opposite them, thus cutting the archers' line of retreat and leaving them defenseless against the determined Spartan assault; the Persian army was thrown into disarray and took flight. A brilliant strategic design that was objectively bound to succeed was ruined by operational and tactical ineptitude.[56]

Aspects of Grand Strategy: Military and Non-Military Components

Given that the concept of grand strategy is central to our analysis, we need to elaborate on it a little further.[57] Essentially, grand strategy is a state's theory about how it can 'cause' security for itself, namely preservation of its sovereignty, territorial integrity, and relative power position.[58] Indeed, the way states choose to ensure security for themselves forms the very core of grand strategy, and their success in so doing is the crucial test of any particular grand strategy. In other words, the validity of a grand strategy can be empirically tested. Ideally, grand strategy must include an explanation of why this security-producing theory is expected to work in a given environment. Grand strategy can be understood as a state's response to specific threats to its security; it must identify potential threats and devise political and other remedies for them. Grand strategy should be viewed as a politico-military means-ends chain in which military capabilities are linked to military strategies that are in turn connected with political objectives. In theory, grand strategies exploit the advantages that the state possesses and aim to minimise those of the opponent. It has already been mentioned that strategy is labouring under scarcity of resources, and grand strategy is no exception. In an anarchic international environment the number of possible threats is great and resources to meet them are bound to be scarce; consequently, priorities must be established among both threats and remedies.

An elaborate treatment of the concept of grand strategy, containing an excellent description of the various means grand strategy employs, both in peacetime and in wartime,[59] has been given by Liddell Hart. According to him:

[T]he role of grand strategy–higher strategy–is to co-ordinate and direct all the resources of a nation, or band of nations towards the attainment of the political object of the war–the goal defined by fundamental policy. Grand strategy should both calculate and develop the economic resources and man-power of nations in order to sustain the fighting services. Also the moral resources–for to foster the people's willing spirit is often as important as to possess the more concrete forms of power. Grand strategy, too, should regulate the distribution of power between the services and industry. Moreover, fighting power is but one of the instruments of grand strategy–which should take account of and apply the power of financial pressure, of diplomatic pressure, of commercial pressure, and, not least of ethical pressure, to weaken the opponent's will.[60]

Since we have already dealt extensively with the military component of grand strategy, let us also briefly comment on its other important, non-military components.[61] Diplomacy is a component of grand strategy that can contribute to national security by securing allies, minimizing the number of potential antagonists, negotiating with opponents or diplomatically isolating them.[62] A high premium is put on identifying and exploiting opportunities offered by the existing or evolving situation in the international (or regional) system. An eye keen on detecting such opportunities, coupled with a capacity to exploit them, may enable statesmen to achieve extraordinary results.

The Austrian chancellor Clemens Metternich offers an excellent example. The Austrian Empire had been in decline since the mid-eighteenth century; it had suffered badly during the Napoleonic Wars, and its multinational composition was a cause of major concern, especially in view of the emergence of the new concept of nationalism. Nevertheless, not only did Metternich manage to extract substantial territorial gains after Napoleon's defeat, but also ensured Austrian supremacy in both Germany and Italy for many decades to come. The secret of his success was simple: after the turmoil created by the French Revolution and Napoleon's campaigns, the watchword among the European great powers was 'stability'.[63] Metternich managed to persuade the two key players, namely Great Britain and Russia, that Austria was the ideal guardian of stability in Central Europe and the Italian peninsula, whilst itself posing absolutely no threat to the balance of power.

The economic component of grand strategy also exercises profound influence on national security. This is done in two ways: a) by supporting military strategy (e.g. enabling arms' procurement, sustaining long periods of mobilization, etc) and diplomacy (e.g. by financing influential groups in foreign countries); b) in an independent capacity, by granting economic aid to foreign countries or conducting economic warfare against them.[64]

Although possession of a strong economic base does not automatically guarantee military prowess (e.g. the Persian Empire *vs.* Alexander, or the West Roman Empire *vs.* the barbarians), nevertheless the connection between the two is too well-known to require elaboration. Similarly, the idea of paying one's way to an alliance is probably as old as the mountains. In early modern history, Cardinal Richelieu set a pattern by offering subsidies to the Swedish king Gustavus Adolphus in order to secure the support of the mighty Swedish army against the German Emperor. In the same manner, the British subsidised Frederick the Great of Prussia so that he could preoccupy not only the Austrians, but the French as well. Economic aid is another familiar concept. The Napoleonic Wars witnessed an interesting case of reciprocal economic warfare: Napoleon forbade the Europeans to trade with Great Britain, whereas the British, by means of a naval blockade, tried to make sure that the Europeans would trade *solely* with Great Britain. The British blockade was irksome and not altogether in compliance with international law, but trading with Great Britain carried many attractions, since the advanced British economy had many valuable goods to offer. Thus, the temptation to break with the Napoleonic 'Continental System' was too great. Actually, Russia's decision to opt for trade with Great Britain was one of the reasons the French emperor undertook the disastrous Russian campaign.[65]

Apart from the military, economic and diplomatic power (alliances, etc), that constitute the so-called 'hard power', states also possess and employ in their grand strategies the so-called 'soft power'.[66] Cultural, ideological or religious affinity or influences are different forms of this power, while nowadays a state might enjoy a certain amount of influence by participating in some key international organizations (e.g. EU, NATO).

Soft power is not to be underrated. In fact, it can play an important role in securing the legitimacy of a grand strategy both home and abroad. This is indeed the political component of grand strategy. The Byzantine Empire provides a textbook case of exploitation of soft power, namely the conversion of various barbarian nations to Christianity, with a view to minimizing the number of opponents and extending the Empire's influence.[67] The exploitation of Communist ideology by the Soviet Union is another case in point whereas, in the same vein, Iran's exploitation of Islamic fundamentalism enabled that state to achieve an international influence out of all proportion to its hard power.

Typologies of Grand Strategies

We have already encountered a typology of military strategies according to their ends-means mix, namely offensive, defensive, deterrent and compellent strategies. There has been no dearth of typologies of grand strategies as well. A particularly important typology that will be used extensively in our study, is the one devised by the prominent German historian Hans Delbrück, based on the means that a strategy employs.

Delbrück outlined two basic forms of strategy: the strategy of annihilation (*Niederwerfungsstrategie*) and the strategy of exhaustion (*Ermattungsstrategie*).[68] The aim of the strategy of annihilation is that of the decisive battle (*Vernichtungsschlacht*),[69] whereas the strategy of exhaustion employs the battle as but one of a variety of means, such as territorial occupation, destruction of crops, blockade, etc. In general, the concept of economic damage to the enemy plays a key role in this strategy. The strategy of exhaustion is neither a variation of the strategy of annihilation, nor inferior to it. On the contrary, such a strategy can often be the only way for a state to achieve its political aims. It must be noted that these two strategies are ideal types; in practice, one often encounters a mix between them.

Although Delbrück referred to military strategies, not necessarily mentioning grand strategies, his distinction between a strategy of annihilation and a strategy of exhaustion may be invaluable to the study of grand strategies. One must also note that in Delbrück's time the term grand strategy was used in a much more restrictive sense than at present; that is, as only covering the overall war policy of a state. Nowadays, a grand strategy by definition makes use of all available means and does not restrict itself to the traditional military ones. Nevertheless, a distinction between a grand strategy of annihilation and a grand strategy of exhaustion can still be made, depending on which means feature most prominently in a grand strategy. In a grand strategy of annihilation the state depends mainly on military strategy; all other strategies (economic, diplomatic, etc) are essentially subservient to it. On the other hand, a grand strategy of exhaustion makes simultaneous use of all possible means so as to achieve the aims set by state policy.[70]

The Napoleonic campaigns constitute classic examples of the strategy of annihilation. They culminated in decisive battles (e.g. Marengo, Austerlitz, Jena, Friedland, Wagram), in which the French emperor completely crushed the armed forces of his enemies, forcing them to sue for peace.[71] On the other hand, the grand strategy that Great Britain adopted from the seventeenth century onwards was a typical example of a strategy of exhaustion. The so-called 'British way of warfare' can be described as entailing: a) blockade of continental ports, b) distant maritime operations directed against the colonies and the overseas trade of the rival continental powers, c) subsidies to allies, d) nominal ground forces' commitment to the continent, and e) peripheral raiding around the continental littoral to exploit the flexibility of sea power for surprise maneuver.[72]

In effect, the Napoleonic campaigns created the second typology of grand strategies that will be used in this study, namely, of the direct and indirect approach. It must be noted that these concepts are not confined to the grand strategy level, but extend to all levels of strategy; nevertheless, we will focus on their application at the level of grand strategy.

The campaigns of Napoleon formed the basis of the theory of war that Clausewitz promulgated shortly afterwards. Clausewitz laid emphasis on the direct approach, namely the direction of one's war effort primarily towards the main opponent and/or the 'centre of gravity' (i.e. the strongest component) of the enemy war effort. In most instances, this centre of gravity was the armed forces of the enemy; consequently, these forces had to be destroyed. Obviously, the strategy of annihilation occupies a central position in Clausewitz's theory and it is no wonder that it continues to be associated with him, as well as with Napoleon to this day.[73] However, 'strategy of annihilation' and 'direct approach' are not identical concepts, as shall be illustrated later.

In contrast, and throughout his work, Liddell Hart has argued in favour of the advantages of the indirect approach.[74] The term 'indirect approach' has had a turbulent history and Liddell Hart's repeated elaborations of it have rendered it practically meaningless.[75] However, we believe that something of use can still be salvaged from the conceptual mess: 'indirect approach' generally denotes the sidestepping of the enemy's strong points and the avoidance of attrition warfare. At the level of grand strategy, the indirect approach may be regarded as the evading of the main opponent by directing one's war effort against the secondary opponent(s), postponing the decisive strike in favour of a more suitable moment.

Planning and Evaluating Grand Strategy

Taking into account the analysis so far, one reaches the conclusion that, in order to be considered successful at the level of grand strategy, planning needs to address the following four dimensions[76] (see Table 1.3):

1. Assessment of the international environment, so as to identify potential or actual threats to national security, as well as the various

18

constraints and opportunities for the implementation of the grand strategy that may be present in this environment. Clearly then, the crucial test for a grand strategy in this dimension is international strategic fit.

2. Identification of the ends that the grand strategy is to pursue, in view of the means available, plus the aforementioned threats, constraints, and opportunities. In view of the ever-present scarcity of resources, there are certain limits to the ends pursued. As already mentioned, priorities must be established among the various aims but one must make sure that the aims set do not exceed the means available. This would lead to the phenomenon of overextension on which we shall elaborate later. The avoidance of overextension is one important indicator of the performance of a grand strategy.

3. Allocation of resources so as to achieve the objectives outlined by grand strategy. The means have to be tailored to the ends so as to avoid both wasting scarce resources and marshalling inadequate resources for the tasks ahead. Thus, the avoidance of redundancy or inadequacy of means is the critical test that a grand strategy has to meet.

4. Shaping the 'image' of the grand strategy both at the domestic and international level, so that: a) the society actively supports the grand strategy of the state; b) all parts of the state structure work towards the same purpose; c) the grand strategy of the state is viewed as legitimate by the international community. In other words, to be successful in this dimension, a grand strategy has to be accepted both at home and abroad.

Table 1.3: Planning of Grand Strategy

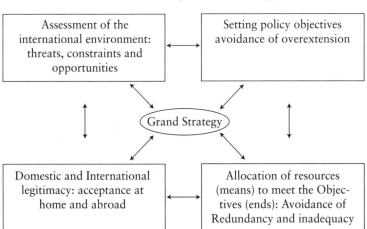

19

We have already pointed out that grand strategy is a security-producing theory whose validity can be empirically tested. In addition, we outlined the crucial tests that this theory has to meet to prove its validity. There are, however, five more criteria that are used for evaluating grand strategies.[77]

The first is the external fit criterion, namely the degree to which a grand strategy fits in with the international and domestic political environment. Thus, the advent of a bipolar world in 1945 made it difficult for small states to pursue a grand strategy based on shifting their allegiance among the various great powers as they saw fit; instead, they had to choose camp (if they were in fact allowed to) practically once and for all.[78] As far as the domestic political environment is concerned, increased public concern about foreign policy, that began with the French Revolution, has made it difficult for decision makers to follow a policy of constantly shifting alliances, where yesterday's friend becomes today's enemy.

The second criterion is the relation between means and ends, namely the degree to which the objectives of a grand strategy correspond to the available means and vice versa. This has to do with the traditional problem of how to avoid overextension (i.e. pursue aims beyond one's capabilities),[79] while at the same time not unduly reducing one's objectives (see Table 1.4). As noted, this is a very important criterion of grand strategy.

The third criterion is that of efficiency, namely whether a grand strategy makes the best use of the available resources. This leads to the issue of cost-benefit assessment. Each of the alternatives of strategic designs available to a state at a given moment leads to different calcu-

Table 1.4: Linking Means and Ends of a Grand Strategy

		Political Commitments (Ends)	
		Few	Many
Available Means (Capabilities)	Few	Passivity	Overextension
	Many	Reduction of Objectives	Strategic Sufficiency

lations of costs and benefits. Thus, the task of the strategist is to hit upon the optimum strategy, the most efficacious one, the one that yields the best results in this cost-benefit analysis.

The fourth criterion is internal coherence, namely that one element or one means of the grand strategy does not hamper the function of another. Indeed, this is what happened to Israel in 1973, prior to the Yom Kippur War. Israeli military strategy, that gave emphasis on striking first, was in conflict with the state's diplomatic strategy, which emphasised enlisting US support. However, if Israel, by striking first, gave the impression of being the aggressor, then it would forfeit American support and thus invalidate its diplomatic strategy.[80]

Finally, the fifth criterion is durability to mistakes, namely the ability of a grand strategy to withstand coincidental mistakes and mishaps without prohibitively high costs. The aforementioned example of the Persian invasion of Greece is a typical example of a grand strategy with low durability to mistakes. On the other hand, the American grand strategy during the Cold War proved durable enough to sustain the mistakes and/or mishaps associated with the involvement of the US in Vietnam.

We shall now proceed to the examination of Thucydides' contribution to the study of strategy, and in doing so we shall be assisted by the concepts outlined above.

2

ATHENS AND SPARTA

POWER STRUCTURES, EARLY CONFLICT AND THE CAUSES OF WAR

Introduction

In this chapter we will provide an overview of the background of the strategic rivalry between Athens and Sparta. The chapter begins with an outline of the domestic structures, the strategic culture and the power bases of the two strategic opponents, where the 'hegemony' of Sparta is contrasted with the 'empire' of Athens. Then, we will briefly outline the earlier phase of the conflict between Athens and Sparta during the so-called *Pentecontaetia*, namely the interval of roughly fifty years between the end of the Persian Wars and the beginning of the Peloponnesian War. It must be noted that we do not intend to give a detailed account of the *Pentecontaetia*. Rather, as Thucydides himself did, we will only focus on the most salient, strategically significant events.[1] We must also point out that our analysis will not deal with the events directly leading to the Peloponnesian War.[2] As will become evident in both the present chapter and Chapters Three and Four, we wholeheartedly endorse Thucydides' view that the causes of the war were structural, namely the growth of Athenian power and Sparta's concomitant attempt to check that growth.[3] Hence, we contend that the final pre-war crises over Potidaea and Corcyra played a comparatively minor role in the outbreak of the war. Those crises did influence the timing of that outbreak, but nothing more; the crucial role was played by the structure of the international system, which made it likely that war would break out.[4] In fact, the overall issue of Thucydides' explanation of the causes of the war between Athens and Sparta, and his contribution to the study of the causes of war in general, will be tackled at the end of the present chapter.

Spartan Hegemony versus Athenian Empire: Domestic Structures and Strategic Culture

The clash between Sparta and Athens was a conflict between two different power structures and two societies organised in very different ways. The domestic structures of each of these two societies exerted a profound influence on what modern analysts call the strategic culture or national style of the two belligerents.[5]

As is well-known, Athenian polity was the archetypal democracy. Central to this was the citizen assembly (*Ecclesia*). This was the most important decision-making body where all Athenian adult males were eligible for participation. The *Ecclesia* convened at least forty times a year, debated openly, and took decisions by majority vote. *Every* state issue, even details of military planning, was decided by the *Ecclesia*. To be sure, ten generals were elected annually (and could be re-elected indefinitely) but their actions were constantly and carefully scrutinised by the *Ecclesia*, which could and quite often did punish the generals for actual or alleged misconduct.[6]

Although the political organization of direct democracy often resulted in inconsistent decision-making, this was more than counterbalanced by the feeling of active participation in the city affairs that every citizen experienced. This feeling ensured enthusiastic citizen participation in the formulation and implementation of state policy, as well as the mobilization of all available means for the achievement of the various ends set by that policy.[7]

In contrast, the domestic structures of Sparta were completely different.[8] Spartan polity was composed of monarchical elements (two hereditary kings), oligarchic elements (a council of elders, the so-called *Gerousia*, consisting of twenty-eight members elected for life plus the two kings) and democratic elements (a citizen assembly).[9] Another institution with immense powers and steadily increasing importance was that of the five *ephors* (overseers). The *ephors* managed the daily affairs of Sparta and supervised the conduct of its populace, keeping a close eye on the Spartan kings. They were elected for a year, presumably with no right for re-election.[10] Nevertheless, despite the co-existence of all these elements, Sparta was essentially an oligarchic polity.

The Spartans had developed a reputation for disdaining luxury,[11] and devoted their whole life from the age of seven onwards to military training. The outcome of this long and intensive training was to turn the Spartans into arguably the best soldiers in the world.[12] In fact, they had good reason to become such. When the Spartans originally settled in Laconia (the south-eastern part of the Peloponnese) they enslaved the indigenous population, the so-called helots. The helots were forced to cultivate the land and yield part of the product to their Spartan masters. This allowed the Spartans to focus on leading a military life. Moreover, when Sparta also conquered Messenia (the south-western part of the Peloponnese), the number of the helots swelled.[13] Both Spartans and helots acted as if a state of war existed between them.[14] The helots were constantly looking for an opportunity to rebel, whereas the Spartans were continuously trying to suppress them by every conceivable means.[15] In essence, the Spartans had turned their city into an armed camp and lived accordingly.[16]

As for the 'strategic cultures' of Athens and Sparta, one may notice that in contrast to the enterprising Athenians, conservatism and caution were the fundamental characteristics of the Spartans. As their Corinthian allies put it to the Spartans:

An Athenian is always an innovator, quick to form a resolution and quick at carrying it out. You, on the other hand, are good at keeping things as they are; you never originate an idea, and your action tends to stop short of its aim. Then again, Athenian daring will outrun its own resources; they will take risks against their better judgement, and still, in the midst of danger, remain confident. But your nature is always to do less than you could have done, to mistrust your own judgment, however sound it may be, and to assume that dangers will last for ever. Think of this, too: while you are hanging back, they never hesitate; while you stay at home, they are always abroad; for they think that the farther they go the more they will get, while you think that any movement may endanger what you have already.[17]

The difference in strategic culture between Athenians and Spartans was not so much a result of their different 'national characters', although this undoubtedly played a role,[18] as of the different structures of their respective polities. The democratic polity of Athens encouraged citizen participation in the affairs of the state and fostered a spirit of innovation, which at times bordered on recklessness. On the contrary, in Sparta the central role of the elders of the *Gerousia* ensured a relative stability of state policy,[19] but at the same time this led to excessive conservatism and an inability to keep up with external developments.

The conservatism and caution of the Spartans were also bolstered by the continual fear of a helot revolt, which made them view external expeditions with reluctance.

These different strategic cultures were evident in the security policies of the two cities. Thucydides goes to some length to document the rise of Athenian power during the *Pentecontaetia*.[20] To start with, the low fertility of the Attic soil coupled with demographic pressures forced the Athenians to turn to the sea and to become a seafaring nation. Thus, as early as at the time of the Persian invasion, Athens possessed a powerful navy. Its naval power enabled Athens to assume the lead in pushing Persia out of the Greek coastal cities of Asia Minor. However, in the process the Athenians also established a progressively firmer control over their allies; the Athenian Empire was born, and it gradually proved to be a tremendous source of wealth for Athens: tribute from the allies, imperial mines, and increased commercial activity all contributed to the growth of the economic power of the Athenian metropolis.[21] This wealth sustained the efficiency of the Athenian navy, guaranteeing the preservation of the Empire and ensuring more income that would once again augment the naval power of Athens. Thucydides put it succinctly:

Because of this reluctance of theirs [the allies-turned-subjects] to face military service, most of them, to avoid serving abroad, had assessments made by which, instead of producing ships, they were to pay a corresponding sum of money. The result was that the Athenian navy grew strong at their expense, and when they revolted they always found themselves inadequately armed and inexperienced in war.[22]

It was a self-perpetuating system that was producing spiraling gains for Athens, far removed from the agrarian economy of Sparta.[23]

Sparta, on the other hand, did not undertake such vast schemes. Consequently, although Sparta had traditionally been the most powerful Greek state and Spartans the initial leaders of the Greeks in the struggle against the Persians, they quickly withdrew and ceded leadership to the Athenians, who, as discussed, used it to their own benefit.

Sparta was content with control of the Peloponnese. This was ensured by the forging of a web of alliances that has become known as the Peloponnesian League (or Alliance). In addition, Sparta also saw to it that its allies were governed by friendly oligarchic regimes.[24] The Peloponnesian allies provided valuable manpower which assisted the elite but relatively small Spartan army. A major inhibition to Sparta's quest for complete control of the Peloponnese was the existence of the powerful city-state of Argos–a permanent rival that constantly needed to be kept in check.[25]

This examination of the two contending states brings to light an important point: although Spartan power rested on solid foundations, it lacked the dynamism Athens possessed. It would seem that the peculiar Spartan system had reached its limits; it could ensure Spartan independence and control of the Peloponnese, but nothing more than that.[26] Sparta remained an introverted city-state whose livelihood depended upon the agricultural economy of the helots. To make matters worse, in an attempt to preserve their land ownership and possibly increase it through dowries, the Spartans came to limit the number of their offspring. With the Spartan population steadily diminishing, Spartan power was also likely to decline.[27] On the contrary, Athens, by creating a commercial and maritime empire, had opened new avenues and could confidently expect its power to keep growing.

Michael Doyle has come up with an interesting analysis of the different nature of the Athenian and Spartan power structures. According to him, Athens' commercial activities enabled it to acquire immense influence beyond its borders, creating in this way a 'periphery' that was controlled by the Athenian 'metropolis'. In contrast, the international influence of Sparta was based exclusively on its military power. The cost of military power was high for the relatively small Spartan warrior community, thus limiting Sparta's international influence. As a result, whereas Athens had created an 'empire', where a metropolis controlled a periphery, Sparta had to be content with a 'hegemony', where the Spartan metropolis was connected with a network of other, less powerful metropoles.[28] It is interesting that, following the end of the Peloponnesian War, the Spartans attempted to replace the Athenian Empire with an empire of their own. However, as we have already mentioned, their political organization did not enable them to support such an undertaking without resorting to sheer military force.[29] Spartan military power being relatively limited and costly, Sparta was led to overextension. As a result, merely four decades after the Peloponnesian War, the Spartan Empire collapsed and Sparta lost control of the Peloponnese and then of Messenia itself.[30]

Once again, the Corinthians captured the essence of the situation and described it brilliantly to the Spartans: "Your whole way of life is out of date when compared with theirs [the Athenians]. And it is just as true in politics as it is in any art or craft: new methods must drive out old ones."[31]

Athens and Sparta: The Early Phase of the Conflict

The early phase of the conflict between Athens and Sparta begins in 479 B.C. during an expedition against the Persians. On the day of the great Greek victory over the Persians at the battle of Plataea, a Greek expeditionary force under the Spartan king Leotychidas landed at Mycale in Asia Minor, defeated a Persian army and destroyed the Persian fleet stationed there.[32] The Greek cities of Ionia (the Aegean coast of Asia Minor) revolted against the Persians, while the Greeks under the leadership of the Spartan regent Pausanias, the victor of Plataea, soon captured Byzantium and thus assumed control of the Dardanelles.[33] Suddenly, the Greeks had gone over to the offensive; they would continue this offensive for the next thirty years.

However, they would do so under new leadership. The abrasive manner of Pausanias and his treacherous contacts with the Persians had made Spartan leadership unpopular among the rest of the Greeks. In any case, it seems that the Spartans had had enough of distant expeditions. Thus, they withdrew from the alliance together with their Peloponnesian allies and ceded the leadership to the Athenians. Consequently, in 478 B.C. Athens assumed the leadership of the Greeks in the anti–Persian struggle and this heralded the birth of the Delian League.[34] This was a development of tremendous significance, laying the foundations of the Athenian Empire.

The Athenian power position vis-à-vis Sparta was also improved by the rebuilding of the walls of Athens, which neutralised the Spartan infantry. The Athenians started rebuilding the walls of their city after the Persian invaders withdrew. The Spartans tried to prevent the rebuilding, coming up with an ingenious arms control proposal, namely the demolition of the walls of every city outside the Peloponnese, Athens included:

When the Spartans heard of what was going on they sent an embassy to Athens. This was partly because they themselves did not like the idea of Athens or any other city being fortified. [...] The Spartans proposed that not only should Athens refrain from building her own fortifications, but that she should join them in pulling down all the fortifications which still existed in cities outside the Peloponnese. In making this suggestion to the Athenians they concealed their real meaning and their real fears; the idea was, they said, that if there was another Persian invasion, the Persians would have no strong base from which to operate, such as they had in Thebes; and that the Peloponnese was capable of serving the needs of everyone, both as a place of refuge and as a place from which to attack.[35]

The Athenians, under the direction of the brilliant statesman Themistocles, procrastinated in replying to the Spartan suggestion, until the wall had reached sufficient height.[36]

The Athenians proved worthy leaders of the anti–Persian struggle, pursuing the war with vigor. Under the leadership of the splendid Athenian general Cimon, the Delian League continued to defeat the Persians. The most notable success came in 466 B.C. when Cimon inflicted a shattering defeat on the Persian army and navy in the battle of the Eurymedon River, along the southern coast of Asia Minor. The Persians did resort to a military buildup, but the tide of Athenian conquest could not be stemmed; the Athenian Alliance/Empire continued to grow, chiefly at Persian expense.[37] The high point of the Athenian advance was reached in 460 B.C., when the Athenians launched a campaign against Persian-held Cyprus and then proceeded to assist an anti–Persian rebellion in Egypt.[38]

Apart from these overseas successes, in that same year Athens registered a dramatic coup in mainland Greece proper: a clash between Athens' neighboring cities of Megara and Corinth, both members of the Peloponnesian League, made Megara join the Athenian Alliance. The Athenians promptly fortified the Megarid region, effectively barring the route of a possible Peloponnesian invasion.[39]

While Athenian power continued to grow, Sparta was experiencing great difficulties. During the 470s and 460s Sparta was in acute danger of losing its hegemony in the Peloponnese. Powerful anti–Spartan alliances emerged: first, between Argos and the Arcadian city of Tegea, and then between all the Arcadians with the exception of the Mantineans. Sparta faced a critical situation but, in traditional Spartan (and later Clausewitzian) manner, two decisive battles at Tegea and Dipaieis settled matters and Sparta successfully defended its Peloponnesian hegemony.[40] As if these challenges were not enough, in 464 B.C. there was a terrible earthquake that caused horrendous material damage and many fatalities among the Spartans. During the chaos, the helots seized the opportunity and revolted. The rebels captured and fortified a strongpoint, held their own in a ten-year siege and finally evacuated Spartan territory under terms. The Spartans enlisted Athenian help in the siege, since the Athenians were considered experts at siege warfare. However, as the Athenians did not make the expected progress, the Spartans came to distrust them and finally asked them to leave. Furious, the Athenians abandoned the alliance with Sparta, dating since the Persian invasion, and aligned themselves with Argos instead.[41]

At this point in history, a clear picture is emerging. Athens has started to attract former members of the Peloponnesian League into its own alliance and subsequently the power of Athens is growing relative to the power of both Persia and Sparta. Athens expands territorially at Persian expense and is growing richer than Sparta. For Sparta, the alternatives are clear: loss of primacy in Greece or launch of preventive war. Circa 460 B.C. the die was cast and the so-called First Peloponnesian War began.[42]

With the Athenian fortification of Megarid barring invasion, it took the Spartans three years to bring their land forces to bear against Athens. In order to settle a local dispute, a large Peloponnesian force moved on to Central Greece by way of the Corinthian Gulf. However, the Athenian navy quickly established control of the Gulf, thus cutting off the Peloponnesian forces. As a result, the Spartans attempted to return to the Peloponnese via Boeotia and Megarid. The Athenians, considering the situation opportune and backed by an Argive force, met them at the Boeotian town of Tanagra in 457 B.C. However, in the ensuing battle the redoubtable Spartan infantry proved its worth once again, defeating the Athenians and securing the withdrawal of the Peloponnesians through Megarid. Nevertheless, that victory was bought at the price of heavy casualties.[43] Tanagra was not an Austerlitz, but a Borodino.

Actually, Tanagra was relatively insignificant strategically, for the remainder of 457 B.C. proved nothing less than an *annus mirabilis* for the Athenian arms.[44] A mere sixty-two days after that battle the Athenians invaded Boeotia, defeated the combined Boeotian forces at the battle of Oenophyta and in so doing conquered both Boeotia and Phocis. Shortly afterwards the island of Aegina, an old naval rival of Athens, capitulated to the Athenians and became a tributary state.[45] This was the apex of Athenian expansion. To crown their triumph, the Athenians completed the 'long walls' connecting Athens with Phalerum and Piraeus.[46]

However, shortly after this, Athenian imperialism starts producing diminishing returns. An ominous and significant development was the annihilation of the Athenian expeditionary corps in Egypt in 454 B.C.[47] The impact of this was to prompt Athens to renounce further expansion in mainland Greece, reach a compromise with Sparta, tighten control over its Alliance/Empire, and concentrate against Persia.[48] It soon became evident that equilibrium had been reached on both fronts. In 451 B.C. Athens and Sparta concluded the Five Years' Peace (in all probability an acknowledgement of the existing status quo)[49] and two years later, in 449 B.C., after an unsuccessful Athenian campaign in Cyprus, Athens concluded the famous Peace of Callias with Persia.[50] The precise terms of that treaty are still a matter of controversy,[51] but it is reasonably certain that the Persian fleet could not sail in the Dardanelles and the Aegean Sea, as well as in the eastern Mediterranean waters west of Pamphylia, and the autonomy of the Greek cities on the west coast of Asia Minor was formally recognised.[52]

Although the Peace of Callias formalised the equilibrium between Athens and Persia, in Greece proper events were to take a turn for the worse for the Athenians. The Athenian attempt to consolidate control of Boeotia ended in failure at Coronea in 446 B.C. Consequently, Athens was forced to relinquish both Boeotia and Phocis. Shortly afterwards the prosperous island of Euboea defected from the Athenian Alliance and, worse still, the Megarians rejoined the Peloponnesian League, slaughtering their Athenian garrison in the process.[53]

No sooner had the Megarid route opened and the Five Years' Treaty expired, than the Spartan infantry entered the fray: the Peloponnesians under the Spartan king Pleistoanax invaded Attica in 446 B.C.[54] However, the invasion was brief and the Peloponnesians withdrew before penetrating deep into Attica.[55] The Spartan political leadership obviously considered the withdrawal premature, because on returning to Sparta Pleistoanax was accused of having been bribed by the Athenians and was forced to go into exile.[56] One cannot be certain of the actual events, but shortly afterwards, namely in 446/445 B.C., Sparta and Athens concluded the Thirty Years' Peace. Athenian control over Aegina was confirmed, but Athens ceded all other territories of the Peloponnesian League still under Athenian occupation.[57] To all intents and purposes, the Thirty Years' Peace put an end to Sparta's pretensions of being the sole hegemon in Greece.

Thus, by 445 B.C. all the pieces of the strategic jigsaw puzzle had been put in place. Although unable to retain the maximum gains it had achieved, Athens had freed itself from Persian occupation to create and

31

consolidate a highly profitable maritime empire. The events of 446 B.C. had ensured that the Athenian Empire would not expand further into the Greek mainland, but on the other hand, together with the Peace of Callias, they had ensured that Athenian naval and commercial supremacy within the Aegean Sea and the greater part of the eastern Mediterranean would remain unchallenged. This strategic background would remain unaltered until the eve of the Peloponnesian War, namely until 433 B.C., when Athens would further enhance its naval mastery by enlisting the support of Corcyra, an important maritime power which had remained neutral until then.[58]

Thucydides on the Causes of War

This is an issue that will recur in the next two chapters, in the discussion of the causes of the 'proper' Peloponnesian War; however, having examined the rise and the course of the early conflict between Sparta and Athens, this is the appropriate point to deal with the theoretical issues involved.

Thucydides makes it clear that the growth of Athenian power which took place immediately after the Persian Wars, sharply altered the political landscape of the eastern Mediterranean in general, and ancient Greece in particular. Athens continued to expand territorially and to grow stronger in both economic and military terms, in relation to Sparta and indeed every other Greek state. Sparta felt threatened and this led to the outbreak of the First Peloponnesian War circa 460 B.C.

This is a classic instance of what nowadays is referred to as 'power transition', leading to 'hegemonic war':[59] The second greatest power in the system registers higher rates of growth compared to the hegemonic power in the system, eventually casting doubts on the hitherto accepted systemic hierarchy. The old hegemon not only refuses to concede its primacy without a fight, but actually launches a preventive war.

This Thucydidean explanation of the causes of war between Sparta and Athens broke new ground in the study of international conflict, and international relations in general. According to Robert Gilpin, Thucydides discovered the 'law of dynamics' in international relations, namely the law of uneven development.[60] A mere generation earlier, Herodotus had been content to explain the Greek-Persian conflict solely on the basis of mythical incidents and human passions. The explanation of Thucydides marks a gargantuan leap in the transition from mythology and crude psychology to International Relations theory. The Thucydidean notion that wars are the result of underlying systemic forces rather than the result of the will of the gods or the whims of individuals, lies at the very core of modern International Relations theory. Through Hobbes, Hegel, and Marx,[61] to the modern structural theories of Kenneth Waltz and Robert Gilpin,[62] systemic explanations of international outcomes remain powerful analytical tools.

However, these systemic explanations of the causes of war have not convinced everybody. A number of analysts have remained skeptical about explanations founded on the underlying causes of wars, focusing instead on the 'proximate' causes of wars, namely the handling of the very crises that immediately precede wars–whenever such crises exist. In the specific context of the Peloponnesian War, the argument that its 'proximate' causes were more important than the 'underlying' ones will be examined in detail in Chapters Three and Four.[63] Nevertheless, we would at this point like to make some comments on the overall issue of underlying vs. proximate causes, using as an example the work of Richard Ned Lebow.[64]

Lebow rejects the notion of inevitability that accompanies explanations based on the systemic causes of wars. He believes that international crises may well constitute important intervening variables that affect in crucial ways both the likelihood of war and the overall evolution of relations between the contending parties. He points out that, had the Cuban missile crisis (1962) ended up in war, as did the Sarajevo crisis (1914), there would have been plenty of analysts ready to attribute that war to underlying causes, the foremost being the systemic antagonism between the United States and the Soviet Union. The fact that there was no war in 1962, or in 1898, when Great Britain and France got embroiled in the Fashoda crisis, shows, according to Lebow, that alternative outcomes are indeed possible and that underlying causes fail to tell the whole story, or even the most important part of it.

Though we strongly disagree with the opinion that the events directly leading to the Peloponnesian War were more important than the systemic background of that war, we do not feel that 'proximate'-cause explanations ought to be entirely dismissed. In general, specific wars are not inevitable. Nevertheless, when hegemonic rivalry is paramount, the states involved would appear to be on an inevitable collision course. Sparta and Athens, like Great Britain and Germany before the First World War, were clearly bent on systemic primacy; hence the wars between them did have an aura of inevitability. On the other hand, France was not a would-be hegemon in 1898, hence she could and did back down in the Fashoda crisis.[65]

It may be argued that the Cuban missile crisis seems to disprove what has just been said about the inevitability of hegemonic war. However, by quoting an example from the nuclear age in order to disprove the conclusions of the pre-nuclear era, one may be comparing apples with oranges. States will fight for systemic supremacy through hegemonic war, provided they reckon that the cost of the war will be acceptable. Thucydides makes this clear, incidentally anticipating what nowadays is called 'expected utility theory':[66]

No one is forced into war by ignorance, nor, if he thinks he will gain from it, is he kept out of it by fear. The fact is that one side thinks that the profits to be won outweigh the risks to be incurred, and the other side is ready to face danger rather than accept an immediate loss.[67]

Occasionally, this estimate proves to be a miscalculation (e.g. the First World War); in fact, Thucydides, anticipating Martin van Creveld, points out that men, especially young ones, possessing an inner desire to fight, are all too prone to misjudge the costs of war.[68] However, in the nuclear age such miscalculations are unlikely, the cost of carnage being clear.

In light of the above, the following conclusion emerges: the antagonism between two states seeking pre-eminence in an international system is a necessary condition for the outbreak of a hegemonic war. When the cost of that war is deemed acceptable, as was generally the case in the pre-nuclear age, then this condition becomes a sufficient one as well.

This concludes the examination of the background to the strategic rivalry between Athens and Sparta. We shall now proceed to conduct an examination of the grand strategic designs of the two opponents during the Peloponnesian War.

3

PERICLEAN GRAND STRATEGY

Introduction

It is customary to regard the Peloponnesian War as a conflict between a land power and a sea power.[1] However, this is a highly distorting view, since the Spartans quickly understood the need to rival Athenian naval strength, and eventually did so. It is much more accurate to view the war as a contest between two opposing grand strategic designs. The use of the ideal types of the strategy of annihilation and exhaustion (see Chapter One) will be particularly pertinent in this respect. One may recall that the strategy of annihilation aims at the destruction of the enemy's armed forces through decisive battle, whereas in the strategy of exhaustion the battle goes side by side with the economic damage that ensues from territorial occupation, destruction of crops, naval blockade, etc.

In Thucydides' text, one can see both of these grand strategies at work: while Sparta employed a grand strategy of annihilation, Athens, initially at least, resorted to a grand strategy of exhaustion. The present chapter will examine the grand strategy of exhaustion that Athens employed against Sparta during the first years of the Peloponnesian War (under the direction of the leading statesman and general Pericles).[2] We shall henceforth refer to this strategy as 'Periclean grand strategy' since he not only conceived it but also supervised its implementation. The four dimensions of grand strategic planning presented in Chapter One will constitute the conceptual framework through which this grand strategy will be analysed.

35

Assessment of the International Environment

The Greek City-State System: Power Distribution and Future Trends

The Greek city-state system[3] in terms of modern international relations theory has been commonly described as 'bipolar', its two opposed poles being Sparta and Athens.[4] Naturally, everything depends on where one sets the boundaries of the system. For instance, the vast Persian Empire with its ample resources obviously influenced the scene.[5] Nonetheless, if the system is confined to mainland Greece or the Greek world in general, then it makes sense to talk about a bipolar system; this is certainly how contemporaries viewed the situation. According to W.R. Connor, at the beginning of the Peloponnesian War, there existed three additional players of importance in terms of the distribution of power: Thebes, Magna Graecia (the Greek colonies of southern Italy and Sicily), and Corcyra.[6] Although these players tried to exploit the conflict between Sparta and Athens to their own advantage, each ended up siding with one of the central protagonists of the conflict. Hence, the distribution of power was essentially bipolar. Nonetheless, one should always keep in mind that the relative position of Sparta and Athens vis-à-vis the other Greek states did not remotely resemble that of the United States and the Soviet Union vis-à-vis the rest of the world during the Cold War.[7]

Apart from the static analysis of power distribution within the Greek city-state system, the dynamic one, i.e. the identification of the various trends in the distribution of power, is of crucial importance as well. Thucydides' famous explanation of the cause of the Peloponnesian War is that "what made war inevitable was the growth of Athenian power and the fear which this caused in Sparta".[8] Thucydides' statement reveals that the emerging power of Athens was growing in strength at a faster rate than Sparta, the traditional hegemon in Greece. Indeed, this seems plausible, given that Athens had founded an extensive empire based on naval strength and maritime trade, whereas Sparta remained an agrarian economy.

In the previous chapter it was shown how Athens managed to create an extensive and lucrative maritime empire in the Aegean: initially, due to its naval power (and following the withdrawal of Sparta), Athens assumed leadership of the anti–Persian struggle and gradually increased control over its allies, in effect turning them into tributary states. The obvious difference in wealth that this created would eventually become apparent. Fully aware of the economic power of Athens, Pericles, while outlining the balance of power to his fellow citizens, provided them with an extensive account of the economic resources of Athens–ample resources indeed.[9] Notwithstanding this, Pericles confined his account to state funds, and did not mention the immense private wealth that was amassed in the city. With trade and allied revenues continually adding to this wealth, it was evident that Athenian power would soon reach frightening proportions. Since economic power constitutes the enabling force behind military power and especially naval power,[10] the picture that emerged for the opponents of Athens was a highly alarming one.

In view of these developments, the claim of the distinguished American historian Donald Kagan that the "Athenian power did not grow between 445 and 435"[11] is hard to understand. Kagan has been led astray by the territorial losses the Athenian Empire sustained in the last phase of the First Peloponnesian War, and by the fact that Athens did not acquire any new allies until the conclusion of the defensive alliance with Corcyra in 433 B.C. At the same time, however, he does not appear to have taken into account the continuous growth of the Athenian economic power during that period. Relative economic power is an extremely important dimension of state power.[12] Even in the absence of territorial acquisitions, changes in the economic power of states may bring about profound shifts in the balance of power over time. In fact, Thucydides has pointed out precisely this, namely that the growth of Athens' economy enabled it to more than counterbalance its recent territorial losses:

Athens [...] had in the course of time taken over the fleets of her allies (except for those of Chios and Lesbos) and had made them pay contribution of money instead. Thus the forces available to Athens alone for this war were greater than the combined forces had ever been when the alliance was still intact.[13]

Thucydides shows an incisive grasp of the link between wealth and power.[14] In this respect, he must be regarded as the originator of a long political realist tradition that paid due attention to the economic sources of national power.[15]

Athens and Sparta: the Bilateral Balance

As demonstrated, Sparta and Athens were the two strongest states of Ancient Greece and the prospects in terms of distribution of power

were clearly balanced in favour of Athens. However, what was the cor-
relation of forces between the two combatants at the time of the outbreak of the war? It seems that Athens was at worst invulnerable to
Sparta and its allies, and at best superior to them. Three elements of
Athenian power accounted for this assessment: the navy, the financial
power, and the Alliance/Empire. This was highlighted by Pericles and
acknowledged by the Spartan king Archidamus. Their statements are
of particular interest and well worth citing. Pericles, trying to persuade
the Athenians that they did not need to fear the outcome of a war
against the Peloponnesians, stated the following:

Now, as to the war and to the resources available to each side I should like you
to listen to a detailed comparison and to realise that we are not the weaker
party. The Peloponnesians cultivate their own land themselves; they have no
financial resources either as individuals or as states; then they have no experience of fighting overseas, nor of any fighting that lasts a long time, since the
wars they fight against each other are, because of their poverty, short affairs.
Such people are incapable of often manning a fleet or often sending out an
army, when that means absence from their own land, expense from their own
funds and, apart from this, when we have control of the sea. And wars are
paid of by the possession of reserves rather than by a sudden increase in taxation. [...] In a single battle the Peloponnesians and their allies could stand up
to all the rest of Hellas, but they cannot fight a war against a power unlike
themselves. [...] But this is the main point: they will be handicapped by lack of
money and delayed by the time they will have to take in procuring it. But in
war opportunity waits for no man. [...] And as for seamanship, they will find
that a difficult lesson to learn. [...] Seamanship, just like anything else, is an
art. It is not something that can be picked up and studied in one's spare time;
indeed it allows one no spare time for anything else. [...] If they invade our
country by land, we will invade theirs by sea, and it will turn out that the
destruction of a part of the Peloponnese will be worse for them than the
destruction of the whole of Attica would be for us. For they can get no more
land without fighting for it, while we have plenty of land both in the islands
and on the continent. Sea-power is of enormous importance.[16]

Pericles' speech reveals his confidence in the outcome of the war. The
economic and naval power of Athens guaranteed that it would not
lose, save through errors of its own making.[17] Peloponnesian land
power was largely inadequate against a maritime power, while lack of
economic resources would impede Peloponnesian operations.

This was no empty boasting on Pericles' part. A surprisingly similar
picture emerged on the other side of the hill. Shortly before Pericles
had made the speech cited above, in an attempt to dissuade his compa-

triots from voting in favour of war with Athens, the Spartan king
Archidamus had made an identical outline of Athenian power at the
Spartan Assembly. According to him:

When we are engaged with Peloponnesians and neighbours, the forces on both
sides are of the same type, and we can strike rapidly where we wish to strike.
With Athens it is different. Here we shall be engaged with people who live far
off, people also who have the widest experience of the sea and who are
extremely well equipped in all other directions, very wealthy both as individuals and as a state, with ships and cavalry and *hoplites* [heavy infantry], with a
population bigger than that of any other place in Hellas, and then, too, with
numbers of allies who pay tribute to them. How, then, can we irresponsibly
start a war with such a people? What have we to rely upon if we rush into it
unprepared? Our navy? It is inferior to theirs, and if we are to give proper
attention to it and build it up to their strength, that will take time. Or are we
relying on our wealth? Here we are at an even greater disadvantage: we have
no public funds, and it is no easy matter to secure contributions from private
sources. Perhaps there is ground for confidence in the superiority which we
have in heavy infantry and in actual numbers, assets which will enable us to
invade and devastate their land. Athens, however, controls plenty of land outside Attica and can import what she wants by sea. And if we try to make her
allies revolt from her, we shall have to support them with a fleet, since most of
them are on the islands. What sort of war, then, are we going to fight?[18]

The strategic deadlock is apparent in Spartan strategy. To put it
metaphorically, in a contest between a lion and a shark, the lion cannot force a decision, since it cannot reach the sources of the shark's
strength.

Thus, the net assessment of the relative balance of power indicated
that the situation was not unfavourable to Athens, to say the least. The
famous motto "we have the ships, we have the men, we have the
money too" could well have been uttered by the Athenians, twenty five
centuries before it was coined by the British jingoists.[19]

Policy Objectives

Policy Objectives and Grand Strategic Designs

Setting the political objectives is the next important step in the formulation of a grand strategy. For Athens, these objectives were simply the
maintenance of the status quo. The preserved existence of the empire
guaranteed the prosperity and power of Athens, both in absolute terms
and in comparison to the other Greek states. Moreover, the Thirty
Years' Peace of 446/5 B.C. acknowledged the equal status of Athens

and Sparta. It was perfectly satisfactory for the Athenians to be placed on an equal footing with what had traditionally been the leading Greek state.[20] This does not necessarily mean that Athens did not aim at achieving primacy in Greece. In fact, considering the fast rates of growth of the Athenian power, one may well argue that a status quo policy on behalf of Athens was the best vehicle for establishing Athenian hegemony over the Greek world. Simply put, Athens merely had to wait and allow the law of uneven growth to work in its favour.[21] The differential rates of growth would eventually produce significant shifts in the balance of power. For Athens, a particularly welcome eventual change to the territorial status quo would be the reacquisition of Megara; as we saw in Chapter Two, the possession of the Megarid conferred enormous strategic advantages to the Athenians.

In view of the above, it is clear why Sparta did not have any particular reason to be happy with the status quo. Consequently, it resorted to preventive war in order to dissolve the Athenian Empire and thus cripple Athenian power, precisely as it had unsuccessfully attempted to do thirty years earlier. Earlier on, Sparta had revealed its intentions by presenting the Athenians with an ultimatum: as war was approaching, a Spartan embassy informed the Athenians that "Sparta wants peace. Peace is still possible if you will give the Hellenes their freedom."[22] This amounted to saying that the Spartan aims were unlimited: acceptance of the Spartan ultimatum would have clearly led to the dissolution of the Athenian Empire. Since the Spartans could not hope to achieve their aims by peaceful means, they had obviously decided to launch war.

An important point emerges here. Thucydides' analysis of the Spartan motives and their relation to the outbreak of the war makes it evident that he was fully cognizant of the relation between war and politics. Obviously, for Thucydides the Peloponnesian War was an act of force on behalf of Sparta to compel Athens to comply with its will. Sparta's political objectives could not be attained by peaceful means, therefore, to use Clausewitzian terms, war came as "the continuation of policy by other means". Bernard Brodie has stated that the idea expressed in this famous dictum by Clausewitz must really be an old one.[23] It would seem that the first detailed expression of this idea is to be found in Thucydides.[24]

The grand strategies of the two competing states were shaped by their respective political objectives. Athens, the status quo power, formed a defensive grand strategy whose aim was to dissuade its opponent from attempting to change the status quo. This would be achieved by convincing the enemy that Athens was unbeatable militarily and that the state possessed ample resources to continue the struggle long after the opponent would be exhausted. In other words, Athens formulated a grand strategy of exhaustion, in which non-military dimensions such as economic strength played a crucial role.[25]

On the other hand, Sparta, the revisionist power, resorted to an offensive, more 'Clausewitzian' grand strategy, based on Spartan military might. Initially the Spartans attempted to persuade the Athenians to make concessions under the threat of military defeat (viz. compellence). Following the failure of forceful persuasion, they resorted to actual warfare attempting to secure victory through a decisive land battle.

The respective grand strategic designs of both Sparta and Athens correspond remarkably to the model types that Sir Basil Liddell Hart has named the acquisitive and the conservative states. According to Liddell Hart:

The acquisitive State, inherently unsatisfied, needs to gain victory in order to gain its object–and must therefore court greater risks in the attempt. The conservative State can achieve its object by merely inducing the aggressor to drop his attempt at conquest–by convincing him that 'the game is not worth the candle.' Its victory is, in a real sense, attained by foiling the other side's bid for victory.[26]

In other words, Athens did not have to beat Sparta in military terms. If the Spartans were made to abandon their quest to overthrow the Athenian Empire, this would signify the victory of the Athenian grand strategy. It is amazing that Liddell Hart's analysis, perceptive though it is, has in fact added nothing novel to the one produced by Thucydides twenty five centuries earlier. Apart from anticipating Liddell Hart, Thucydides may be said to operate on the same wave length as his near contemporary, Sun Tzu.[27] Simply put, instead of defeating the might of Sparta, Athens chose to foil the Spartan plan for victory–what Sun Tzu has called the highest form of strategy.[28]

To reiterate, Athens was satisfied with the status quo, whereas Sparta was bent on overthrowing it. Consequently, Athens formulated a grand strategy of exhaustion, aiming to make Sparta acknowledge the futility of trying to change the status quo, while the latter formulated a strategy of annihilation, trying to force a land battle where its powerful infantry would prove decisive.

Athenian Grand Strategy: Two Underlying Principles

An underlying principle of the Athenian grand strategy was rejection of appeasement. Pericles insisted on securing equal status between Athens and Sparta. Any unilateral Athenian concessions, no matter how trivial they might seem, would erode this status. Thus, immediately before the outbreak of the war, the Spartans stated that peace could be preserved, provided the Athenians revoked the famous Megarian Decree, which excluded the citizens of Megara from the ports of the Athenian Alliance and the Agora (marketplace) of Athens.[29] Even on this relatively minor issue, Pericles was not prepared to make unilateral concessions. For him, this Spartan request was nothing but a test of the Athenians' determination and will. If Athens conceded on that issue, then Sparta was sure to come up with further demands. As Pericles himself put it:

I am against making any concessions to the Peloponnesians. [...] It was evident before that Sparta was plotting against us, and now it is even more evident. [...] They come to us with a proclamation that we must give the Hellenes their freedom. Let none of you think that we shall be going to war for a trifle if we refuse to revoke the Megarian decree. [...] For you this trifle is both the assurance and the proof of your determination. If you give in, you will immediately be confronted with some greater demand, since they will think that you only gave way on this point through fear. But if you take a firm stand you will make it clear to them that they have to treat you properly as equals. [...] When one's equals, before resorting to arbitration, make claims on their neighbours and put those claims in the form of commands, it would still be slavish to give in to them, however big or however small such claims may be.[30]

Consequently, Pericles asked the Spartans to offer a *quid pro quo* for the revocation of the Megarian Decree, namely that they would abandon their practice of periodic expulsion of foreigners from their territory (*xenelasia*), which was hampering the trading activities of Athenians and their allies.[31] These terms were rejected by the Spartans and thus war became inevitable. Rather than submit to coercive demands, Pericles chose war.

Here we are provided with as good an analysis of the dangers of appeasement as any in modern literature. The lessons that the Western democracies had to learn painfully while dealing with Hitler in the 1930s[32] had already been understood by Thucydides. Naturally, this does not conclude the discussion about appeasement. Appeasement has negative connotations in the West because of the Munich Pact of

1938, but sometimes it can actually be a very useful instrument. The Byzantines, for example, often resorted to appeasement in order to close secondary fronts and deal with the primary threat unhindered.[33] However, when a state, especially a hegemonic power, utilises the tool of appeasement, it runs two risks. First, that its behavior may invite further demands and challenges by its adversary. Second, that it may be perceived as a sign of weakness by its own allies and thus jeopardise the hegemonic supremacy. It was precisely for these reasons that Pericles rejected appeasing the Peloponnesians.[34]

Another underlying principle of Periclean strategy was the avoidance of overextension. Pericles advised that Athens should not try to expand its dominions. During a period of competition with one's principal adversary, war with a third party ought to be avoided.[35] The fact that Pericles rejected the opportunity of further territorial aggrandisement is clear evidence that he had grasped what has now become widely accepted, namely that the collapse of great powers can be brought about by overextension.[36] Under this practice, a state sets objectives and undertakes commitments beyond the means available to it. Consequently, the costs it incurs in pursuing these objectives and sustaining these commitments are often greater than the benefits it extracts from its endeavours (e.g. a costly war in a far-off place that produces little in return) and in the long run its power diminishes.

We have examined the international situation prior to the outbreak of war, the political objectives of Athens and Sparta, and the grand strategic plans these objectives generated. Let us now turn our attention to the means employed by the grand strategy of Athens under the direction of Pericles.

The Means of the Periclean Grand Strategy

Periclean grand strategy made use of a variety of means. Apart from the traditional military means, it employed economic, diplomatic, technological, and psychological ones. The particular combination of these means (policy mix) was guided by the following principles:

a. Balance the power of the enemy.
b. Exploit competitive advantages and negate those of the enemy.
c. Deter the enemy by the denial of his success and by the skilful use of retaliation.

43

d. Erode the international power base of the enemy.

e. Shape the domestic environment of the adversary to your own benefit.

Balance the Power of the Enemy

The first aim of the Periclean grand strategy was the balancing of the power of Sparta and its allies. Balancing can be done either by utilizing power from abroad (external balancing), and/or by mobilizing and exploiting domestic resources (internal balancing).[37] External balancing is achieved primarily through alliances.[38] Athens drew upon the collective resources of its free allies, Chios, Lesbos, and Corcyra. These allies provided ships in wartime.[39] In one instance, Thucydides mentions that in the first year of the war, the expedition around the Peloponnese by an Athenian fleet consisting of 100 ships was assisted by a powerful squadron of fifty ships from Corcyra.[40]

As far as internal balancing is concerned, it has already been demonstrated that Athens was drawing support from within its empire. If the free allies provided Athens with ships, the subordinate ones or, as Thucydides put it, "cities in the tribute-paying class"[41] supported Athens financially and provided a pool of trained sailors in addition to those possessed by Athens itself.[42]

Athenian internal balancing drew upon the resources of both its imperial holdings and the state of Athens itself. Thus, the Athenians created a financial and naval reserve to be used only in extreme emergency:

> They also decided to set aside and keep intact a special fund of 1,000 talents from the money in the Acropolis. The expenses of the war were to be paid out of other funds, and the death penalty was laid down for anyone who should suggest or should put to the vote any proposal for using this money in any other way except to defend the city in the case of their enemies coming to attack them with a fleet by sea. To go with this money they set aside a special fleet of 100 triremes, the best ones of each year, with their captains. These, too, were only to be used in the same way as the money and to meet the same danger, if it should ever arise.[43]

One cannot fail to grasp the link between wealth and power, in this case naval power. The decision to create this iron reserve is significant for it suggests that the Athenians had begun mobilization for a long war and wanted to hedge against the possibility of serious depletion of their reserves.[44]

Finally, Pericles also paid attention to the ongoing training of the Athenians in maritime affairs, which provided the city with a constant number of sailors, whose mastery of their craft was superior to that of their enemies.[45]

In sum, in order to achieve its goals in wartime, balancing within the Periclean grand strategy basically consisted of the mobilization and deployment of both the Athenian wealth and manpower together with that of the free allies and the imperial subjects.[46]

Exploit your Competitive Advantages and Minimise those of the Enemy

A second principle of Pericles' grand strategy was to exploit the competitive advantage of Athens and to diminish that of Sparta. One such advantage was provided by the existence of a comprehensive urban fortification complex, namely the walls around Athens. The story of the rebuilding of these walls after the Persians withdrew and their subsequent expansion to cover the ports of Phalerum and Piraeus was mentioned in the previous chapter. These walls were to have a significant impact on relations between Athens and Sparta in general and the conduct of the Peloponnesian War in particular, by neutralizing the advantage the Spartans derived from their highly trained land forces. As Josiah Ober observed, "Pericles' strategy radically altered the use of force in Greek international relations. The physical obstacle represented by stone and brick fortifications effectively stymied the deployment of military force by human agents who lacked the technological means to overcome the obstacle."[47] Essentially, these walls made Athens a safe haven, an island, which was indeed what Pericles himself suggested:

Suppose we were an island, would we not be absolutely secure from attack? As it is we must try to think of ourselves as islanders.[48]

This brings us to the second source of Athenian competitive advantage that the Periclean grand strategy put in good use, namely the navy.[49] In essence, Pericles suggested that, instead of fighting a pitched battle with the Spartan infantry, the Athenians should use their navy for launching commando raids on enemy territory. Thus, they would make the war costlier for the Spartans without suffering serious casualties themselves. We have already seen Pericles (and Archidamus) highlighting the importance of the Athenian navy in the forthcoming war. At a later stage, Pericles gave his fellow citizens a more general account of the importance of sea power. His statement has retained its validity throughout history:

Now, what you think is that your empire consists simply of your allies: but I have something else to tell you. The world before our eyes can be divided to two parts, the land and the sea, each of which is valuable and useful to man. Of the whole of one of these parts you are in control–not only of the area at present in your power, but elsewhere too, if you want to go further. With your navy as it is today there is no power on earth–not the King of Persia nor any people under the sun–which can stop you from sailing where you wish.[50]

Interesting analogies may be drawn with later eras. For instance, one may easily argue that the maritime strategy of Athens is a direct predecessor to the similar and renowned strategy that was used many times by Great Britain to such good effect.[51] Paul Kennedy has given the following definition of naval mastery:

a situation in which a country has so developed its maritime strength that it is superior to any rival power, and that its predominance is or could be exerted far outside its home waters, with the result that it is extremely difficult for other, lesser states to undertake maritime operations or trade without at least its tacit consent.[52]

Great Britain enjoyed such a fortuitous situation from the end of the seventeenth century until the end of the First World War. Athens was certainly in such a situation from the end of the Persian Wars until the destruction of its expeditionary force at Sicily in 413 B.C. The only problem with the Athenian maritime strategy was that the financial costs were considerable.[53] A strategy that focused upon naval warfare was much more demanding upon resources than a strategy that was reliant upon the traditional methods of a land campaign. Nonetheless, Athens proved that it could well sustain the relevant cost.

Deter the Enemy by Denial of his Success and by the Skilful Use of Retaliation

The third principle of the Periclean grand strategy envisaged the use of what in modern terminology we call deterrence (see Chapter One). Athenian deterrence had two dimensions. The first was what would nowadays be referred to as deterrence by denial. The formidable walls of Athens plus the easy supply of the city by sea ensured that Athens would not be conquered, no matter how powerful Sparta and its allies were on land. In the meantime the Athenians would avoid decisive battle with the enemy, irrespective of how much damage an invasion of Attica might cause–this later became known as the 'Fabian strategy'.[54] Pericles argued that it would be suicidal for the Athenians to abandon their walled defenses and offer battle on land against the invading Peloponnesians. To begin with, the Spartans and their allies were more numerous.[55] In addition, the superior quality of the Spartan infantry was only too well known. Simply put, the Peloponnesians were invincible (or, as the Spartan defeat at Sphacteria revealed, near-invincible) on land a point that Pericles repeatedly emphasised.[56] Even if by a miracle the Athenians managed to win a land battle, the war would still not be over; the following year would once again feature a Peloponnesian invasion. If, alternatively, the outcome was the likely one of an Athenian defeat, then Athens would lose both the war and the empire at a stroke, since it would be unable to retain control of its allies. In Pericles' words:

We must abandon our land and our houses, and safeguard the sea and the city. We must not, through anger at losing land and homes, join battle with the greatly superior forces of the Peloponnesians. If we won a victory, we should still have to fight them again in just the same numbers, and if we suffered a defeat, we should at the same time lose our allies, on whom our strength depends, since they will immediately revolt if we are left with insufficient troops to send against them. What we should lament is not the loss of houses or of land, but the loss of men's lives. Men come first; the rest is the fruit of their labour.[57]

In Periclean strategy, the distinction between deterrence by denial and defense was a clear-cut one. Defense is directed against the enemy's hostile actions. Pericles rejected it and suggested instead a strategy addressing Sparta's aims–its motivation in undertaking offensive action. Defense seeks to prevent harm to one's self; denial seeks to prevent enemy gains. While these two strategies are frequently similar, they are not synonymous.[58]

With the hindsight of history, Pericles' rationale may appear sound, but one has to understand that it ran counter to the prevailing Greek ethos from Homer onwards, namely the glory of war.[59] Having the Spartans outside the walls destroying the land, and suggesting that nothing should be done about it, leaves one open to accusations of cowardice, an accusation far more potent in Ancient Greece than in our era. In this respect, the post-heroic strategy suggested by Pericles was an extremely difficult one to expound. However, Pericles stuck to his strategy, for he sincerely believed that it was the only one that could bring victory: to avoid critical battle and let time work to the detriment of the adversary. In the meantime, the Athenian navy would keep the empire together, thus enabling Athens to continue the war indefinitely, precisely as Pericles (and Archidamus) envisaged, in contrast to those in Sparta who were thinking in terms of a short war.[60]

There is an interesting psychological aspect in the deterrence by denial as encountered in Periclean grand strategy. Since the avoidance of battle implicitly consented to the destruction of the Attic mainland, it constitutes an interesting variation of the 'scorched earth policy' that is generally construed as an indication of determination to continue the struggle without sparing any sacrifices.[61]

The second dimension of Athenian deterrence, namely 'deterrence by retaliation', is a more familiar one. As Pericles had made clear, any Peloponnesian invasion of Attica would provoke reprisal raids on the Peloponnesian coast by the Athenian navy. This was of particular importance to the credibility of the Athenian deterrence, since it carried the threat of imposing costly retribution on Sparta and its allies. Such a powerful threat was lacking in the case of pure defense behind the walls. For, although such a strategy guaranteed the impregnability of Athens, it did so without inflicting any punitive costs on the invading Peloponnesians. This is precisely what Liddell Hart had in mind when he rejected static defense as a military strategy for conservative states and instead stated that "economy of force and deterrent effect are best combined in the defensive-offensive method, based on high mobility that carries the power of quick riposte."[62]

As to the retaliatory dimension of Athenian deterrence, it is interesting to note that retaliation was of relatively moderate proportions at the beginning of the war. As we will see later on, this has led to accusations of weakness and lack of strategic purpose that persist to this day. In reality, Athenian retaliation was foreboding and progressively escalating. Thus, in the second year of the war (430 B.C.), Pericles, in what was an important organizational innovation, transferred about 300 cavalry to the Peloponnese by sea on special horse-transports. "These horsemen had virtually free rein for the Spartans possessed no mounted force to impede them."[63] Even more important, that Athenian expedition featured the storming and sack of the Laconian coastal town of

Prasiae.[64] This escalation threatened the already fragile stability of Sparta's social order, since it encouraged a revolt of the restless helots. If Sparta did not comply with the Athenian desire but persisted with the war, retaliation was bound to escalate to a further point.

In this respect, the capture and fortification of Pylos and the subsequent Spartan defeat at Sphacteria in 425 B.C., far from constituting deviations from the Periclean grand strategy,[65] were in fact its logical corollary. As was demonstrated at Prasiae, Pericles was willing to attack and seize anything located on a coast, but does not seem to have been bent on permanent conquest and fortification; that could wait until later. When the progressive Athenian escalation reached that point and Pylos was seized and fortified, the Spartans were thrown out of balance and were induced to commit the blunder of sending a force to the small island of Sphacteria, opposite Pylos. This presented the Athenians with a golden opportunity that they were quick to exploit–to blockade and then capture the Spartan force. As Pericles himself had stated: "In war opportunity waits for no man."[66]

One might ask why Sparta would ever be compelled by retaliation to yield when it had not been deterred by the threat of retaliation in the first place. Pericles, however, was determined to demonstrate to the Spartans that the marginal benefits of their aggression were bound to decline over time, whereas the marginal costs of retaliation were bound to increase over time. This was clearly demonstrated by events at Prasiae, Pylos, and Sphacteria–Sparta could not defeat Athens, while continuing to hemorrhage losses and incur costs in the war. As a result, the Spartans sued for peace–a clear vindication of the Periclean strategy.[67]

Erode the International Power Base of the Enemy

Another principle of the Periclean grand strategy was the erosion of the international power base of the enemy. The primary weapon in promulgating economic warfare and intimidation was the use of the Athenian navy. The damage inflicted by its deployment was twofold; first, it inflicted damage on the Peloponnesian coast, second, it hampered the trading activities of the Peloponnesians. This was particularly damaging for such states as Corinth and Megara, which depended considerably on maritime trade.[68] Thus, the Peloponnesians were forced to cope with the means provided by the agricultural sector of their economies, in other words with financial means inferior to those possessed by Athens.[69] In addition, the international power base of Sparta was weakened by intimidating both its actual and potential allies. Among the various instances of this policy, the most famous one occurred after Pericles' death, namely the Melian Dialogue. Even neutral states that were leaning towards Sparta had to be intimidated in disproportion to what they were doing.[70]

Shape the Domestic Environment of the Adversary to your own Benefit

Finally, another principle of the Periclean grand strategy was that Athens should try to shape the domestic environment of Sparta in a way that would benefit Athenian interests. For this to happen, Athens needed to wage psychological warfare on its enemy. Pericles intended to convince the Spartans that war against Athens was futile; even though they might ravage Attica at will, it would become evident to them that they could not force a decision, while in the meantime the Peloponnesian coasts would lie at the mercy of the Athenian navy.[71] This situation would eventually bring about a shift in the domestic balance of power in Sparta; moderate leaders would emerge, who would understand that the war did not make any sense, and they would sue for peace. This was actually how the two opponents reached peace after the tenth year of the war, when King Pleistoanax, the commander of the invading force of 446 B.C. and a supporter of peace, became the principal figure in Sparta.[72] In terms of modern strategic theory, this attempt of Pericles to influence the domestic balance of power in Sparta by the controlled use of Athenian offensive forces constitutes an example of environment-shaping strategy. Such a strategy enables a state to cope with the reality that its decisions affect the political environment. Environmental shaping entails using power to help create security conditions that render it unnecessary to fight in order to protect one's interests.[73]

These were the principles that governed the policy mix of the various means (military, economic, diplomatic, technological and psychological) employed by the Periclean grand strategy in order to attain Athens' political objectives. Thus, a pretty clear outline of the Periclean grand strategy emerges. Aiming at the maintenance of the status quo, Periclean grand strategy attempted to dissuade the opponent through a strategy of exhaustion. In military terms, this grand strategy rested upon the deterrent effect that impregnable fortifications and naval commando raids would have on the enemy (see Table 3.1). It now remains for us to deal with the important dimension of legitimacy, both domestic and international.

Table 3.1: The Grand Strategies of Athens and Sparta

	Athens	*Sparta*
Political Objectives	Limited aims—maintenance of the status quo preservation of the Athenian Empire	Unlimited aims—change of the status quo dissolution of the Athenian Empire
Grand Strategy	Dissuasion by exhaustion	Persuasion by threatened or actual military annihilation
Military Strategy	Deterrence by denial and retaliation	Offense, decisive land battle

The Issue of Legitimacy

It is fundamentally important that the grand strategy of a state must be perceived to be grounded in legitimacy, both at home and abroad. The American experience in Vietnam should suffice to prove this point; the loss of domestic legitimacy exercised a crippling effect on American grand strategy. How, then, did Pericles cope with the problem of ensuring domestic legitimacy for his grand strategy?

Domestic Legitimacy

One may recall that the Periclean grand strategy was inherently unpopular. The fact that Pericles actually managed to persuade the Athenian public to adhere to an unpopular policy speaks volumes for his talent as a statesman. It is for this reason that Hans Delbrück has called Pericles one of the greatest statesmen and military leaders in history.[74] Nevertheless, even Pericles himself did not find it easy. The Athenians, who had felt that moving behind the walls and thus abandoning their property to the mercy of the enemy was difficult enough, were shattered to see this property being destroyed:

Their land was being laid waste in front of their very eyes–a thing that the young men had never seen happen and that the old men had seen only at the

51

time of the Persian invasion. Naturally enough, therefore, they felt outraged by this and wanted, especially the young, to march out and stop it.[75]

Pericles became a convenient scapegoat and a fine was imposed on him–a characteristic example of the erratic decision-making of the Athenian polity.[76] Nevertheless, the Athenians remained true to the strategy devised by Pericles and did not seriously depart from it until long after his death.[77] Therefore, to put the matter differently, domestic legitimacy is a *conditio sine qua non* for the success of a grand strategy. All strategies, all strategic designs will collapse unless there is domestic legitimacy, and this is particularly true for democracies. In this respect, Pericles' *Epitaph*, his speech in memory of those who fell during the first year of the war, deserves special attention. This speech is a tribute to the Athenian way of life, aiming to persuade the Athenians to rally round the war effort of their city.[78]

The question of domestic legitimacy also included another dimension in the Athenian grand strategy. This was the attempt to undermine the domestic power base of Sparta by efforts to foment a revolt of the helots. The raids of the Athenian navy were providing the helots with excellent opportunities to wreak havoc on their Spartan masters and the visible possibility of achieving liberation.[79]

International Legitimacy

International legitimacy can also be helpful to a cause. Obviously, under conditions of international anarchy, i.e. in the absence of a supreme authority that regulates interstate antagonism, relations between states are fundamentally conflictual.[80] Consequently, one cannot expect much good will from the international environment. Nevertheless, if the grand strategy of a state is internationally acknowledged as legitimate, this might at least spare that state some potential enemies and thus enable it to economise on its resources.

Unfortunately for Periclean Athens, things were not promising in this respect. What had begun as the Delian League, an alliance wrought to defend against the Persian threat, had turned into the Athenian Empire which, as demonstrated earlier, was primarily a source of revenue for Athens. All legitimacy had disappeared, and the coercive power of the Athenian navy was the sole factor responsible for holding the alliance together. The Athenians were well cognizant of this fact. Athenian ambassadors visiting Sparta shortly before the outbreak of the war had no trouble acknowledging that the Athenians faced "immoderate hostility from the Hellenes–especially so far as our empire is concerned".[81] Pericles himself went as far as calling the Athenian Empire a tyranny, yet a tyranny that it would be unsafe to abandon:

> You cannot continue to enjoy the privileges unless you also shoulder the burdens of empire. And do not imagine that what we are fighting for is simply the question of freedom or slavery: there is also involved the loss of our empire and the dangers arising from the hatred which we have incurred in administering it. Nor is it any longer possible for you to give up this empire. [...] Your empire is now like a tyranny: it may have been wrong to take it; it is certainly dangerous to let it go.[82]

What was weakness for Athens constituted strength for Sparta. The Spartans presented themselves as the liberators of the Greeks from Athenian oppression, thus gaining considerable support.[83]

This point concludes the examination of the Periclean grand strategy. A more or less complete picture of the relative strengths and weaknesses of each side (see Table 3.2), as well as the way in which Athens tried to exploit its strengths and minimise the impact of its weaknesses, has been gained. Let us now attempt to evaluate the Periclean grand strategy.

Table 3.2: Athens and Sparta: Relative Strengths and Weaknesses

Athenian Strengths	*Spartan Strengths*
• Naval Mastery	• Powerful Land Forces
• Economic Strength	• International Legitimacy
• Overseas Empire	• Low-Cost Strategy
• Impregnable Fortifications	
Athenian Weaknesses	*Spartan Weaknesses*
• Weak Land Forces	• Weak Naval Forces
• Lack of International Legitimacy	• Limited Financial Resources
• High-Cost Strategy	• Danger of Internal Revolt
• Erratic Decision-Making and Precarious Domestic Legitimacy	• Difficulty of Long and Distant Campaigns

Evaluation of the Periclean Grand Strategy

In Chapter One it was pointed out that grand strategy, the theory of a state about how to produce security, is empirically tested against political outcomes (viz. the survival and well-being of the state). Athens lost the Peloponnesian War. How then should the Periclean grand strategy be rated? Was it a failure? Literature is divided. We have already cited Delbrück's statement about Pericles being one of the greatest statesmen and military leaders in history. On the other hand, some analysts have called the Periclean strategy "a form of wishful thinking that failed"[84] and have stated that "as a strategist he [Pericles] was a failure, and deserves a share of the blame for Athens' great defeat".[85] Clearly, this calls for a more detailed evaluation of the Periclean grand strategy.

As explained in Chapter One, there are five criteria used for the evaluation of grand strategies, namely; external fit, relation between means and ends, efficiency, internal coherence, and durability to mistakes and mishaps. Undoubtedly the Periclean grand strategy did remarkably well according to these criteria. To start with, it fitted properly in with the international environment. The territorial and political status quo was perfectly satisfactory for Athens, while at the same time Athenian power was continually growing. Consequently, Athens had no need for an offensive strategy; after all, it had already alienated many states and there was no reason to increase its considerable list of enemies.[86] If anything, with the Aegean Sea being solidly under Athenian control, the targets of an offensive strategy could only be directed towards the mainland, and that meant dealing with the Spartan infantry. Rather than doing this, the Athenians chose a competitive strategy, a strategy where their strengths were applied over the enemy's weaknesses (e.g. naval raids directed against the delicate Spartan domestic structure). Pericles explicitly analysed the comparative strengths and weaknesses of each side (see Table 3.2) and prepared a strategy to exploit them in favour of Athens. As to the domestic political environment, the Periclean grand strategy did not run counter to any of the norms or premises of the Athenian polity per se.

The Periclean grand strategy also scored well in terms of the relation between means and ends. While the important Athenian objectives were achieved, overextension was carefully avoided; the resources of Athens were certainly considerable, but not unlimited. Pericles understood both sides of the link between economic resources and political ends: "First, not by downplaying but by accurately emphasizing the great expense at war; and second by implying that such expense was not unanticipated and that Athens had ample funds to meet it."[87]

It is obvious that under the leadership of Alcibiades the Athenians abandoned the Periclean principle of balancing means and ends in order to avoid overextension.[88] The outcome was the costly Sicilian expedition that aimed at extending Athenian control to the remote and populous lands of Sicily (and even beyond) and ended in an unmitigated disaster for Athens.[89] This expedition changed the whole course of the war and, according to Thucydides, this great departure from the Periclean grand strategy was the very reason for the Athenian defeat.[90]

Regarding the criterion of efficiency, one can see that the Periclean strategy once again performed well. First, all available means were utilised; in other words, the strategy was total. What is striking is that, although Athens was in the midst of a great war, the military element did not dominate its grand strategy. In addition to military strategy, the Athenian grand strategy featured economic strategy, diplomacy, psychological pressure, and domestic legitimacy. Second, without suffering undue casualties, the Athenians were able to beat off the challenge of the Peloponnesians (as well as some of their own allies) and retain their empire in Greece, at least until the disaster in Sicily. The destruction of Attica was insignificant in comparison. Only in financial terms were the costs appreciable. However, this was intrinsic to the capital-intensive maritime strategy that Athens had followed since the days of the Persian Wars, in contrast to the labour-intensive continental strategy of Sparta. Moreover, Athenian resources were equal to the task of sustaining the war effort.

The Periclean grand strategy also had no difficulty at all in meeting the criterion of internal coherence. All the components of this grand strategy reinforced each other and none of them restricted the influence of another. For instance, the military dimension (naval commando raids) was never allowed to interfere with the diplomatic one (tacit bargaining with the enemy).

Finally, the Periclean grand strategy proved startlingly durable to mishaps, though these mishaps were uncommonly severe. In 430 B.C. Athens was hit by a plague that raged for two years, then subsided, and then, in the winter of 427–426 B.C., flared up again for one more year. According to modern estimates, the plague wiped out one-third of the Athenian population.[91] Even though Thucydides finds it impossible to ascertain the total number of fatalities, he makes it clear that it was a major calamity.[92] A disaster of this magnitude would normally suffice to undermine any grand strategic design; indeed even coping with such an eventuality seems too much to ask of a grand strategy. Nevertheless, Periclean grand strategy proved durable enough to overcome these impediments.

A grand strategy that scores so well against these criteria can be expected to score well when put into operation, and this is indeed what happened with the Periclean grand strategy. All its components created a grand total which was victory through the exhaustion of the enemy. After ten years of war, the Spartans admitted that they had had enough, and abandoned their quest for victory. In fact, Athens could have achieved even more. According to Arther Ferrill:

In the first six years of the war (431–426) Periclean strategy had worked to Athens' advantage. To be sure, Platea had fallen to Thebes and Sparta, and Attica had been at the mercy of the Spartan army, while the plague took a heavy toll; but around Corcyra and the Corinthian Gulf Athens had held its own and inflicted losses on the Peloponnesians. [...] Athens remained strong, and the Spartans seemed unable to use their land power effectively against the naval giant.[93]

Then, in 425 B.C. there followed the astonishing Athenian success in Sphacteria. Had the Athenians been more astute in exploiting this triumph, they would have emerged victorious, since the Spartans were clearly willing to make concessions.[94] "In the first six years Periclean strategy had very nearly worked, but the Athenians refused to negotiate."[95] As if this were not enough, the Athenians suffered two serious defeats on land; at Delium in 424 B.C. against the Boeotians, and at Amphipolis in 422 B.C. against a Peloponnesian expeditionary force under the Spartan general Brasidas.[96] Nonetheless, even the Peace of Nicias in 421 B.C. can be regarded as favourable to Athens.[97] Athens retained its profitable empire and discouraged further Spartan attacks, until Alcibiades decided upon the Sicilian expedition.

Critiques of the Periclean Grand Strategy

Finally, we must examine the specific criticisms directed against the Periclean grand strategy. It has been primarily criticised on four counts:[98] first, that by rejecting even minor concessions to the Peloponnesians, Periclean grand strategy brought about war and as such it was a high-cost strategy. Second, that it was unforeseen by the enemy; hence it lacked credibility and, consequently, its deterrent value was low (i.e. it provoked war–high-cost strategy again). Third, that it was too feeble to exploit any opportunities and increase the cost the enemy had to bear (misuse of available means). Finally, that it depended on Pericles for its execution and thus was bound to be abandoned after his death (in fact, this criticism does not question the soundness of the strategy itself). Let us deal with each of these criticisms in turn.

The first criticism, namely that Pericles' rejection of appeasement (viz. refusal to revoke the Megarian Decree) brought about the Peloponnesian War,[99] brings us once again to the issue of underlying vs. proximate causes of the war (see Chapter Two). As far as this criticism is concerned, it should be noted that it is unjustified to put all of the blame on Pericles. The international situation at the time was very tense, and no one can say with confidence that the war could have been avoided, one way or another. David Baldwin presents a more balanced view:

Although Pericles' action failed to deter war, the probability of war was fairly great to begin with; and perhaps nothing he could have done would have avoided it. Given the tense and complex situation, the imposition of economic sanctions may well have been the policy option with the highest probability of success–even though it was very low. Taking into consideration the difficulty of the task, the policy alternatives available, and the complexity of the situation, it seems as plausible to say that the Peloponnesian War occurred *despite* Pericles' prudent–perhaps even ingenious–attempt to head it off via the Megarian Decree as it does to say that the decree "precipitated" the war.[100]

In addition, refusal by Sparta to give the *quid pro quo* asked for by Pericles, that it stop applying *xenelasia* to Athenians and their allies, is an indication that Pericles' assessment of the true nature of the Spartan request may have been correct. It seems that Sparta had unlimited objectives, and was essentially impossible to appease; had the Athenians backed down in the face of the Spartan demand, they would probably have faced more pressure from Sparta in the future.

With regard to the second criticism, namely that the Periclean grand strategy was unforeseen by the enemy and thus could not deter him, we have seen that the avoidance of battle, a core principle of the Periclean strategy, was in sharp contrast to the prevailing Greek ethos of the era. Donald Kagan has made much of the contrast between the prescriptions of Periclean strategy on the one hand and the predominant Greek culture on the other, arguing that this contrast made it unlikely in the eyes of the enemy that the Athenians would actually follow such a strategy. Consequently, this strategy, though reasonable, lacked credibility as a deterrent.[101]

Nevertheless, Kagan has overstated his case. To start with, Archidamus had thought it improbable that the Athenians would become "the slaves of their own land";[102] Spartan policy-makers, therefore, had no difficulty in anticipating that the Athenians would avoid battle. In addition, there had been an even more striking precedent in the past where the Athenians had behaved similarly: in 480 B.C., during the Persian invasion, not only did the Athenians avoid battle with the Persians, but in fact they abandoned their city and continued the war with their navy. It is true that the Periclean grand strategy was a difficult one to envisage let alone implement. However, this is a long way from saying that it was completely unanticipated by the enemy and therefore of limited deterrent value. Furthermore, the strategy of avoiding battle in Attica was never seriously questioned, even after the death of Pericles. Clearly, it had been endorsed by the Athenians, precisely as Archidamus had predicted.

In order to counter the third criticism, namely that the Periclean grand strategy was too feeble to exploit any opportunities and inflict additional costs on the enemy,[103] one needs to elaborate upon the deterrent dimension of the Periclean grand strategy, which, for all its importance, has often been misunderstood. Deterrence is a form of coercion that attempts to influence the enemy's behavior in a manner conducive to the interests of the coercer.[104] Coercion involves affecting the relative attractiveness of the various courses of action open to an opponent. This is precisely what the Athenians under Pericles did: they manipulated the threat of negative sanctions (retaliation) that Athens could impose on Sparta. The threat of retaliation is the threat to inflict pain unrelated to the non-desirable activity of the opponent, until the opponent complies.[105] Recall Pericles:

If they invade our country by land, we will invade theirs by sea, and it will turn out that the destruction of a part of the Peloponnese will be worse for them than the destruction of the whole of Attica would be for us.[106]

The strategy of Pericles threatened Sparta with the certain prospect of *greater pain* in the event of Spartan invasion. The infliction of this pain, however, was not a once and for all administration; instead, it was part of an ongoing bargaining process (gradual turning of the screw).

This explains Athenian relative moderation in inflicting damage during the first year of the war and its escalation thereafter.[107] In modern strategic jargon, Pericles was using a strategy of graduated escalation in inflicting pain as a bargaining tool.[108]

Obviously, badly designed, impulsive retaliation (e.g. massive raids and immediate occupation of outposts, as various critics of Pericles have suggested) might have had the exact reverse impact: moving the Spartan political leadership from a cool and rational calculation of marginal costs and benefits to impulsive conduct permeated by revanchism. As an author otherwise critical of Pericles admits:

The offensive actions were deliberately unimpressive, for they were intended only as evidence that an extended war would be damaging to the Peloponnesians. To engage in offensive actions which were more vigorous would, in fact, conflict with the plan. Offensive actions, while unable to bring about victory, might enrage the enemy.[109]

As to the fourth criticism, namely that the Periclean grand strategy depended solely on Pericles for its execution,[110] one must recall that Athenian reliance on fortifications and naval power existed long before Pericles.[111] In formulating his grand strategy, Pericles built upon past experience and took into account the geopolitical realities (structural imperatives). Consequently, it is wrong to attribute this particular element of Athenian strategy solely to his influence and thus reach the conclusion that with Pericles gone this strategy would necessarily be abandoned. In contemporary parlance, Athens' maritime strategy was a core strategy, viz. a state strategy consisting of all elements of policy that remain constant regardless of the international environment in which the state finds itself.[112]

To reiterate, the Periclean grand strategy cannot be blamed for the outbreak of the war; it was not at all unforeseen, and consequently constituted a sound strategy of deterrence; it coerced the enemy with escalating retaliation as a part of a bargaining process, and therefore it was neither weak nor lacking in strategic intent; finally, to a large extent it reflected structural imperatives that coexisted with or without the presence of Pericles.

Why Athens Lost

In evaluating the Periclean grand strategy, it might be pertinent to quote the opinion of Thucydides, who would have been well positioned to make an accurate judgment. Thucydides asserts that Athens lost the war because it abandoned the strategy devised by Pericles. He goes on to say that had Athens kept following that strategy, it could have beaten the Peloponnesians.

Pericles had said that Athens would be victorious if she bided her time and took care of her navy, if she avoided trying to add to the empire during the course of the war, and if she did nothing to risk the safety of the city itself. But his successors did the exact opposite. [...] So overwhelmingly great were the resources which Pericles had in mind at the time when he prophesied an easy victory for Athens over the Peloponnesians alone.[113]

Colin Gray has summarised the anatomy of the Athenian failure in the Peloponnesian War as follows:

For Sparta to succeed, Athens had to be weakened by plague, had to suffer irreparable losses in men and prestige in the expedition to Sicily (415–413 B.C.) and, having effected a partial recovery from these calamities, then had to commit major errors in lack of vigilance in the naval campaign for control of the Dardanelles. No less important, massive financial subsidies from Persia were required for Sparta to acquire the naval power that it needed.[114]

Persia, it must be said, did not dare subsidise Sparta's naval buildup against the powerful state of Athens before the Athenians ruined themselves by overextension in Sicily (see next chapter).

It therefore becomes evident that the Athenians lost the war only when they dramatically reversed the Periclean grand strategy that explicitly disdained further conquests. Pericles had not only outlined a theory of victory to his fellow citizens, but had also laid down the conditions under which his grand strategy was not expected to work:

I could give you many other reasons why you should feel confident in ultimate victory, if only you will make up your minds not to add to the empire while the war is in progress, and not to go out of your way to involve yourselves in new perils. What I fear is not the enemy's strategy, but our own mistakes.[115]

The fact that the Athenians chose to bring about these very conditions is not Pericles' fault.

We have seen that in Thucydides' opinion the Periclean grand strategy would have brought victory to Athens if meticulously followed. This is an important tribute to the author of this strategy, Pericles, who not only devised it, but made sure that it was followed, if less than wholeheartedly, by the Athenian public. The present study is in complete agreement with Thucydides' praise of Pericles.

4

SPARTAN GRAND STRATEGY

Introduction

As repeatedly illustrated, strategy is never conducted in a vacuum; it is always directed against one or more opponents who in turn formulate their own strategy. Consequently, no strategic analysis of the Peloponnesian War–or in fact any other war–can be complete without examining the interaction between the strategic designs of both belligerents, i.e. the 'horizontal' dimension of strategy. Therefore, it is necessary to examine not only the grand strategy of Pericles and Athens in general, but also the grand strategy of Sparta.[1] As was pointed out in the previous chapter, Sparta followed a grand strategy of annihilation whereas Athens initially, under the direction of Pericles, followed one of exhaustion. However, the Sicilian expedition (415–413 B.C.) marked Athens' turn to a grand strategy of annihilation, which it would continue until the end of the war.

The analysis in the previous chapter ended with the Peace of Nicias (421 B.C.), which represented the victory of Periclean grand strategy. In this chapter, our examination will span the whole duration of the war. Naturally, bearing in mind what has been mentioned above, we will not be confined to a static analysis of the Spartan grand strategy, but we will also analyze its constant interaction with the grand strategy of Athens.

Sparta and Athens: The Bilateral Balance of Power

The bilateral balance of power between Sparta and Athens has been extensively analyzed in the previous chapter. The case presented was that Sparta and Athens were the two most powerful states in Greece, that the power of Athens was growing faster than that of Sparta

61

(chiefly because of its more developed economic system) and that at the time of the outbreak of war, the economic power, the navy and the empire of Athens made it at worst immune to Sparta and its allies and at best superior to them. As made evident by Archidamus' speech to the Spartan Assembly, Spartan grand strategy had reached a deadlock: whereas Athenian power was growing and Athens was encroaching upon Sparta's allies,[2] undermining in this way a basic element of Spartan security, Sparta lacked the means to strike at the centre of gravity of Athenian power, namely the navy.

For Archidamus, the problem of the growth of Athenian power and the threat that this created for Spartan security could not be immediately solved. Sparta needed to redress the balance with Athens first. Apart from internal mobilization (marshalling their domestic resources), Sparta and its allies needed to resort to external balancing, namely securing allies, Greeks or Persians, that could provide the two things the Peloponnesian League lacked–navy and money:

What I do suggest is that we should not take up arms at the present moment; instead we should send to them [the Athenians] and put our grievances before them; we should not threaten war too openly, though at the same time we should make it clear that we are not going to let them have their own way. In the meantime we should be making our own preparations by winning over new allies both among Hellenes and among foreigners–from any quarter, in fact, where we can increase our naval and financial resources. No one can blame us for securing our own safety by taking foreigners as well as Greeks into our alliance when we are, as is the fact, having our position undermined by the Athenians. At the same time we must put our own affairs in order. If they pay attention to our diplomatic protests, so much the better. If they do not, then after two or three years have passed, we shall be in a much sounder position and can attack them, if we decide to do so.[3]

Unfortunately for Sparta, it was not Archidamus' counsel, but the belligerent speech of *ephor* Sthenelaidas that carried the day with the Assembly. Sthenelaidas did not counter any of Archidamus' arguments. Instead, he concentrated on the injuries that the Athenians had inflicted on the Peloponnesian League. The closing sentences of his speech are characteristic:

Therefore, Spartans, cast your votes for the honour of Sparta and for war! Do not allow the Athenians to grow still stronger! Do not entirely betray your allies! Instead let us, with the help of heaven, go forward to meet the aggressor![4]

This shows that, although both Archidamus and Sthenelaidas agreed that Athens' power was growing in relation to Sparta's, they differed in their assessment of the existing balance of power. While Archidamus considered Athens to be stronger, Sthenelaidas and, as it turned out, the majority of the Spartans, considered Sparta to be stronger.[5] This misperception was to remain evident in Spartan grand strategy for the next ten years. It seems that Sthenelaidas and his followers expected a short war, believing that a Spartan invasion of Attica would lead to a quick victory,[6] while also thinking that Sparta could wage a low-cost war without suffering much itself. Events were to prove them wrong on both counts: the destruction of Attica did not bring about the capitulation of Athens, whereas Sparta was far more vulnerable to Athenian sea power than previously thought.

Thus, the net assessment of the relative balance of power indicated that the situation was, to say the least, not unfavourable to Athens. However, the majority of Spartans thought otherwise. The enormous disparity between the (unlimited) political objectives assigned to it and the (inadequate) means available was to the serious detriment of the Spartan grand strategy.

A change in the balance of power occurred only after the destruction of the Athenian expeditionary force in Sicily in 413 B.C. At that point, apart from its traditional advantage on land, Sparta had also obtained parity at sea, whereas the Athenian Empire was collapsing. Furthermore, the Persians had started giving financial aid to Sparta.[7] The only hope for Athens was a change in Persian policy. As the Athenian states-man Pisander put it to his fellow citizens in 411 B.C.:

Now that the Peloponnesians have as many ships as we have ready to fight us at sea, now that they have more cities as their allies, and now that the King and Tissaphernes are supplying them with money, while ours is all gone, have you any hope that Athens can survive unless someone can persuade the King to change sides and come over to us?[8]

As we shall see, the Persians, far from changing policy, in fact intensi-fied their aid to the Spartans. The massive Persian support had dramati-cally tilted the balance in favour of Sparta. With the continuation of this support, Sparta's victory was, essentially, a matter of time.

Political Objectives

As mentioned in the previous chapter, under Pericles' direction, Athens had limited political objectives, merely aiming at the preservation of the status quo, in contrast to Sparta that had unlimited objectives, i.e.

the dissolution of the Athenian Empire. Nevertheless, bearing in mind the strategic culture of Sparta, resorting to a war with unlimited objectives must have been a novel experience for the Spartans. As already pointed out, Athens, the status quo power, formed a defensive grand strategy of exhaustion aiming to convince the enemy that Athens was an unbeatable military power and thus make the enemy abandon the effort of overthrowing the Athenian Empire. On the other hand, Sparta, the revisionist power, resorted to an offensive grand strategy of annihilation, based on Spartan military might. The Spartans initially attempted to achieve their policy objectives through compellence and, failing that, through actual warfare in which they attempted to secure victory through a decisive land battle.[9]

Archidamus favoured a strategy of annihilation–of complete annihilation both on land and at sea.[10] Nevertheless, he believed that Sparta lacked the means to pursue such a strategy, and therefore recommended that it make preparations and secure allies. Sthenelaidas too favoured annihilation, but, in contrast to Archidamus, he thought that Sparta *did* have the means to implement it, at least on land.[11] However, a grand strategy of this kind was highly demanding: whereas Athens had merely to make the Spartans abandon their quest for overthrowing the Athenian Empire, nothing short of a complete victory would suffice for Sparta in order to achieve its policy objectives.[12]

The political objectives of the Athenian grand strategy underwent a dramatic change in 415 B.C. when the Athenians at the instigation of Alcibiades undertook the Sicilian expedition. All of a sudden, Athens had set unlimited aims, domination of the entire Hellenic world plus the western Mediterranean. Alcibiades himself, after defecting to Sparta, gave the Spartans the following account of the Athenian war aims:

We sailed to Sicily to conquer first, if possible, the Sicilians, and after them the Hellenes in Italy; next we intended to attack the Carthaginian Empire and Carthage itself. Finally, if all or most of these plans were successful, we were going to make our assault on the Peloponnese, bringing with us all the additional Hellenic forces which we should have acquired in the west and hiring as mercenaries great numbers of native troops [...]. In addition to our existing fleet we should have built many more triremes, since Italy is rich in timber and with all of them we should have blockaded the coast of the Peloponnese, while at the same time our army would be operating on land against your cities, taking some by assault, and others by siege. In this way we hoped that the war would easily be brought to a successful conclusion and after that we should be the masters of the entire Hellenic world.[13]

As a result, Athenian grand strategy was readjusted based on the revised objectives set by policy. To achieve these objectives, Athens had to revert to a grand strategy of annihilation: crushing its enemies on the battlefield and then conquering them. In addition, Athens followed a direct grand strategic approach by turning against Syracuse, the strongest city in Sicily.

However, the Sicilian expedition ended in complete disaster for Athens (see next chapter). Its expeditionary force was totally annihilated in 413 B.C. At the same time in Greece, the Spartans had reopened hostilities and some of the Athenian allies had revolted. In its attempt first to retain what had not been lost from its empire and then to recover what had been, Athens relied on the strategy of annihilation. Since Sparta's challenge of the Athenian maritime empire had to be repelled, the Athenians were seeking decisive encounters at sea. Consequently, a war that had started as a clash between a status quo and a revisionist power employing a grand strategy of exhaustion and one of annihilation respectively, ended with both combatants pursuing unlimited objectives and employing grand strategies of annihilation. Nonetheless, the approach of both sides continued to be direct: since the navy was the enemy's chief asset, it was the navy that had to be sought and destroyed.

The Means of Spartan Grand Strategy

In the previous chapter we mentioned that the grand strategy of Athens employed a variety of means in addition to the traditional military ones. The same was true for Spartan grand strategy, although in Sparta's case the military means played a relatively greater role. There was constant interaction between the means employed by one side and those employed by the other. Using the means at one's disposal in order to achieve one's political objectives entailed to a considerable degree countering the means at the enemy's disposal. The analysis that follows will try to capture the interaction between those strategic designs, i.e. the horizontal dimension of strategy.

Spartan grand strategy did not presuppose the actual outbreak of hostilities; the Spartans would have been perfectly happy if they could have achieved their objectives by the mere threat of war. Archidamus, especially, had a masterly understanding of the workings of coercive diplomacy and consistently tried to achieve Spartan objectives through the threat of force, holding the actual use of force in reserve. As he urged his fellow citizens:

You must think of their land [the Athenians'] as though it was a hostage in your possession, and all the more valuable the better it is looked after. You should spare it up to the last possible moment, and avoid driving them to a state of desperation in which you will find them much harder to deal with.[14]

Spartan coercive diplomacy featured the issuing of a series of demands to the Athenians. The revocation of the Megarian Decree was one of these, whereas the final Spartan ultimatum asking the Athenians to "give the Hellenes their freedom" was nothing but a blunt demand for the dissolution of the Athenian Empire.

What made the Spartans so confident that they could achieve their aims through ultimata? As already mentioned, the majority of Spartans believed that they were holding a trump card, namely that of their ability, through their superiority in land forces, to invade Attica at will. This ability entailed two potential evils for Athens. The first was a crushing defeat in a major land battle, were the Athenians to take the customary step of marching to oppose the invading Peloponnesians. The second was the devastation of Attica. Spartan conventional wisdom had it that these two threats would be enough to cow the Athenians into submission. In fact, as was seen in Chapter Two, there had been a precedent in the First Peloponnesian War, when a similar advance of a Peloponnesian army to Attica in 446 B.C. had quickly made the Athenians sue for peace.[15]

The aforementioned incident and the lessons the Spartans drew from it are extremely interesting. To start with, it illustrates that the past behavior of a state determines to a very great extent the other states' expectations about its future behavior. Thus, the majority of the Spartans expected that the Athenians would be cowed by the threat of a Peloponnesian invasion of Attica, in exactly the same way as they had been previously. This clearly shows how important it is for a state to possess a 'good face', namely to have a reputation for displaying determination and behaving uncompromisingly over any issue of vital importance.[16] It is precisely in a failure to retain such a reputation that we can trace the greatest danger of appeasement. If the adversaries get accustomed to securing concessions from our side, they will not believe that at some point we will be determined not to back down and such a miscalculation may result in war.[17] It is highly probable that Sthenelaidas and the majority of the Spartans made this error of judgment.

The flawed analysis of the Spartans also illustrates the difficulty of extracting 'lessons from the past'. It is true that in 446 B.C. Athens sought a compromise in light of the Peloponnesian invasion, but the international situation in 432 B.C. was different. In 446 B.C. Athens had suffered a serious military defeat in Boeotia, had lost Megara and was faced with a revolt in Euboea. Athens' attempt to create a land empire on the Greek mainland had failed and the compromise reached in 446–445 acknowledged the fact that the Athenian Empire would from then on be exclusively confined to the Aegean.[18] In 432 B.C. however, Athens had no reason at all to back down, since its imperial territories were immune to Spartan land power. This important change of the situation was overlooked by the majority of the Spartans.

Consequently, as shown in the previous chapter, Pericles, rejecting appeasement, did not submit to the Spartan demands and thus did not allow the Spartans to gain any advantage from their powerful land forces. No such advantage was to be gained in wartime either, since the walls of Athens completely neutralised the Peloponnesian infantry, and the Athenians did not come out to offer battle. At the same time, Athens was drawing freely upon the resources of the empire and the rest of its allies, while continually escalating its reprisals against Sparta, culminating in the incidents of Pylos, Sphacteria and Cythera. As a result, Sparta sued for peace.

This makes it evident that the Spartan compellent military strategy could only work in peacetime, i.e. by threatening devastation of Attica and thus cowing the Athenians into submission without resorting to actual hostilities. If the Athenians chose to disregard the Spartan compellent threat, then the execution of that threat, although undoubtedly damaging to the Athenians, could not bring about victory in war. In other words, the Spartan military strategy constitutes another example of a military strategy suitable for compellence in peacetime but unsuitable for victory in war (see Chapter One).

The adoption of such a strategy does not mean that Sparta had merely stood and watched the Athenian naval and financial power increasing. Sparta kept conscientiously trying to thwart the effective employment of these means possessed by Athens. One may recall that Archidamus advised the Spartans that they needed to restore the balance of power with Athens before attempting to go to war by seeking allies that could provide the Peloponnesians with money and a navy. He also pointed out that the Peloponnesians would have to tap into their own resources as well, but that alone would be inadequate.[19] Archidamus had just provided the universal theory of victory over a maritime power: creating an economic unit that can afford to build a navy equal or superior to that of this power.[20]

However, the premature start of the war by Sparta rendered that plan unlikely to succeed. Simply put, Sparta's chances at sea were not rated particularly highly; consequently, few third parties were prepared to risk their naval and financial assets by backing a Peloponnesian navy. For instance, the Spartans tried to secure naval and financial aid from the Greek colonies in southern Italy and Sicily.[21] No help came from that quarter.[22] The Persians, who alone could tilt the balance, were also unhelpful.[23] Even worse, the Persians concluded a treaty of friendship with Athens in 424–423 B.C. This treaty acknowledged the bilateral status quo as it stood following the Peace of Callias. The Athenians, true to the Periclean grand strategy, avoided war with a third party while the Peloponnesian War was raging. At the same time, the recently established Persian King Darius II had more pressing problems at home, where he faced a series of revolts, and thus had no taste for hostilities with an evidently unbeatable Athens.[24] Only rebel subjects of the Athenian Empire were willing to provide resources for the Peloponnesian navy.[25] Clearly, Sparta's attempt to match Athens' sources of strength in terms of naval strength and financial wealth, had failed.

However, this was not the only way that Sparta used the various means at its disposal. A central element of Spartan grand strategy was to try and make the war as costly as possible for the Athenians. In the previous chapter it was pointed out that the Athenian maritime strategy cost a lot in terms of finances. In contrast, the Peloponnesian land forces were relatively cheap to maintain. Spartan society being continually prepared for war, actual warfare made but little difference.[26] For the rest of the Peloponnesian allies, sending their armed contingents to an excursion in Attica for some two to six weeks a year, also implied little cost.[27]

The aim, however, was to increase the cost Athens had to incur. This attempt had three dimensions: a) destruction of Attica; b) dissolution of the Athenian Empire; c) exploitation of every secondary front opened by the Athenians. The destruction of the Attic land, apart from the immediate financial cost, would also inflict some social cost to the Athenians; the whole social fabric of Athens would be upset, as the farmers and the social strata associated with the land would be displaced and forced to seek refuge behind the walls.[28]

The second dimension of Sparta's cost-raising strategy was the attempt to cause the dissolution of the Athenian Empire. This would be done through either encouraging defection or aiding revolts of the Athenian allies. The Spartans had been working towards this long before the outbreak of the war.[29]

The revolt of Mytilene, an island allied to Athens, in 428–427 B.C. provides an excellent example of Sparta's attempt to raise the cost of war for Athens and exploit the situation. After the Mytilenians revolted, the Spartans prepared to attack Athens both by land and by sea, whilst also preparing a fleet to help the rebels. They obviously believed that the Athenians could not simultaneously sustain the blockade of Mytilene, the costly siege of the city of Potidaea, the raids on the Peloponnesian coast, and at the same time be able to take care of the defense of their city. According to Thucydides:

> The Athenians were aware that these [Sparta's] preparations were being made on the theory that they themselves were weak, and wished to make it clear that the theory was a mistaken one and that they could easily beat off any attack from the Peloponnesian fleet without recalling their own fleet from Lesbos. They therefore manned 100 ships with their own citizens (excluding the knights and the Pentacosiomedimni) and with their resident aliens, sailed out to the Isthmus, where they made a demonstration of their power and carried out landings just as they pleased on the Peloponnesian coast.[30]

Obviously, Athens' resources were yet to be depleted. Nevertheless, a Peloponnesian fleet did eventually sail for Mytilene. Although the island had capitulated before the fleet arrived, there were still plenty of opportunities either to recapture it or to spread revolt all around the Ionian coast. However, Alcidas, the Spartan commander of the fleet, must have been extremely ill-at-ease at sea and declined to exploit these opportunities.[31] Nonetheless, the message was obvious: Sparta was keen on undermining the Athenian Empire.

A much more vigorous attempt at this was undertaken by the Spartans in 424 B.C., when they sent a force under the valiant general Brasidas to Macedonia and Thrace. Brasidas, using a blend of military prowess and diplomatic skill, proceeded to dismantle the Athenian Empire in that area. The Spartans embarked upon this horizontal escalation of the war in order to create a diversion that would make the Athenians more amenable to peace proposals. Not only was this successful, but it also created the preconditions for the eventual ousting of the Athenians from Macedonia and Thrace.[32]

Finally, the third dimension of the Spartan cost-raising strategy was the exploitation of every secondary front the Athenians had opened. True to the adventurous and sometimes reckless spirit that their political organization promoted, the Athenians were eager to exploit opportunities, actual or perceived, in various places. However, wherever the Athenians appeared, the Spartans would soon follow; they would simply not let the Athenians claim easy gains.[33]

The greatest of these Athenian ventures was the expedition in Sicily. In this expedition Athens was using its financial and naval power not only to deter the enemy as it had been doing until that point, but also to expand territorially. This expedition also involved, for the first and last time during the Peloponnesian War, a major Athenian commitment of land forces.

Sparta's attempt to counter this aggressive employment of Athenian means did not take long. The Spartans once again resumed their efforts to make the war costlier for the Athenians, albeit in a more systematic fashion. Thus, instead of periodically invading Attica, they established a permanent garrison there by fortifying Decelea in 413 B.C. This had disastrous consequences for Athens.

> Ever since Decelea had been first fortified [...] Athens had suffered a great deal. Indeed, the occupation of Decelea, resulting, as it did, in so much devastation of property and loss of manpower, was one of the chief reasons for the decline of Athenian power. The previous invasions had not lasted for long and had not prevented the Athenians from enjoying the use of their land for the rest of the time; now, however, the enemy were on top of them throughout the year; sometimes there were extra troops sent in to invade the country; sometimes it was only the normal garrison overrunning the land and making raids to secure supplies; and the Spartan King Agis was there in person, treating the whole operation as a major campaign. The Athenians therefore suffered great losses. They were deprived of the whole of their country; more than 20,000 slaves, the majority of whom were skilled workmen, deserted, and all the sheep and farm animals were lost. [...] Then the supplies of food from Euboea, which previously had been brought in by the quicker route overland from Oropus through Decelea, now, at great expense, had to go by sea round Sunium. Every single thing that the city needed had to be imported, so that instead of a city it became a fortress.[34]

A frequently asked question is why it took the Spartans so long to establish a permanent fort in Attica. The fortification of Decelea is often attributed solely to the advice of Alcibiades,[35] whereas some scholars go so far as to claim that this delay in the creation of a permanent fort proves that Sparta did not have a strategy during the Peloponnesian War.[36] We consider both these claims to be wrong. The idea of establishing a permanent fort in Attica pre-existed in Spartan strategy. The Corinthians had mentioned it in their speech at the Assembly of the Peloponnesian League in 432 B.C., that is, before the outbreak of hostilities. Moreover, the Spartans during the negotiations that led to the Peace of Nicias threatened the Athenians with the creation of a permanent fort in their territory.[37] The Spartans did not embark upon this scheme earlier simply because they had not felt the need for it. As mentioned, the majority of them believed that the war would be short. In contrast to the annual invasions that lasted only a few weeks, the establishment of a fort in Athens and its manning on a permanent footing was an action entailing serious costs. The commitment of a substantial part of their workforce had important consequences for the economies of the Peloponnesian states (with the exception of Sparta), whereas the logistic support of a multitudinous army permanently stationed on enemy territory was impossible with the means of fifth century B.C. It was precisely for this reason that the Peloponnesians were forced to "overrun the land and make raids to secure supplies." The fortification of Decelea was a highly costly measure, suitable for a long war; since the majority of Spartans expected the war to be short, they did not initially feel the need to undertake it.[38]

Furthermore, the Spartans counterbalanced the Athenians in Sicily by offering aid to the city of Syracuse, Athens' chief enemy on the island. According to Thucydides, this aid was instrumental in preventing Athenian victory and allowing Syracuse to recover from its initial reverses.[39] From then on, the Athenians were forced to conduct a strategy of 'two-and-a-half wars'; one war against Syracuse, another against Sparta, plus a possible allied revolt. As a result, they were soon faced with spiraling financial costs.[40]

The disaster in Sicily put an end to Athenian ventures and, consequently, to Spartan countermoves. However, the other two dimensions of Sparta's cost-raising strategy were working at full force. Decelea was depleting Athenian strength, while the empire was all but liquidated. Athens had reached the limit of its resources; it only had to sustain a single great defeat at sea for the final collapse to come.

However, that was not all. The Athenian disaster in Sicily enabled the Spartans to put in practice the Archidamian theory of victory that called for securing allies who could help them match Athenian naval and economic strength. All of a sudden, everybody rushed to help Sparta.[41]

Ships and money were finally forthcoming. The Peloponnesian League embarked on an ambitious shipbuilding program; a powerful contingent of fifty-five ships came from Sicily to assist the Peloponnesians, while the Spartans forcibly collected money from various states of Central Greece.[42]

The real coup though was Persia. The Spartans entered into profitable agreements with the Persian satraps Tissaphernes and Pharnabazus. Although the relationship with them, especially Tissaphernes, was not strewn with roses, it marked an important turning point in the war.[43] Finally, in 407 B.C. the Spartans found a staunch ally in the Persian court, i.e. Cyrus, son of the Persian king, who was given an extensive command in Asia Minor.[44] Persian money started flowing freely, enabling Sparta to make up for various naval reverses.[45] Archidamus' scheme was, after all, implemented, and the battle of Aegospotami settled the issue.

The Athenians did try to hang onto their empire after the defeat in Sicily, by rebuilding a fleet and reducing public expenses.[46] In addition to these traditional means of Athenian grand strategy they also utilised diplomacy, attempting to win the Persians over to their side.[47] Thucydides points out that both sides tried to enlist Persian support, even before the outbreak of the hostilities.[48] However, although initially the Persians were willing to reach a compromise with the Athenians (viz. the Treaty of Epilycus), following the Sicilian expedition a Persian alliance could be secured–either by Sparta or by Athens–only at the price of abandoning the Greek cities of Asia Minor to Persian control. Since most of these cities were part of the Athenian Empire, it was easier for Sparta and more difficult for Athens to pay this price. Athenian and Persian interests were clearly conflicting and, as a result, Athens' attempt to coax the Persians was doomed. The continuation of Persian support for Sparta ensured that ultimately Athens could not avoid defeat.

Here we conclude the examination of the means utilised by the two competing grand strategies. One realises that the employment of the various means was not a static process set in stone within one's grand strategy. Interaction with the opponent was continuous, influencing and shaping the means employed.

The Issue of Legitimacy

Both Athens and Sparta tried to ensure the legitimacy of their grand strategies. Interestingly enough, the horizontal dimension of strategy is evident here as well. Once again, there was continuous interaction between the two opponents, each of them trying to ensure the legitimacy of their own grand strategy while undermining that of the opponent's. International legitimacy played a central role in Sparta's grand strategy during the Peloponnesian War. It has already been demonstrated that the one-time allies of Athens had become tributary states and were looking forward to an opportunity to revolt. Athens' considerable weakness, as far as international legitimacy was concerned, constituted one of the advantages of Spartan grand strategy. Sparta had built a reputation of being an enemy of tyranny and had often overthrown tyrants of Greek cities, Athens included.[49] In addition, Sparta had been the leader of the Greeks against the Persians during the crucial, defensive phase of the Persian Wars. Consequently, at the outbreak of the Peloponnesian War it was easy for the Spartans to present themselves as the liberators of the Greeks from Athenian oppression, thus gaining widespread support. According to Thucydides:

> People's feelings were very much on the side of the Spartans, especially as they proclaimed that their aim was the liberation of Hellas. States and individuals alike were enthusiastic to support them in every possible way, both in speech and action.[50]

One may recall that the Spartans had presented the Athenians with an ultimatum demanding that they give the Hellenes their freedom. Apart from a statement revealing Sparta's unlimited aims, this was also a shrewd propaganda ploy; Sparta had just gone on record demanding the liberation of Hellas and, most importantly, was willing to fight for that cause. This was a ploy the Spartans would skillfully use throughout the war. Brasidas, for instance, during his brilliant campaign in northern Greece, repeatedly emphasised his role as a liberator; this, coupled with his just and moderate behavior, created a most favourable attitude towards Sparta in that area.

> The chief factor in creating a pro-Spartan feeling among the allies of Athens was the gallantry of Brasidas and the wisdom which he showed at this time—qualities which some knew from experience of them and others assumed because they had been told of them. He was the first [Spartan] to be sent out in this way, and by the excellent reputation which he won for himself on all sides he left behind a rooted conviction that the rest also were like him.[51]

Besides exploiting the lack of international legitimacy of the Athenian grand strategy, Sparta also tried to undermine Athens' domestic legitimacy. Apart from (or even in contrast to) the direct approach favoured by Archidamus, namely that of matching Athenian financial and naval strength, the Spartans also adopted an indirect approach to further their political objectives. Ravaging Attica constituted this indirect approach, which was aimed–apart from the economic and social cost that has already been mentioned–primarily against Athenian morale. Archidamus, showing a remarkable knowledge of the domestic structure of the enemy, tried during his expedition in Attica to exploit the internal divisions of the Athenians so as to undermine the internal legitimacy of the Athenian grand strategy.[52] His conduct during the first invasion is characteristic:

They say that Archidamus had a planned policy in remaining at Acharnae with his army all ready for battle, and not on this invasion descending into the plain. [...] When they [the Athenians] had made no move against him at Eleusis or in the Thriasian Plain, he wanted to see whether they would come out against him if he made a camp at Acharnae. Acharnae itself seemed to him a good position for a camp, and at the same time he thought it likely that the Acharnians, who, with their 3,000 *hoplites*, were an important element in the state, would not allow their own property to be destroyed, but would force all the others as well to come out and fight for it. If, on the other hand, the Athenians did not come out and fight during this invasion, the Peloponnesians would in future invasions have all the more confidence in laying waste the plain and advancing right up to the walls of Athens. By that time the Acharnians would have lost their own property and would be much less willing to risk their lives for the property of other people; *consequently there would be a lack of unity in the counsels of Athens*. This was the policy of Archidamus which accounted for his remaining at Acharnae.[53]

The blow to Athenian morale was tremendous. Given the erratic decision-making of the democratic Athenian polity, where everything depended on the shifting attitudes in the *Ecclesia*, the indirect approach of the Spartans might indeed have been successful. In fact, Thucydides mentions that after the second Peloponnesian invasion and the total devastation of Attica, the Athenians sent ambassadors to Sparta to sue for peace. Spartan demands must have been excessive, or so they must have appeared to the Athenians, because the ambassadors did not achieve anything.[54]

However, Pericles did manage to persuade the Athenian public to stand by the unpopular strategy of withdrawing behind the walls. The Athenians remained true to this strategy and neither attempted to offer battle to the Peloponnesians[55] nor sued for peace again. Moreover, as shown in the previous chapter, Pericles counterattacked and tried to shape the domestic environment of Sparta in a way compatible with the Athenian interests: if the Spartans could be convinced that war against Athens was futile, the grand strategy that prescribed war with Athens would lose its domestic legitimacy and moderate leaders would emerge. This was in fact the way the two opponents reached peace after the tenth year of the war, when Pleistoanax became the key figure in Sparta.[56]

The two opponents, apart from attempting to shape each other's domestic environments to serve their own interests, also tried to exploit the divisions that existed between democrats and oligarchs in most Greek cities.[57] However, Sparta was in the unique position of being able to exploit such divisions in Athens itself, while Athens enjoyed no similar opportunity.[58] The Spartans tried to capitalise on the oligarchic sentiments of some prominent circles in Athens. When an oligarchic coup took place in Athens in 411 B.C. the Athenian oligarchs tried to reach an agreement with Sparta, and it is even possible that they might have conspired to lead the Peloponnesian army into the city.[59] This internal strife aggravated an already difficult strategic situation and, according to Thucydides, drove the final nail into Athens' coffin.[60]

To summarise, Sparta formulated a grand strategy of annihilation,[61] aiming at the destruction of the Athenian power and the dissolution of the Athenian Empire. The threat of a decisive land battle was central to the Spartan grand strategy, while at the same time there was a continuous effort to make the war as costly as possible for Athens. Great importance was placed on international legitimacy, with Sparta appearing as the liberator of the Greeks from Athenian oppression, while at the same time the Spartans attempted to undermine the domestic legitimacy of the enemy's grand strategy. Finally, diplomacy played a decisive role enabling Sparta to conclude an alliance with the Persians and thus balance the naval and financial power of Athens. Although the military dimension was clearly central to the Spartan grand strategy, none of the other dimensions were ignored. What remains to do is examine how this grand strategy actually worked in practice.

Athenian and Spartan Grand Strategies: Results

An evaluation of the Spartan grand strategy during the first phase of the Peloponnesian War, the so-called Archidamian War (431–421 B.C.), would reveal glaring weaknesses. We have repeatedly pointed out that, as far as the relation between means and ends was concerned, the Spartan grand strategy was highly problematic: the ends pursued were unattainable with the means at hand. Additionally, there was remarkable inefficiency in the use of the available resources. The Spartans neglected establishing a permanent fort in Attica, resorting to the comparatively ineffectual annual invasions instead, while their attempts to stir trouble within the Athenian Empire were either belated (Brasidas' expedition) or half-hearted (Alcidas' Mytilenean adventure). Finally, the mistake/mishap at Sphacteria was enough to deliver a crushing blow to Spartan grand strategy.

However, turning to its positive elements, the Spartan grand strategy possessed internal coherence, and performed well in terms of the external fit criterion: since Sparta could not conceivably be content with the status quo, it would sooner or later have to resort to compellence and, failing that, preventive war. In fact, the difference between the policy recommendations of Sthenelaidas and Archidamus was specifically in the timing of the preventive war. The Spartan grand strategy also fitted well with Sparta's domestic political environment; the idea of preventive war may nowadays be ethically unacceptable in quite a few countries,[62] but fifth-century-B.C. Spartans found nothing wrong with it.[63] Be that as it may, the positive aspects of the Spartan grand strategy were unable to salvage it; its weaknesses were so prominent, that it was bound to fail.

This was indeed what happened. The Spartans did invade Attica and wreak havoc, but the Athenians did not submit. In the meantime, Athenian retaliation progressively escalated, culminating in the events of Pylos, Sphacteria, and then Cythera. These events were enough to throw the conservative Spartan leadership off balance, make it abandon its bid for victory, and try to obtain peace at almost any cost. By turning against their primary opponent, the Athenians achieved decisive results. However, as was pointed out in the previous chapter, the Athenians misused their successes and refused to negotiate, thus missing the chance to extract substantial profits.

The Athenian refusal to negotiate made the Spartans embark upon two ploys they had not felt the need to use up to that point: a) the attempt to dismantle the Athenian Empire in northern Greece (viz. Brasidas' expedition); and b) the threat to establish a fort in Attica.[64] These developments did temper the Athenian attitude and bring about peace, albeit a favourable one to Athens.[65] The Spartans failed to achieve their war aim of overthrowing the status quo, did not dare resume aggression against Athens, and by and large ignored the grievances of their allies.[66] Ten years of futile war, accompanied by terrible setbacks both in terms of morale and material losses was the price Sparta paid for the mismatch between means and ends in its grand strategy.

During the Peace of Nicias (421–415 B.C.) the most important development was the re-emergence of Argos as a player in the international arena after the expiration in 421 B.C. of the Thirty Years' Treaty with Sparta. According to Thucydides, "Argos was very well off in every direction, having taken no part in the Attic war, indeed having profited greatly from her position of neutrality."[67] Since Sparta had been forced to ignore the grievances of its allies during the conclusion of peace with Athens, a great number of these allies defected and sought security through an alliance with the Argives. Obviously, Argive power was on the rise. Moreover, Athens seized the opportunity to develop a 'continental strategy' by aiding Argos and its allies against Sparta. This represented an increase in the efficiency of the Athenian grand strategy; Sparta could be harmed with limited impact on Athenian resources.

All of a sudden the situation became critical for the Spartans, who found themselves in danger of losing control of the Peloponnese. To counter this threat, they once again resorted to the combination of the strategy of annihilation and direct approach. In a truly Napoleonic/Clausewitzian fashion, Sparta crushed the Argive army in the Battle of Mantinea in 418 B.C., regaining its pre-eminence in the Peloponnese.

By this one action they [the Spartans] did away with all the reproaches that had been levelled against them by the Hellenes at this time, whether for cowardice, because of the disaster in the island, or for incompetence and lack of resolution on other occasions. It was now thought that, though they might have been cast down by fortune, they were still in their own selves the same as they always had been.[68]

The Battle of Mantinea provides us with the opportunity to further elaborate on the concept of the decisive battle, which occupies a central position in the Napoleonic/Clausewitzian concept of war. It has been persuasively argued that this concept has its origins in Ancient Greece. An offensive campaign in Ancient Greece, in order to cause the greatest possible damage to the enemy, had to be conducted during the limited period of the year when the wheat crops were vulnerable to arson. This, combined with the fact that the armies of the Greek city-states consisted of farmers that would soon have to return to their fields, made the Ancient Greeks seek a quick settlement of the issue in a single, decisive battle.[69] Probably the most important of the decisive battles of the Ancient Greeks was the Battle of Plataea, already discussed in Chapter One.

However, one great problem with battles of this kind is that their outcome is often determined by minor details or unforeseen developments, thus exponentially increasing the risk incurred by those who resort to them.[70] Hence, many of history's decisive battles could have had different outcomes from the actual ones.[71] This could have happened in Mantinea, provided the Athenians and the Eleans had intervened at the right moment on the Argives' side. In general, decisive battles are 'high-risk ventures'.[72]

The year 415 B.C. proved to be the turning point of the war, since Athens embarked on an attempt to conquer Sicily. The Spartans were quick to perceive this window of opportunity; it was clear to them that Athens had overextended.[73] Consequently, they abandoned their earlier caution and renewed hostilities in Greece while sending aid to Athens' enemies in Sicily. These actions contributed to a great extent to the Athenian disaster in Sicily, which changed the whole course of the war. Sparta shown its ability to exploit the enemy's mistakes.

An evaluation of the Spartan grand strategy during the final phase of the war, the so-called Decelean War (413–404 B.C.), shows that the Spartans had learned their lesson. Without doubt the new grand strategic design satisfied the external fit criterion, as indeed the previous one had done. However, marked improvements can be noted regarding the relation between means and ends. It was clear that after Sicily the balance of power had shifted. This new balance made it possible for the Spartans to successfully pursue their initial aim of overthrowing the status quo.[74] Now, for the first time, the means at their disposal matched their policy objectives. It is interesting to note that the final phase of the war was chiefly naval, conducted in the eastern Aegean. In other words, the Spartans were now capable of challenging Athens in its own element and striking at the centre of Athenian power, namely its navy. Thus, the indecisive clash between the 'lion' and the 'shark', turned into a clash between two 'sharks', where decisive results could be obtained.

In addition, the Spartans came to display ruthless efficiency in using their assets. The fortification of Decelea showed that this time they meant business, while their very willingness to turn against the Athenian navy, made it evident that they would not squander their resources in 'sideshows'.

A particular problem that arose in the Spartan grand strategy was that there was a fundamental incoherence between Sparta's proclaimed role as liberator of Greece and the Persian alliance, which effectively meant abandonment of the Greeks of Asia Minor to Persian control. This could and did lead to friction between the Spartans and the Asian Minor Greeks, but the Spartans somehow managed to keep the issue subdued until the end of the war.[75]

Finally Spartan grand strategy displayed remarkable durability to mistakes/mishaps. The Peloponnesian navy sustained severe defeats at Cyzicus (410 B.C.) and Arginusae (406 B.C.)–actually, at Cyzicus it was completely annihilated.[76] However, Persian aid enabled the Spartans to make good these losses. Consequently, the situation augured well for Sparta.

The Athenians, on their own part, immediately understood that they had to cut down on spending, maintain a decent navy, and secure the allegiance of their allies.[77] In all this they did quite well. Thus, the Athenian post-Sicily grand strategy performed well in terms of efficiency. It also fitted well with the highly threatening international political environment, was not contrary to the domestic one, while at the same time being internally coherent. As a result, though the greater part of the empire had gone for good, Athens managed to preserve some important places like Samos and Euboea, while inflicting severe defeats on the Peloponnesian navy at Cyzicus and Arginusae.

These naval battles provide an illuminating insight on the interaction between the various levels of strategy. Although the situation at the levels of grand and military strategy was clearly favourable to Sparta, nevertheless the Spartans could not achieve their objectives due to persistent failure at lower levels. This becomes even more striking if one considers that the Peloponnesian navy had come to enjoy an advantage at the *tactical* level. High pay, provided by Persian funds, had attracted the best seamen to the Peloponnesian navy, while the Athenians, having lost the elite of their naval personnel in Sicily, were increasingly dependent on raw recruits. Therefore, the Peloponnesian ships "were sailing better" than the Athenian ones.[78] Nevertheless, until the arrival of Lysander, the Spartan admirals were plainly incompetent in the handling of fleets. Thus, ineptitude at the operational level blunted both grand strategic dexterity and tactical excellence.

What the Spartan admirals could not achieve, the Athenian strategic culture handed over to Sparta on a silver plate. It seems that, in spite of the difficult strategic situation, the Athenian aims were once again unlimited. This is evident since Athens twice rejected Spartan peace proposals. The story of these proposals is highly interesting. They came after Cyzicus and Arginusae respectively. Both called for recognition of the status quo as it stood at the time, i.e. Athenian recognition of the losses their empire had sustained, and abandonment of the forts each combatant had on the other's territory, namely Pylos and Decelea.[79] In fact, at the time of the second peace proposal the Athenians had abandoned their fort in Pylos; in other words, the Spartans were unilaterally willing to abandon Decelea, something that is highly indicative of the conservatism of the Spartan political leadership. In the same vein, Athens' rejection of the Spartan proposals speaks volumes about Athenian adventurism.

Actually, as far as Athens was concerned, everything was hanging by a thread; one major defeat of the Athenian navy would spell the end. In other words, Athenian grand strategy had extremely low durability to mistakes/mishaps. The day of reckoning came when the Spartan admiral Lysander captured the Athenian fleet at Aegospotami in 405 B.C.[80] Athens was now blockaded by sea as well as by land. It capitulated the following year, signifying the final triumph of Spartan grand strategy.

The terms imposed on Athens were relatively generous: the long walls and the Piraeus fortifications would be destroyed, Athens would retain no more than twelve ships, receive back the oligarchic fugitives and join the Peloponnesian League. Interestingly enough, despite Corinthian and Theban demands for the total destruction of Athens, the Spartans did nothing of the sort. Clearly, with the Athenian threat eliminated, Athens could be a useful tool in Spartan hands for manipulating the balance of power in Greece.[81]

THUCYDIDES AND STRATEGY IN PERSPECTIVE

Introduction

In the current chapter, we shall proceed to review the contribution made by Thucydides to the study of strategy and we shall examine the conclusions that can be drawn from his analysis and their possible relevance today. In addition, we will trace how some key strategic concepts that were first analyzed by Thucydides have developed through history and how they are likely to endure into the future. We open the chapter with an examination of some general conclusions and then we will proceed to explore how the analysis of Thucydides can shed light on the determinants of a grand strategy. We will then explore the concepts of the strategy of annihilation and exhaustion, and finally examine the enduring theme of underestimating the enemy.

Athenian and Spartan Grand Strategies: Conclusions

Thucydides asserts that the Athenians lost a war they could have easily won, since the balance of power was in their favour.[1] Obviously, therefore, Athens courted defeat by making some flawed strategic choices. On the contrary, Sparta, despite the initial unfavourable balance of power, managed to achieve total victory by eventually choosing a strategy that maximised its advantages and minimised those of its opponent. Thus, the choice of strategy may make the difference between victory and defeat.[2]

The text of Thucydides contains the first detailed presentation of a theory of grand strategy. This has been acknowledged, but only insofar

as the Periclean grand strategy is concerned. In effect, Pericles is cred-
ited with the first detailed grand strategic plan in history, and Thucydides with the presentation of this plan.[3] However, this only tells half
of the story. Thucydides did not present only one, but two detailed
grand strategic designs that clashed with each other. Athens was not
alone in having formulated a grand strategy; Sparta had its own. The
task facing Athens was twofold: first, Athens had to implement its own
grand strategy; second it had to contend with the Spartan grand strategy. Thucydides was fully cognizant that strategic implementation
involves the interaction of two opposing wills (viz. the horizontal
dimension of strategy).

The fact that this aspect of Thucydides' analysis has not been adequately understood is reflected in the publicity that some of the protagonists of his *History* have received. Pericles has rightly been praised
for the grand strategy he designed and formulated, and has been
acknowledged as one of the greatest statesmen and military leaders in
history.[4] Archidamus however, a remarkable general and statesman in
his own right, has been ignored by contemporary scholars.[5] This is
unwarranted, since he too had a profound understanding of strategy,
as evidenced by both his outline of a theory of victory in dealing with
a maritime power, and the ingenuous way in which he used coercive
diplomacy. It was Sparta's loss that Archidamus had less influence on
the formulation of Spartan grand strategy than Pericles had on the
formulation of the Athenian one. Whereas Pericles managed to achieve
domestic legitimacy for his grand strategy, Archidamus could not
achieve the same for the grand strategy he contemplated.

Another conclusion is that a grand strategy must adapt to the existing balance of power. It has been acknowledged that strategy is always
addressed against one or more opponents. The means that can be used
against an opponent are determined by the relative balance of power
with the said opponent. If the means are lacking, certain ends are
beyond achievement and must not be pursued. The above analysis
demonstrates that both Sparta and Athens at certain instances misjudged the balance of power, setting policy objectives (dissolution of
the Athenian Empire; conquest of Sicily; recovery of the Athenian
Empire) that they could not achieve with the means available to them.
This overextension virtually condemned their grand strategies to failure, despite the fact that those grand strategies scored well when measured against the other criteria of evaluation. On the contrary, grand

strategies that set objectives not at variance with the balance of power (Periclean grand strategy, Spartan grand strategy after the Sicilian expedition) were generally successful (see Table 5.1).

Table 5.1: Evaluation of Athenian and Spartan Grand Strategies

Grand Strategy/ Criteria	External Fit	Means- Ends	Efficiency	Internal Coherence	Durability to Mistakes	Result
Athens, 431–421	+	+	+	+	+	Success
Sparta, 431–421	+	−	−	+	−	Failure
Athens, 415–404	+	−	+	+	−	Failure
Sparta, 415–404	+	+	+	−	+	Success

An analysis of Athenian and Spartan grand strategies can still offer valuable lessons to the modern strategist. The increasing relevance of the Periclean grand strategy of exhaustion will become evident in ensuing sections. As to the Spartan grand strategy, it is an excellent example of the Clausewitzian approach to war; the direct approach and destruction of the enemy's armed forces. Archidamus knew, and the rest of the Spartan political leadership eventually came to understand, that decisive results could only be obtained by turning against Athens and focusing on the strongest point of Athenian power structure, i.e. what Clausewitz called the 'centre of gravity' of the Athenian power. This was the navy. The indirect approach of ravaging Attica would not enable Sparta to strike at this centre of gravity; only an alliance with Persia made this possible. The fact that the Spartans consciously turned against the Athenian navy as soon as they obtained the means necessary to strike against it, demonstrates that they had a clear belief in the advantages of the direct approach. Interestingly enough, Athenian grand strategy also demonstrates the merits of the direct approach. It was only by hurting Sparta itself (Pylos, Sphacteria, Cythera) that Athens could secure its objectives; while at the last stage of the war it was only by striking at the Peloponnesian navy that the Athenians could hope to beat off the grave threat facing their city and salvage what they could from their empire.

Sir Basil Liddell Hart has argued extensively in favour of the indirect approach (see Chapter One), going so far as to attribute virtually every successful military action to the adoption of an indirect approach, and every unsuccessful one to the adoption of a direct approach.[6] Numerous are the criticisms levied against his theory[7] and one might think that to add to them we are flogging a dead horse. However, our criticism intends to highlight the very merits of Liddell Hart's thesis. One of the weaknesses of his argument is that he usually neglects the interplay between the various levels of strategy. Thus, he cites the fact that the indirect approach was employed at the tactical or the operational level as evidence for the superiority of this approach, while at the same time ignoring the fact that at the strategic level the approach adopted was direct. For instance, he has called Lysander's victory at Aegospotami "a tactical indirect approach at sea, which was itself the sequel to a fresh indirect approach in grand strategy".[8] The second part of this statement is, of course, mistaken; we have repeatedly pointed out that Sparta's turn against the Athenian navy is a characteristic case of the direct approach. Demonstrably, Liddell Hart's attempt to attribute all the military successes in history to the indirect approach seriously weakens his analysis. However, the first part of the statement is correct; Lysander did use the indirect approach at the tactical level.[9] Generally, the grand strategies of Sparta and Athens seem to provide arguments in favour of a direct approach at the levels of grand strategy and military strategy. Indirect approach may be used and in fact it may even be advisable at lower levels, namely at the operational or tactical levels of war.

The Determinants of Grand Strategy

An examination of Thucydides' text offers valuable insights regarding the determinants of grand strategy. It appears that in the analysis of Thucydides one can find at least the rudiments of a theory of the causes of grand strategic choices, based on a combination of both structural and perceptual factors.[10]

It has been pointed out that grand strategy aims at producing security for the state (see Chapter One). Consequently, the formulation of a state's grand strategy is bound to be determined by two factors: a) the balance of power between the state and its strategic opponent; b) the severity of the threats posed to the state by its strategic opponent. Thucydides was well cognizant of this, paying great attention to both power and fear.[11] These two factors will be examined in turn.

Obviously, an assessment of the existing balance of power with a strategic opponent is an important determinant of a state's grand strategy. However, apart from appraising the existing balance of power, states also attempt to forecast what the future balance of power will be. Their appraisal of trends in the distribution of power is highly likely to influence their choices at the grand strategic level: as a general principle, they will try to arrest and reverse unfavourable trends, while attempting to accelerate and exploit favourable ones. In other words, the trends in the distribution of power (i.e. the dynamic analysis of the balance of power) are another determining factor in deciding a state's grand strategy, at least as important as the current distribution of power (i.e. the static analysis of the balance of power).[12]

The combination of static and dynamic analyses of the balance of power may lead to two possible assessments: a) the state is growing stronger relative to its strategic opponent; b) the state is growing weaker relative to its strategic opponent.[13] These two possibilities form the structural background against which a state's grand strategy is formulated.

A warning is in order here: although we have found it convenient to say that states examine the balance of power, it is obviously the political leadership of a state that makes that appraisal; hence one might argue that what is relevant is not the structure of the international system per se, but what the political leadership perceives it to be. Without examining at length the complex issues of perception in international politics,[14] let us point out that, although perceptions of the balance of power are significant and often feature within the analysis of Thucydides (*viz.* the Spartans' belief in a quick victory prior to the war), structural realities cannot be ignored or misperceived for long. As both the Spartans and the Athenians discovered, the actual balance of power will eventually make itself felt.

The other determinant of grand strategy, namely the threat posed by a state's strategic opponent, is primarily perceptual in character. What chiefly matters here is how a state's political leadership perceives the hostile intentions of its foe. It has been pointed out that the very issue of treating separately the capabilities and the intentions of a strategic opponent implies we feel safe enough to do so; if the capabilities of a specific strategic opponent appear considerable, states normally do not pause to analyze its intentions.[15] Be that as it may, foreign intentions, as they are perceived by a state's political leadership, do matter.[16] For instance, although Egypt is more powerful than Syria, Israeli decision makers are currently much more concerned about the latter; Egypt is perceived as relatively benign, Syria is perceived as threatening. There have even been instances where threat perception was almost completely divorced from the other side's capabilities. Thus, by 146 B.C. Carthage could by no stretch of the imagination possess the capability to challenge Rome. Defeated in three wars in succession, the once mighty Carthaginian Empire had been reduced to a tributary state. Nevertheless, the Romans still felt threatened, a perception that resulted in the total destruction of Carthage, the extermination of its adult male population and the enslavement of its women and children.[17]

The emphasis placed upon the perception of threat does not mean that foreign threats are merely a matter of perception, lacking any foundation. Still, while the balance of power is, as has been pointed out, bound to become apparent sooner or later, perceived threats may or may not actually exist and even if they do, may not necessarily materialise. That is why primary importance is given to how a political leadership perceives foreign intentions; regardless of actual Athenian intentions the Spartans felt threatened, and that is what mattered. Still, it is clear that a state is better off if the threat perceptions of its political leadership correspond to reality; erroneous threat perception results either in waste of resources and unnecessary provocation (if one is making preparations to ward off nonexistent threats) or strategic surprise (if an unanticipated threat materialises).[18]

Since strategy by definition deals with situations of actual or potential conflict, it has to estimate the degree of threat posed by various strategic opponents. Depending on the extent of the national interests threatened, the impact of a foreign threat may be perceived as high or low. These two possibilities constitute the perceptual background of grand strategy. This background is more volatile than the structural one; perceptions change more quickly than capabilities. This occasionally results in violent fluctuations in a state's grand strategy. For instance, the sudden abandonment of appeasement by Great Britain after Hitler occupied Prague in March 1939, came as a result of a shift in the perception of the threat posed by Germany.[19]

The combination of the structural and perceptual determinants of grand strategy gives the following matrix (see Table 5.2).

This framework can be applied to strategic relationships between great or small powers, as well as between a great and a small power.[20] In the latter case, however, given that the power gap is normally huge, differential rates of growth have often little relevance, even if they

Table 5.2: The Determinants of Grand Strategy

		Balance of Power	
		Rise	Decline
Threat	High	I	III
	Low	II	IV

I: Expansion, Intransigence
II: Expansion, Benevolence
III: Buck-Passing or Balancing or Preventive War or Appeasement
IV: Buck-Passing or Appeasement

favour the small power. For the framework to be applicable, unequal growth must be significant enough to influence bilateral relations, without necessarily threatening to alter the overall balance of power. Thus, although Athens had no chance of overpowering the Persian Empire, the relative growth of its power enabled it to gain the upper hand over Persia on the western coast of Asia Minor and the waters west of Pamphylia. Let us now examine the grand strategic outcomes of the combination of the balance of power and the threat perceptions of the political leadership.

Intransigent and Benevolent Expansion

It has been persuasively argued that whenever a state's power rises compared to that of its strategic opponent, that state will seek to change the status quo until the costs of so doing exceed the benefits; at which stage an equilibrium will be reached. This does not necessarily imply that rising powers are necessarily intent on territorial expansion. The change of the status quo may take various other forms, such as extension of one's influence (viz. the enlargement of NATO) or establishing advantageous rules in the international economy (viz. British and later American emphasis on free trade).[21] Occasionally it takes some time before the relative rise of a state's power versus a strategic opponent produces a significant shift in the bilateral balance. Thus, in such cases we may expect the rising state to basically mark time, proceed cautiously in relation to that particular strategic opponent, and instead concentrate its efforts on other, more manageable strategic opponents.

Thus, the structural determinant of grand strategy would prompt a rising state to expand until it reaches a point of diminishing returns,[22] irrespective of the threatening environment that it finds itself in. Nevertheless, the intensity of the threats faced by that state is bound to influence the pattern of its expansion. Rising powers facing high threats have no incentive to compromise, but as a rule try to weaken the source of threat as much as possible or eliminate it altogether. On the other hand, a rising power operating in a low-threat environment normally does not feel the need to exert itself. For certain, rising powers facing low threats may prove as expansionist as any, especially if they feel the need to restore a favourable status quo or are simply bent on achieving 'greatness'. Still, however, the threat environment does make a difference.[23]

Buck-Passing, Balancing, Preventive War, and Appeasement

The greatest challenge to a grand strategy comes when a state is growing weaker relative to its strategic opponent. The adverse shift in the balance of power is a harsh reality that requires remedial action. Once again, the perceptual determinant of grand strategy plays a key role. While rising states are likely to expand irrespective of what the threat environment looks like, the grand strategic choices of declining states depend heavily on the magnitude of the threats perceived by their political leadership. To begin with, the preferred course of declining states against rising strategic opponents, regardless of the magnitude of the perceived threat, is buck-passing, i.e. trying to get another state or states to check the rising power, while they remain on the sidelines.[24] However, buck-passing is often impossible (e.g. in a bipolar international system), and even when it is possible, it may not guarantee the desired outcome.

Declining states facing low threats have a rather strong incentive to appease their strategic opponents, appeasement defined as neutralization or at least reduction of a threat by making concessions.[25] In this particular instance, assuming that buck-passing is impossible or ineffective, this is the least risky as well as the least costly grand strategic course. An intransigent policy may simply provoke the rising adversary to adopt a similar stance and possibly increase his demands. In the same vein, the low threat posed by the strategic opponent means that appeasing him is not likely to have any dire consequences in the future (viz. Hans Morgenthau's classic recommendation to compromise on one's peripheral interests and staunchly defend the core ones).[26] On the contrary, compromise reached in a low-threat environment may lay the seeds for bilateral cooperation.[27]

Thus, when a declining state faces low threats, appeasement seems to provide a comparatively risk-free and cost-free grand strategic choice. However, events are much more difficult when a declining state faces high threats; in other words, when vital national interests are perceived to be under threat, and the state's power is diminishing relative to that of its strategic opponent. In this case, appeasement does not provide an easy solution, since states, particularly great powers, normally do not compromise on what they regard as their vital national interests (but see below).

Normally, the preferred course of action is the aforementioned buck-passing. Assuming that buck-passing is impossible or ineffective, another course of action is balancing behavior. As was pointed out in Chapter Three, balancing can be done either by utilizing power from abroad (external balancing), and/or by mobilizing and exploiting domestic resources (internal balancing). Internal reform with a view to the more effective utilization of available means has been a popular course of action for old and declining empires. On the other hand, external balancing is chiefly done through alliances, formal or informal. A declining power as a rule welcomes new allies, whereas a rising power is generally in lesser need of them.

However, buck-passing and balancing behavior are not the only grand strategic options available to a declining state facing high threats. Preventive war is another option as well, provided that the declining state still perceives itself as being stronger than its strategic opponent (see Chapter One). It may or may not actually be stronger, but in this case it is perception that matters. One may recall that prevention entails fighting early and creating a *fait accompli* while it is still possible, that is before the balance of power tips in any decisive way and the strategic opponent becomes strong enough to be threatening. A grand strategy of preventive war implies the choice of the lesser evil: war today against destruction tomorrow.

Nevertheless, a declining state facing high threats may perceive itself so irreparably weak relative to its strategic opponent that neither preventive war nor balancing are an option. The balance can no longer be redressed and the power gap is growing to the detriment of the declining state. In such instances, appeasement is probably the most rational option: the declining state is inclined to concede what, in view of the increasing power differential, it is likely to lose anyway. Obviously, appeasement in a high-threat environment as a rule entails higher costs than in a low-threat one; hence it is encountered less often as a grand strategic option. Still, as Thucydides made apparent in the Melian Dialogue, concessions, however huge, are preferable to destruction.[28]

Thucydides and the Determinants of Grand Strategy

Returning to the analysis of Thucydides, an examination of the strategic turning points of the period 479–404 B.C. will confirm what has been said so far (see Table 5.3).

To begin with, the expansion of the Greek cities and later Athens at Persian expense fits with the profile of what rising states facing high threats are likely to do. The Persian invasion united the Greek city-states and persuaded them to effect a massive military (chiefly naval) build-up. On the other hand, as far as the Persians were concerned, the disaster in Greece was an enormous blow for two reasons: first, it led to a significant diminution of military power, since a considerable part of the Persian armed forces was decimated;[29] second, the Persian king suffered a great loss of prestige that weakened his authority and destabilised his rule.[30] Thus, Persia was unmistakably in decline compared to the Greek cities in general and Athens in particular. As outlined in Chapter Two, the Persians did attempt to check decline and stave off the high threat by resorting to a military build-up, but this attempt at internal balancing failed.[31]

The Athenian expansion in Greece proper constitutes another example of a rising power facing high threats and as a result expanding uncompromisingly. The Athenians knew that the creation and expansion of their empire was not likely to gain them anything but 'immoderate hostility' among the other Greeks. However, since Athenian power was in ascendancy, Athens could beat off the challenges and continue its expansion.

The Spartan resort to preventive war circa 460 B.C. is also consistent with what we have come to expect of a declining power perceiving a high threat, having no opportunity of buck-passing (viz. the bipolar

Table 5.3: Strategic Turning Points, 479–404 B.C.

Date	Event	Strategic Player(s)	Balance of Power/Threat	Grand Strategic Choice(s)
479	Greeks defeat Persians at Plataea and Mycale.	Greek cities–Persia	RH—DH	Expansion–Balancing
478	Athenians assume Greek leadership. Creation of the Delian League.	Athens	RH	Expansion
466	Battle of Eurymedon—Persians routed.	Athens	RH	Expansion
ca. 460	Athenian expedition to Cyprus and Egypt.	Athens–Persia	RH–DH	Expansion–Balancing
ca. 460	Megara joins Athenian Alliance.	Athens	RH	Expansion
ca. 460	Outbreak of First Peloponnesian War.	Sparta–Athens	DH–RH	Preventive War–Expansion
457	Athenian conquest of Boeotia and Aegina.	Athens	RH	Expansion
ca. 454	Athenian expeditionary corps destroyed in Egypt.	Athens	RH	Diminishing Returns
451	Five Years' Peace.	Athens–Sparta	RH–DH	Equilibrium
449	Peace of Callias.	Athens–Persia	RH–DH	Equilibrium
446	Athenian defeat at Coronea. Megarian revolt.	Athens	RH	Diminishing Returns
446	Thirty Years' Peace.	Athens–Sparta	RH–DH	Equilibrium
431	Outbreak of the Peloponnesian War.	Sparta–Athens	DH–RH	Preventive War–Intransigence
425	Battle of Sphacteria–Spartans surrender. Spartan peace offer.	Athens–Sparta	RH–DH	Expansion–Appeasement

424	Battle of Delium–Athenians defeated.	Athens	RH	Diminishing Returns
423	Treaty between Athens and Persia.	Athens–Persia	RL–DL	Benevolence–Appeasement. Cooperation
422	Battle of Amphipolis–Athenians defeated.	Athens	RH	Diminishing Returns
421	Peace of Nicias.	Athens–Sparta	RH–DH	Equilibrium
418	Battle of Mantinea–Spartans defeat the Argives.	Argos–Sparta	RH–DH	Expansion–Balancing
415	Athenian Expedition to Sicily.	Athens–Syracuse	RL–DH	Expansion–Balancing
413	Athenian expeditionary corps destroyed in Sicily.	Athens	RH	Diminishing Returns
412–411	Alliance between Sparta and Persia.	Sparta–Athens	RH–DH	Expansion–Balancing.
		Persia–Athens	RL–DH	Expansion–Appeasement
410	Battle of Cyzicus–Spartans annihilated. Spartan peace offer.	Sparta	RH	Diminishing Returns
407	Massive Persian help to Sparta.	Persia	RL	Expansion
406	Battle of Arginusae–Spartans defeated. Spartan peace offer.	Sparta	RH	Diminishing Returns
405	Battle of Aegospotami–Athenian fleet captured.	Sparta	RH	Expansion
404	Athens capitulates. Spartans do not destroy the city.	Sparta	RL	Expansion, Benevolence

R = Rising Power D = Declining Power H = High Threat L=Low Threat ancient Greek city-state system), but also believing it is still strong enough to eliminate the source of threat by force. However, as was seen in Chapter Two, Sparta was unable to check Athenian expansion (viz. the Athenian conquest of Boeotia and Aegina) and equilibrium was reached, resulting in the Five Years' Peace.[32]

In the meantime, as the reverses in Egypt and later in Cyprus demonstrated, Athenian expansion vis-à-vis Persia had reached the point of diminishing returns. The interaction between expansion to the point of diminishing returns on the one hand and balancing on the other resulted in the equilibrium reflected in the Peace of Callias.

The same process was repeated in mainland Greece, after the Athenian mishaps in Coronea and Megara in 446 B.C. Of course, Athens had safely retained its empire and consequently was still growing stronger relative to its Greek adversaries, but further expansion on land was simply unprofitable, or even unattainable. This was the state of affairs codified in the Thirty Years' Peace.[33]

The process of Sparta's resorting to preventive war in 431 B.C. has been the subject of detailed analysis earlier in this book: declining in power, perceiving a high threat, but considering the combination of itself and its allies stronger than Athens, Sparta chose war (see Chapters Three and Four). The Athenian reaction is interesting, since it constitutes the only example in Thucydides' analysis where a rising power did not resort to outright expansion, and remained content to maintain the status quo. In all probability, Pericles estimated that Athens, the growth of its power notwithstanding, was not strong enough to engage in profitable expansion, especially since, as was pointed out in Chapter Three, the targets of this expansion could only be located on the mainland. In other words, in Pericles' mind the equilibrium of 446/5 B.C. had not shifted in Athens' favour. However, Athens retained the intransigence expected from rising powers facing high threats, as was shown by its rejection of even minor concessions to the Spartans.[34]

The battle of Sphacteria made it evident to both belligerents that Athens *could* now pursue an expansionist grand strategy. The Spartans accepted the fact that their attempt to check the growth of the Athenian power had failed and that the situation could only worsen. Hence, willing to make huge concessions, they resorted to appeasement, as was pointed out in Chapter Three. However, by now the Athenians were even more intransigent and refused to enter into any negotiations.[35]

Yet the point of diminishing returns for Athenian expansion was not far off. The defeats at Delium and Amphipolis drove the point home and the Peace of Nicias codified the equilibrium reached between the two belligerents.[36]

The treaty between Athens and Persia in 423 B.C. provides the only instance in Thucydides' analysis where both parties in the strategic relationship perceived the other side as presenting a low threat. Both Athens and Persia had more important things to do than attack each other, and both understood that. This treaty may be interpreted as displaying benevolence on the part of the Athenians, who satisfied themselves with the gains registered with the Peace of Callias, and appeasement on the part of the Persian king, who acquiesced to those gains. Obviously, once this issue was settled, a genuine pattern of bilateral cooperation emerged.

The grand strategy of Argos after 421 B.C. and the subsequent defection of some of Sparta's allies to Argos provide yet another example of a rising power facing high threats from a traditional rival and expanding at its direct expense.[37] In defense, Sparta attempted to check its decline by securing the loyalty of its remaining allies and enlisting their support against Argos. The outcome of the battle of Mantinea bears testimony to the success of the Spartan grand strategy.[38]

The Athenian expedition in Sicily proves that a rising power will tend to expand, even when faced with a low threat from its strategic opponent. The Athenians did not embark on the Sicilian expedition because they felt threatened by the Syracusans, but simply because they wanted to conquer Sicily (see previous chapter and the discussion below). The Syracusans, in response, resorted to both internal and external balancing by making war preparations and enlisting Spartan support. The situation soon became critical for the Athenians, as their enormous expeditionary corps in Sicily found itself under serious threat, while they were simultaneously facing renewed and efficiently conducted hostilities in Greece proper. The annihilation of the Athenian expeditionary corps in Sicily showed that, once again, Athenian expansion had reached the point of diminishing returns.[39] However, this time, Athens could not recover and was condemned to permanent decline in contrast to its two great strategic opponents, Sparta and Persia.

Spartan grand strategy after Sicily completely conforms to the expectations of what a rising power is likely to do when perceiving high threats, namely expand uncompromisingly until it reaches the point of diminishing returns. In the mind of the Spartan political leadership this point was reached twice, namely after the battles of Cyzicus and Arginusae. Hence the Spartans came up with peace proposals to codify the existing equilibrium (see Chapter Four).

Persian grand strategy after Sicily presents the second instance in Thucydides' analysis where a rising power facing low threats chooses to expand.[40] In their quest to restore the status quo ante in western Asia Minor, the Persians were intransigent in their demand for re-incorporation of the Greek cities area's to the Persian Empire.[41]

Athens responded differently to each of the two challenges it faced. The Spartan challenge was met with an Athenian attempt at internal balancing; the declining state facing a high threat was not prepared to compromise.[42] However, in relation to Persia, Athens was willing to compromise. As was highlighted in the previous chapter, the Athenians after Sicily made strenuous efforts to win the Persians over to their side. Those efforts were certain to entail some concessions. In other words, since Athens could not hope to improve its power position vis-à-vis Persia, it resorted to appeasement.[43] The threat posed by Persia was high and appeasement was bound to entail important concessions, but these paled in comparison to the Spartan threat and its possible consequences: while the Persians only wanted the Greek cities of Ionia, the Spartans and their allies could conceivably go as far as razing Athens to the ground and selling its inhabitants into slavery.

Finally, the relatively generous terms Sparta granted Athens in 404 B.C. also conform to the pattern of 'benevolent expansion' expected from rising states facing low threats. The elimination of the Athenian threat meant that, although the Spartans would definitely expand at Athens' expense, they would also exercise some restraint.

Applicability of the Theory

The above demonstrates that Thucydides' analysis of the determinants of grand strategy is able to explain the events of the period (479–404 B.C.). Is this analysis universally applicable? Well, a number of other examples would seem to validate it. Let us begin with the grand strategic outcomes of a rising power within a high and low-threat environment, namely intransigent and benevolent expansion respectively. The previously cited example of Rome vis-à-vis Carthage shows what a rising power can do when perceiving high threats. Great Britain from the end of the seventeenth century until the defeat of Napoleon offers another such example. The British responded to this strategic situation (favourable trends in the distribution of power plus high threats) by ruthlessly expanding at the expense of the sources from where the threat emanated, first the Netherlands and then France. Hard-nosed and aggressive, the British had little taste for compromise. The War of American Independence (1775–1783) signified the fact that British expansion had reached the point of diminishing returns, but with the advent of the Industrial Revolution British power continued to rise. After a long struggle with a resurgent France, Great Britain finally emerged victorious, powerful, and safe in 1815. A long period of intransigent expansion was crowned with success.

At this stage, a remarkable change took place. Since it took some time for other countries to match the Industrial Revolution developments of Great Britain, British power kept growing compared to that of the other great European states for some time after Waterloo. Operating in a low-threat environment, British grand strategy lost the element of intransigence that characterised it until then. Great Britain continued to effect favourable changes on the status quo, such as the liberalization of international trade, but at the same time showed greater willingness to compromise: the British ceased to usurp the colonies of the other European powers, while playing a conciliatory role in the Concert of Europe.[44]

The United States offers a similar example of a rising state that expands yet modifies the pattern of its expansion according to the intensity of the threats it faces. The Americans have repeatedly proved ferocious strategic adversaries, bent on securing the unconditional surrender of their defeated opponents. If the American public can be persuaded that a situation is threatening enough, the United States is able to exert tremendous effort to achieve unlimited objectives. The fate of Imperial and Nazi Germany, as well as that of Japan, testify to that. However, as soon as the source of threat was eliminated, American grand strategy adopted a benevolent stance. Although the Americans generally continued to change the status quo (viz. the 'recasting' of the domestic structures of West Germany and Japan after 1945), they dropped their earlier intransigence and proved magnanimous victors.

The evolution of American strategic rivalry with the Soviet Union seems to confirm this pattern. By the second half of the 1980s the United States clearly had the upper hand. The existence of nuclear weapons notwithstanding, Washington missed no chance to obliterate the Soviet threat. Unequal arms' control agreements, intensive propaganda aiming to delegitimise the Soviet model, and the encouragement of secession of the non-Russian nationalities, were all employed to this end (see also below). However, the present American stance towards Russia is markedly different. It goes without saying that American expansion has not stopped; NATO enlargement and military action in the Balkans, coupled with increased American presence in former Soviet territories, testify to this. However, this goes side by side with generous financial assistance to Russia, plus recognition of certain Russian interests, such as Moscow's right to combat secession within the Russian Federation. Obviously, what makes the difference is the low threat posed by Russia, at least until recently.[45]

Concerning buck-passing as a response to declining power, regardless of the magnitude of the perceived threat, the response of both Great Britain and the United States to the rise of Germany before both world wars provides a characteristic example. In each case, the 'offshore balancers' tried to shift the burden of checking Germany onto others, i.e. France and Russia/Soviet Union, committing themselves to balancing Germany only when the buck-catchers failed to accomplish their mission.[46]

Regarding appeasement as the outcome of declining power in a low-threat environment, the grand strategies of a number of declining great powers help illustrate the point. One of the earliest examples is that of Spain *vis-à-vis* France at the turn of the seventeenth century. Spain was a great power of long standing. Spanish hegemony in Europe and tremendous expansion overseas endured for more than a century, beginning in the 1490s and formally ending with the Treaty of the Pyrenees in 1659. Although Spanish arms had repeatedly proved victorious against the French during that period, by the mid-seventeenth century France had become stronger than its opponent. However, after a series of victories and territorial acquisitions at Spain's expense, the French turned their attention elsewhere and stopped posing a grave threat to Spain. The impact of this course of action was understood in Madrid, and thereafter the Spaniards changed strategic course vis-à-vis France, becoming a virtual French satellite (viz. the accession of a French prince to the Spanish throne in 1700).[47]

British policy towards the United States at the turn of the nineteenth century constitutes a most important case of a declining state choosing to appease a strategic opponent deemed to present a low threat. From the 1890s the burgeoning United States started following an assertive if not high-handed policy towards British interests on the American continent. The Americans, invoking the Monroe Doctrine, insisted on mediating in a border dispute between Venezuela and British Guyana, effected a favourable modification of the border between Canada and Alaska, and established exclusive control over the Panama Canal Zone which they then fortified, although an earlier Anglo-American treaty (1850) had called for common construction and control of the canal. The British chose to accede to the American demands on these issues, ignoring the American naval expansion program, and in due course made a 'complete strategic abandonment' of Central and North America, leaving Canada defenseless in the process.[48] Apart from a mystical belief in 'Anglo-American racial brotherhood', prevalent in certain circles of British society, there were sound reasons why Great Britain should opt for a grand strategy of appeasement against the United States. Simply put, the British could ill afford to engage with the Americans about what were after all minor interests, while at the same time facing a dangerous threat close to home, namely the rise of Germany.[49]

It has been argued that declining states facing high threats will often resort to internal and external balancing (see above). Diocletian's administrative division of the Roman Empire into four parts in the late third century A.D., the reform of the Ottoman Empire promulgated in 1856, the transformation of the Austrian Empire into Austria-Hungary in 1867 and the proposed scheme for connecting all the 'white' subjects of the British Empire into a federation, all constitute attempts at reversing decline by means of internal balancing.

In the same context, one can find numerous examples of external balancing as well. Post-1871 France was a typical case of a state growing weaker relative to its chief strategic opponent, the German Empire, which was also perceived to pose a high threat to French national security. The defeat at Prusso-German hands and the loss of Alsace-Lorraine in the war of 1870–1871 were painful enough; the continued hostility of the German Empire and the tremendous growth of its power were none other than alarming. France responded by resorting to both internal and external balancing. Internal balancing came through the reorganization of the French army, while external balancing took the form of alliances with Russia, Great Britain and eventually the United States.[50] Although in bilateral terms France itself continued to grow weaker in relation to Germany, the French balancing effort proved ultimately effective and the First World War was won.[51]

The desperate strategic situation in which Great Britain found itself in 1940–1941 was the result of a long period of decline. By 1941, Great Britain's chief strategic opponent, Nazi Germany, had won European supremacy and was making a credible bid to become the strongest power in the world, while at the same time posing a mortal threat to Great Britain itself. Although the British managed to rally their domestic resources, the situation could only be reversed through external balancing.[52] The Lend-Lease Bill, passed by the American Congress on 11 March 1941, enabled Britain to draw from vast American resources, whereas Hitler's invasion of the Soviet Union on 22 June 1941 provided London with the opportunity to enlist Soviet support, ideological differences with Moscow notwithstanding.[53] As had been the case with France (and Great Britain itself) in the First World War, the grand strategic choice of balancing the power of its strategic opponent enabled Great Britain to cope successfully with the challenge of decline coupled with high threats.[54]

History is littered with examples of preventive war by a declining power that still considers itself stronger than its rising and highly menacing strategic opponent. Austria vis-à-vis Prussia in 1756 provides a case in point. Austria had every reason not to welcome the arrival of Prussia to the club of great European powers; the rise of Prussia posed a grave threat to Austria's position in Germany, a point driven home by the Prussian seizure of the rich Austrian province of Silesia in 1740. Consequently, the Austrians managed to forge a great continental coalition comprising Austria, France, Russia, Sweden, and eventually Spain, in a clear attempt to check Prussian power before it reached unacceptable proportions. However, although Prussia came close to disappearing from the map during the ensuing Seven Years' War, the failure of the Austrian grand strategic plan did not augur well for Austria's future position.[55]

It must also be mentioned that preventive war has been contemplated and launched not only in response to a decline in relative power, but also in anticipation of such a decline. The destruction of the Danish fleet by the British in 1807 is an example. Although Denmark was neutral, Great Britain was afraid of a possible Franco-Danish naval alliance that would immensely increase Napoleon's naval power and thus put British national security in jeopardy. As a consequence, the Royal Navy launched a surprise attack at the port of Copenhagen, seized seventy-five ships, and removed the potential threat conclusively.[56]

Finally, the Soviet Union's relationship with the United States in the mid-1980s provides an example of a declining state facing a high external threat but being unable to counterbalance the source of that threat: the Soviet system could not even keep functioning, let alone sustain an antagonism with the United States for world supremacy. The choice of appeasement developed almost naturally: the Soviet leader Mikhail Gorbachev made enormous concessions to the strategic opponent of the Soviet Union, merely to gain some time to pursue the reforms necessary to stabilise the crumbling Soviet state.[57]

It would be interesting, and perhaps useful, to use the above framework in order to examine the grand strategic choices stemming from the current rise of China, especially regarding China's strategic relationship with the United States.[58] To start with, one should bear in mind that latent and actual Chinese power are two very different things. Though Chinese power grows by leaps and bounds, currently China is basically a rising middle power.[59] Thus, the relative rise of China vis-à-vis the United States has yet to produce a significant enough shift in the bilateral balance. Consequently, though the Chinese may rattle their swords against Taiwan or various Southeast Asian states (viz. the maritime disputes over Spratly and Paracel Islands), overall they proceed rather cautiously vis-à-vis the United States and, to a lesser extent, vis-à-vis Japan and Russia.[60] However, as Chinese capabilities grow, China becomes more assertive and is bound to continue becoming so.[61] For instance, the Chinese military plans for the creation of a blue-water navy after the year 2030 have a distinctly anti–American flavour.[62] Thus, assuming that the present trends will continue, the structural background of the strategic relationship between China and the United States points at expansion of the former at the expense of the latter.

It is here that the perceptual element enters the fray. The United States' perception of China oscillates between viewing it as a 'strategic partner' (i.e. a state that poses a low threat) and viewing it as a 'strategic adversary' (i.e. a state that poses a considerable threat). Accordingly, one sees the United States either as accommodating China (viz. the American assistance to China's entering the World Trade Organization) or balancing it (viz. American military activities in East Asia, closer ties with Japan and rapprochement with India). The American stance will in turn influence Chinese threat perceptions, correspondingly affecting the Chinese incentive to compromise. This is not to say that if the United States appeases China, the latter will not turn intransigent. However, if the Chinese political leadership perceives the United States as posing a high threat to China, then it will most probably turn intransigent.

If the above theoretical presentation, drawn from Thucydides' analysis, is correct, then it becomes possible to outline a theory that may serve as a predictive and explanatory tool regarding the determinants of grand strategic choices. The structural determinant, namely the static and dynamic balance of power between a state and its strategic opponent, needs to be combined with the magnitude of threat posed by that strategic opponent, as perceived by the political leadership of the aforementioned state. This threat perception will influence the pattern of that state's expansion, should its power be on the rise, and also influence the state's choice between buck-passing, balancing, appeasement, or even preventive war, should its power be declining.

This concludes the discussion of the determinants of grand strategy. Let us now deal with the concepts of the strategy of annihilation and exhaustion.

The Strategies of Annihilation and Exhaustion: Past, Present and Future

These two forms of strategic design and their employment during the Peloponnesian War have been analyzed in detail in the preceding chapters. The more widespread of the two has been the strategy of annihilation. It has been repeatedly pointed out that this strategy aims at the destruction of the armed forces of the enemy through a decisive battle, that the most well-known practitioner of this strategy was Napoleon, and that its greatest theoretical exponent is Clausewitz, who combined it with the direct approach.

The grand strategy of Sparta during the Peloponnesian War conforms completely to the Napoleonic/Clausewitzian model. The Spartans were trying for years to bring about a decisive battle on land and, as soon as they acquired the necessary naval power, they followed a similar approach at sea. During the war, Sparta managed to achieve decisive victories both on land and at sea. On land, since the Athenians did not come out of their walls to offer battle, the decisive victory was won against the Argives and their allies at Mantinea in 418 B.C., securing Spartan supremacy in the Peloponnese. At sea, the defeat of the Athenians at Aegospotami in 405 B.C. gave Sparta the final victory in the Peloponnesian War. In other words, one can see in Spartan grand strategy the epitome of the strategy of annihilation, a strategy that was destined to dominate Western strategic thought for a long time.

The supremacy of the strategy of annihilation reached its zenith during the period from the end of the Napoleonic Wars till the end of the Second World War (1815–1945). During that period, it was consciously employed for the first time by the Confederate General Robert Edward Lee during the American Civil War (1861–1865). Lee's great victories at the Second Bull Run (1862) and Chancellorsville (1863) created a severe crisis within the Union's high command. In the long run, however, the Union's material superiority proved enough to ensure victory in the war. It is very interesting, nevertheless, that the strategy of the Union's forces under the command of General Ulysses Simpson Grant was also a variation of the strategy of annihilation. Once again the approach was direct, aiming at the destruction of the enemy's armed forces through attrition, making use of the vast superiority of the Union in manpower and materiel. In general, the combination of direct approach, attrition and material superiority has ever since constituted the way in which the armed forces of the United States approach war.[63]

In Europe, the strategy of annihilation was mastered by the Prussian (and later German) General Staff, under the leadership of Field-Marshal Helmuth von Moltke.[64] Under the political direction of Bismarck, the decisive victories of the Prussian army against the Austrians at Sadowa in 1866, and against the French at Sedan in 1870, led to dramatic changes to the contours of the political map of Europe, culminating in the creation of the German Empire. The campaigns of Moltke are classic examples of the Clausewitzian approach to war. To start with, war was used as a tool for the achievement of political ends which were each time set by the political leadership; the conduct of the war itself was never allowed to jeopardise the achievement of those aims. Furthermore, Moltke consciously aimed at the destruction of the armed forces of the opponent, since it was correctly understood at that time that they constituted the centre of gravity of the war effort of both Austria and France.[65]

The strategy of annihilation was also used during the two world wars. However, the total mobilization of the belligerents made it impossible to win a war through victory in a single battle, no matter how great this victory was. In fact, it is no accident that the very concept of 'battle' was widened in scope during that period: instead of the isolated encounter of the Spartan and Napoleonic eras, the new concept of battle covered extensive operations which went on for weeks or even months, like the Battle of Verdun (1916) or the Battle of Britain (1940–1941).[66] War began to extend beyond the armed forces of the combatants, to include the whole material and moral potential of a country (total war).[67] Consequently, the cost of the use of military force started to increase exponentially and, conversely, a strategy of annihilation became a less attractive tool.

The advent of nuclear weapons completed this process. Since 1945, although the employment of war as an instrument of policy has not disappeared, it has been greatly restricted, especially among nuclear powers. In other words, it was no longer possible to regard a nuclear war as a viable means to achieve political aims,[68] since neither side could avoid devastation. With the current state of technology, this is, to some extent, also true for a protracted conventional war, especially among great powers.[69] Nevertheless, this does not infer that the phenomenon of war is about to disappear. A look at the post-Cold War international system shows that the use of force in both international and domestic relations remains a potent measure. On the other hand, it can be persuasively argued that the idea of a war between great powers, both at the nuclear and the conventional level has become obsolete.[70]

Still, this has not led the great powers to abandon the pursuit of victory, the attempt to prevail at the interstate antagonism. Instead, it led to the revival of the strategy of exhaustion. As previously outlined, this strategy gives emphasis to a number of means beyond the traditional military ones, while relying to a large extent on causing economic damage to the opponent.[71] The strategy of exhaustion already had a glorious past. One may recall the victorious strategy of Pericles in the first phase of the Peloponnesian War (see Chapter Three). The Athenians declined to give battle on land, remaining safely behind their walls. At the same time, with the help of their naval power, they simultaneously quelled the revolts of their allies/subjects, and launched progressively escalating naval reprisals against the Spartans. In addition, the political dexterity of Pericles took care of the domestic legitimacy of his grand strategy. The outcome was that the Spartans recognised that they could not defeat Athens, and abandoned their attempt to overthrow the Athenian Empire (viz. the Peace of Nicias).

Many centuries later, namely from the seventeenth century onwards, another great power, England/Great Britain, adopted a grand strategy of exhaustion similar to that of Pericles; this was the so-called 'British way of warfare' (see Chapter One).

Moving on to the twentieth century one can see that the United States, in order to deal with the Soviet Union during the Cold War, drew from past experience and resorted to a grand strategy of exhaustion. In fact, there are quite a few similarities between the grand strategy of exhaustion that Pericles suggested to the Athenians in order to deal with the Spartans, and the conduct of the U.S. towards the Soviet Union during the Cold War.[72] The American grand strategy against the Soviet Union featured: a) containment of the Soviet power through a complex of alliances around the borders of the USSR; b) economic and technological embargo, through denial of Soviet access to Western economic resources and high technology; c) undermining the domestic legitimacy of the Soviet political system through support of dissidents and encouragement of ethnic movements; d) intensification of the technological arms race (e.g. Strategic Defense Initiative—'Star Wars'), so as to exhaust the opponent financially; e) rejection of appeasement, so as to prevent the USSR from registering gains from possible American concessions, and ensure that the American leadership of the West would not be endangered in the process; f) investment in powerful armed forces and maintenance of high defense budgets for a long period, so as to preserve the balance of power (internal balancing); g) maintenance of qualitative superiority through investment in high technology; h) support of the various opponents of the USSR (e.g. China, Afghan guerrillas); and finally i) undermining the image of the Soviet Union and delegitimization of the Soviet model in the eyes of international public opinion. The result of all this was the gradual exhaustion of the Soviet Union. The Soviet system eventually could not withstand combined American pressures, and the attempt to reform it (*perestroika*) contributed to its total collapse.

The Cold War is not the only contemporary instance of the utilization of the strategy of exhaustion. A cursory examination of the strategy followed by the US and its NATO allies in Bosnia in 1995 will suffice to prove this point; economic warfare, diplomatic isolation, strengthening of the opponent's local adversaries, psychological pressure and other means of grand strategy were used in order to bring about the exhaustion of the opponent. Thus, the air strikes were but one component of that strategy. Prior to these strikes, the power of the Bosnian Serbs had been eroded by economic warfare, while in the meantime they faced diplomatic isolation. In addition, the US helped manipulate the local balance of power, both through arms supplies to Serbia's local antagonists (Croatia, Bosnian Muslims) and through engineering the alliance between Bosnian Muslims and Bosnian Croats. Last, but not least, the US also took good care to rally domestic support for its policies in Bosnia (domestic legitimacy). With these combined elements in operation, the exhaustion of the opponent was ensured. Following that, the application of limited military force of exemplary character was enough to coerce the Bosnian Serbs to submit to the terms imposed by the US and NATO (viz. the Dayton Agreement).

In the coming decades, the employment of the strategy of exhaustion is bound to become more popular. In fact, as the cost of the application of military force increases and the sensitivity of Western societies to casualties grows, the pursuit of victory will become possible to a large extent only through the strategy of exhaustion. Technological trends (viz. the 'revolution in military affairs') based on the ability to collect, transmit, and intercept information, as well as deliver firepower against any target anywhere,[73] facilitate the military dimension of this strategy, in the same way as the technological developments in Ancient Greece (viz. the triremes) made naval raids an important pillar of the Periclean grand strategy.

A similar argument has been advanced by Edward Luttwak, who has argued in favour of a 'post-heroic' concept of war, laying stress on such means as economic embargoes, blockades, and air strikes in an attempt to minimise casualties, even at the expense of a swift decision that involves potentially higher casualty rates.[74] Luttwak, however, mistakenly attributes this concept to the Romans; actually, the Periclean grand strategy is the ideal type of 'post-heroic warfare.' For instance, an analogy may *inter alia* be drawn between the way in which the Athenians were using their navy, and the discussion that is nowadays taking place regarding the utilization of long-range weapons such as bomber aircraft in order to manipulate the cost to the other side without oneself suffering casualties. Another analogy can be found between Pericles' refusal to face the Spartan infantry in battle, and the reluctance of today's Western powers to be drawn into large-scale land operations, even against relatively weak powers. Both Pericles and current Western strategic planners care less about the 'glory of war' and more about the attainment of certain political ends with the smallest possible number of casualties.[75]

However, the increasing popularity of the strategy of exhaustion does not mean that the Clausewitzian approach to war, as exemplified by Spartan grand strategy in the Peloponnesian War, will be relegated to the history books. This is because, even with the adoption of the strategy of exhaustion, the direct approach will continue to be dominant, at least at the higher levels of strategy. In fact, we have already mentioned that even the Periclean grand strategy, the archetype of the strategy of exhaustion, achieved decisive results only when following a direct approach and striking against Sparta itself with the operations of Pylos, Sphacteria and Cythera. Furthermore, the strategy of annihilation is not at all eradicated, especially between opponents of vastly unequal strength.

Evidence from four instances of military force deployment by the US in recent times, lends credence to the applicability of the themes of exhaustion vs. annihilation, combined with a direct approach.[76] In the first case, after Iraq's invasion of Kuwait in August 1990, economic sanctions were placed on Iraq. The hope was that the economic damage inflicted would induce Saddam Hussein to see the error of his ways and withdraw Iraqi forces from Kuwait. Since this pure strategy of exhaustion did not work, a substantial portion of annihilation was added to the mix. The core element of Iraqi power, the Iraqi armed forces, was subjected to a ruthless barrage through every means (military, economic, psychological, etc) at the Allies' disposal. The air strikes took a heavy toll on the Iraqi armed forces, whereas the economic blockade and diplomatic isolation of their country ensured that losses in military hardware could not be replaced. In the meantime the immense psychological pressure demoralised their personnel. Propaganda outlining the inevitability of defeat led to mass surrender of their forces. The killer blow was delivered by large-scale land operations, which constitute another textbook case of destruction of the opponent's armed forces, precisely according to the precepts of Napoleon and Clausewitz. Incidentally, these operations provide an excellent example of the direct approach at the strategic level of war (destruction of the centre of gravity of the enemy power) coupled with the indirect approach at the operational level (the massive westerly movement that preceded the operations and took the Iraqi command and troops by surprise).[77]

The war in Kosovo is another case in point. The emphasis was not on the 'decisive battle' on land, but on the gradual physical emasculation of the Serbian war machine and the psychological dislocation of the Serbian political leadership, thus compelling the latter to comply with the terms imposed by NATO. As was the case with Iraq, the arms embargo prevented the Serbs from replacing losses sustained by the aerial bombardment, whereas the pressure was further increased by aid to the Kosovo Liberation Army (KLA) and economic warfare which laid stress on oil embargo. In the meantime Yugoslavia remained internationally isolated, whereas the Western powers launched a huge propaganda campaign in an attempt to damage the international image of the Serbian leaders, comparing them to the Nazis. Initially, NATO air bombardments took more of an indirect approach, leaving many strategic facilities, such as television stations and power grids, untouched. However, since expectations of swift Serb capitulation proved wrong, NATO gradually escalated the bombing and resorted to a direct approach, turning against the centre of gravity of the Serbian war effort, namely Serbian military power. The prospect of large-scale land operations was held in reserve, and the Serbian political leadership eventually gave way before this could become an actuality. The operations ended with the NATO allies completely achieving the strategic objective set out at the beginning of the campaign: the Serbian forces withdrew from Kosovo and were replaced by NATO ones.[78]

In the campaign in Afghanistan that followed shortly after the 9/11 terrorist attacks, annihilation elements dominated the strategic mix. Due to the political circumstances surrounding that war, it was rather easy for the United States to achieve international legitimacy and completely isolate its opponent. The political-diplomatic measures deployed were also highly promising. The Northern Alliance, the ex–king of the country, and various other tribal leaders were utilised in this respect. The military component of the American strategy resembled that of the Kosovo War (although at much greater intensity), with the important difference that the Taliban and al-Qaeda forces were weaker than those of Serbia, while the Northern Alliance could be molded into a far more formidable force than the KLA. Though the approach adopted by the US armed forces' was decidedly post-heroic,[79] it was also a direct one, striking at the enemy's centre of gravity, i.e. its armed forces. The fact that the Northern Alliance offensive compelled the Taliban to concentrate their armed forces assisted American air power tremendously;

the US Air Force kept striking at the enemy armed forces, actually retargeting areas struck only weeks or days before. The result was a rather speedy collapse of the Taliban regime.[80]

After the end of the Kuwait War in 1991, Iraq had been on the receiving end of a strategy of exhaustion that relentlessly sapped its strength. However, the political objectives of the American invasion of 2003, namely regime change and democratization, once again brought annihilation to the forefront. After an initial attempt at a decapitating strike against Saddam Hussein himself, the US armed forces resorted to the familiar direct approach, striking at the centre of gravity of the enemy power, i.e. the Iraqi armed forces. Once again, this was combined with an indirect approach at operational level: while the Iraqis concentrated on defending certain fortified urban centres (e.g. Al-Nasiriyah), the Americans simply by-passed them and headed for Baghdad. In the meantime, even when land operations temporarily halted, the US Air Force kept pounding the enemy armed forces, eventually paving the way for their swift destruction and the collapse of Saddam Hussein's regime.[81]

Based on the evidence provided by these cases, it seems that one may draw some conclusions regarding the way in which the United States, the strongest power in the present international system, is expected to approach war in the forthcoming years: A central role will be played by the exhaustion of the opponent through economic warfare (destruction of the opponent's base of production, economic embargo) and diplomatic isolation. In this way, the US will attempt to exploit the central position it currently occupies in the international economic and political system. Its position in the international division of labour is such, that its decision to impose measures like economic embargoes against opponents is bound to have disastrous economic consequences for the latter. In addition, at the diplomatic level, the dominant international position of the US enables it to draw a huge number of other countries to its side, thus condemning its opponent to diplomatic isolation.

As far as military strategy is concerned, the approach will be direct, aiming at the destruction of the opponent's armed forces. Here as well, the United States will try to exploit its comparative advantages, namely superiority in firepower and supremacy in sea, air and space.

Finally, great emphasis will be placed on technological superiority, especially in the field of intelligence.[82] This has two dimensions: First, the emphasis on technological superiority aims at minimizing casualties, through the use of technologically advanced weapons systems that the opponent will be unable to strike at effectively (e.g. aircraft and cruise missiles).[83] Second, the emphasis on technology for the collection, processing and transmission of intelligence in real time, often constitutes the only way to counter opponents that do not possess substantial armed forces or a significant economic base (e.g. terrorist groups) or do possess such assets but perform large-scale concealment thereof.

All this shows once again the continued relevance of Thucydides' strategic analysis. The preceding analysis of the grand strategies of Athens and Sparta made it clear that each of the two combatants tried to exploit their comparative advantages and simultaneously to neutralise the respective advantages of the opponent. The US currently tries to do precisely the same thing. The grand strategy that the United States is expected to follow in the forthcoming years is based on the exploitation of comparative American advantages (central position in the international economic and political system, superior firepower, sea, air and space supremacy, technological superiority) and the neutralization of the respective advantages of its potential opponents (better knowledge of the terrain, possibly higher determination for continuation of the war and higher casualty tolerance). Furthermore, the fact that the American technological superiority has enabled the United States, at least on occasion, to operate in a military league of its own, brings to mind the way in which the naval supremacy of Athens enabled it to enter a completely new mode of warfare, transcending the traditional mode which had been based on the infantry phalanx.

Underestimating the Enemy: From Alcibiades to the Present

As highlighted in the previous chapters, Thucydides thought that the turning point of the war was the Athenian expedition to Sicily in 415 B.C., undertaken at the instigation of Alcibiades.[84] Up to now, our analysis has but briefly touched upon this highly interesting phase of the Peloponnesian War. In our opinion, the Sicilian expedition was a strategic blunder of the first magnitude, whose consequences were made even worse by horrendous ineptitude at the tactical level. In the current section, we will concentrate on the strategic plan that brought the Athenians to Sicily, not dwelling much on the tactical aspects of that campaign.[85] Thucydides makes it clear that this plan was fundamentally flawed, since it was based on a considerable underestimation of the enemy the Athenians were to encounter in Sicily.[86]

Underestimating the enemy is something of a recurring theme in history. A frequent example is to estimate the enemy forces as numerically weaker than is actually the case. In the present analysis we will examine a different kind of enemy underestimation. We are interested in instances where the enemy is presented as 'inferior' due to cultural, racial or other factors, but where this supposition lacks any objective foundation. Consequently, using as a starting point Thucydides' analysis of the Sicilian expedition, we will present other cases where the underestimation of the enemy led to strategic failure, and will attempt to offer some insights as to the possible recurrence of this theme in the future.

We have already presented the war aims of the Athenians when they decided to undertake the Sicilian expedition, namely conquest of Sicily and possibly of Italy and other territories around the western Mediterranean littoral, with a view to acquiring overwhelming strength and subsequently establishing dominion of mainland Greece and the rest of the Greek world. If one were to believe Alcibiades' speech to the Athenian *Ecclesia*, the first step in this process, that is the Sicilian expedition, should have been a mere pushover for the Athenians. According to him, the inhabitants of the Greek cities in Sicily, numerous though they were, did not feel they possessed a homeland and were constantly shifting their allegiance from city to city. In addition, the *hoplite* armies of those cities were not particularly strong:

Do not change your minds about the expedition to Sicily on the grounds that we shall have a great power to deal with there. The Sicilian cities have swollen populations made out of all sorts of mixtures, and there are constant changes and rearrangements in the citizen bodies. The result is that they lack the feeling that they are fighting for their own fatherland; no one has adequate armour of his own person, or a proper establishment on the land. What each man spends his time on is in trying to get from the public whatever he thinks he can get either by clever speeches or by open sedition–always with the intention of going off to live in another country, if things go badly with him. Such a crowd as this is scarcely likely either to pay attention to one consistent policy or to join together in concerted action. The chances are that they will make separate agreements with us as soon as we come forward with attractive suggestions, especially if they are, as we understand is the case, in a state of violent party strife. As for their *hoplites*, they have not got so many as they boast of.[87]

This picture of the Greek city-states in Sicily sounds, of course, inherently unlikely. The Athenians ought to know what a Greek city was like, and therefore reject the view that their kindred cities in Sicily were inhabited by shapeless mobs, ready to abandon their allegiance to their city.[88] However, they obviously indulged in an exercise in collective wishful thinking.[89] In fact, that was not all: Alcibiades claimed that the conquest of Sicily was quite likely and that the very undertaking of the expedition would have a depressing effect on the Peloponnesians:

It will have a depressing effect on the arrogance of the Peloponnesians when they see that we despise the quiet life we are living now and have taken on the expedition to Sicily. At the same time we shall either, as is quite likely, become the rulers of all Hellas by using what we gain in Sicily or, in any case, we shall do harm to the Syracusans, and so do good to ourselves and our allies.[90]

This was wide of the mark, to say the least. As illustrated in the previous chapter, far from being disheartened, the Spartans immediately understood that Athens had overextended and that they were themselves presented with a golden opportunity to win the war. The passages just cited should be sufficient to do away with the notion that Alcibiades was a great statesman, as some people still believe.[91] Besides, this notion completely collapses if one examines his claim that Athens was 'quite likely' to conquer that lot of overcrowded, badly governed and weakly armed cities that allegedly comprised Sicily.

In fact, such a state of affairs was simply untrue. Syracuse, a colony of Corinth and the chief opponent of Athens at Sicily, had for long been a powerful city. At the time of the Persian invasion of Greece, Gelon, tyrant of Syracuse, was master of a large part of Sicily and arguably the most powerful Greek ruler. Approached by envoys from Sparta and Athens for aid against the Persians, he promised a force of 200 triremes, 20,000 *hoplites*, 2,000 cavalry, an equal number of archers, slingers and light horsemen, plus corn for the entire Greek army. This force never reached Greece, either because of disputes over the overall command of the anti–Persian struggle or, more likely, because of the Carthaginian invasion of Sicily.[92] Be that as it may, both this episode and the fact that Gelon and the other Greeks of Sicily managed to defeat the Carthaginians, speaks volumes of the power of Syracuse and the general condition of the Greek cities in Sicily.

What about the condition of these cities at the time of the Athenian expedition? Nicias was hardly a brilliant strategist and carries much of the blame for the eventual annihilation of the Athenian expeditionary force, but one must admit that, prior to the expedition, he gave his fellow citizens an accurate picture of the situation:

We are going to set out against cities which are, according to my information, of considerable strength, not subjects of one another and not wanting the kind of change by which they would be glad to escape from some oppressive government on easier terms; very unlikely, in fact, to give up their freedom in order to be ruled by us. The numbers also of the Hellenic cities are very large for one island. Apart from Naxos and Catana, which I expect will join us because of their racial connection with Leontini,[93] there are seven other cities equipped with military and naval forces very much along the same lines as our own, particularly Selinus and Syracuse, our main objectives. They have great numbers of *hoplites* and archers and javelin-throwers, great numbers of triremes, and plenty of men to form the crews. They have money, not only in the hands of private people, but also in the temples of Selinus, and Syracuse also receives the payment of first-fruits from some of the native peoples. But the greatest advantage they have over us is in the number of their horses and in the fact that they grow their own corn and do not have to import any.[94]

Thus, Nicias presents a completely different picture from the one presented by Alcibiades. The Sicilian Greek cities: a) are determined to retain their independence; b) are rich and powerful; c) have a military and naval organization similar to the mainland Greek cities; d) possess two great assets, namely superiority in cavalry and self-sufficiency in foodstuffs. Thucydides makes it clear that this picture was accurate. According to him, when the campaign started going downhill, the Athenians at the expeditionary force:

...wished all the more that the campaign had never been made. These were the only cities they had come up against which were of the same type as their own, democracies like themselves, and places of considerable size, equipped with naval and cavalry forces. They had been unable to make use of a fifth column or to offer the prospect of a change in the form of government as a means for gaining power over them.[95]

The actual course of the campaign vindicated Nicias. The Athenians failed to secure allies in Sicily other than the two cities mentioned by Nicias, Naxos and Catana, plus the majority of the native Sicels.[96] The Syracusan military forces were admittedly not on a par with the battle-hardened troops from mainland Greece, a fact that resulted in initial victories for the Athenians. However, the Syracusans did not lack bravery and it would not be long before they were brought up to standard.[97] In the meantime, however, the complete Syracusan superiority in cavalry created a host of problems for the Athenians.[98] The Athenians tried to exploit their initial successes by besieging Syracuse, but at that point, with the Syracusans about to sue for peace, the Spartans entered the fray sending aid to Syracuse under the brilliant general Gylippus.[99] Soon, the situation was reversed. Gylippus' troops occupied some important outposts, effectively turning the Athenians from besiegers to besieged.[100] As if this were not enough, the Syracusans showed extreme ingenuity and developed a powerful navy.[101] Although initially worsted, the Syracusan navy created a sensation by defeating three times in succession the hitherto undefeated Athenian navy.[102] All of a sudden, and Nicias' superstitious procrastination is much to blame for this, the Athenians were trapped in Sicily.[103] An attempt to escape by land failed and resulted in the total annihilation of the expeditionary force. Those who did not perish were sold as slaves or ended up in the stone quarries.[104]

One might object to the above analysis by pointing out that the Athenians made quite a few mistakes in their conduct of the operations (e.g. they delayed their attack on Syracuse) and that, although they had undoubtedly underestimated the enemy, they were still able to come very close to victory. The answer to this objection is twofold. First, the Syracusans themselves made mistakes. Prior to the arrival of the Athenians at Sicily, the Syracusan statesman Hermocrates had come up with the ingenious proposal that the Syracusan fleet should come out and meet the Athenians in Italy, either at Tarentum or the promontory of Iapygia (the south-eastern tip of Italy). This would make it considerably more difficult for the Athenians to cross the Ionian Sea, since they would have to take pains to keep their force together for fear of being destroyed piecemeal, and thus be compelled to advance very slowly.[105] Hermocrates' plan was not adopted.

Second, and most important, the magnitude of the opposition in Sicily, not to mention the Peloponnesian aid, and the distances involved, made it simply impossible for the Athenians to retain their conquests in Sicily even if they had managed to force the capitulation of Syracuse. To give an example: In the previous chapter we mentioned the Spartan triumph over Argos at Mantinea. Even such a great victory against a nearby opponent, coupled with the help of powerful oligarchic elements inside Argos, was not enough to retain this city within the Spartan sphere of influence.[106] How then, one might ask, could Athens maintain control of such a distant and populous place as Sicily, especially in the face of the renewed Spartan challenge in Greece proper? In fact, the speedy collapse of the Athenian designs in Sicily, as soon as the Peloponnesian aid appeared, should speak for itself. It is ironic that

Nicias, for all his incompetence during the campaign, had captured the essence of the situation prior to it:

Even if we did conquer the Sicilians, there are so many of them and they live so far off that it would be very difficult to govern them. It is senseless to go against people who, even if conquered, could not be controlled, while failure would leave us much worse off than we were before we made the attempt.[107]

The above analysis should leave no doubt with regard to the evaluation of the Sicilian expedition as a strategic move. It was a huge blunder, resulting from frivolous attitudes and an unbelievable underestimation of the enemy.[108] Thucydides' analysis highlights the dangers inherent in such underestimation.

Nevertheless, this is a lesson that has had to be re-learnt numerous times in the course of history. Ancient statesmen were not the only ones prone to underestimating the opponents of their states. Similar instances abound in modern times as well.[109] A most striking example is that of the Russo-Japanese War (1904–1905). The Imperial Russia of the turn of the nineteenth century, although impressive on the map and possessing armies of awesome numerical strength, was hopelessly backward both socially and economically. Its military establishment was plagued by numerous weaknesses, its system of government was corrupt and inefficient, and the whole country was infested by revolutionary groups ready to cause trouble.[110] Territorial expansion was considered a suitable way to escape from the various difficulties. In the Far East, however, Russian ambitions clashed with those of the Japanese. The differences were not necessarily irreconcilable; the Japanese were willing to cede Manchuria to the Russians, provided they would secure Korea for themselves. However, the key Russian decision-makers thought otherwise. According to one of them, Russia needed "a short victorious war to stem the tide of revolution." Czar Nicholas himself was calling the Japanese 'short-tailed monkeys', whereas leading Russian generals were trying to estimate whether one Russian soldier equaled one and a half or two Japanese soldiers.[111]

This underestimation of the enemy was even worse than the one committed by Alcibiades, and was paid for dearly. Japan was fast becoming an industrialised country, was already an important naval power and, most importantly, enjoyed the considerable advantage of geographical proximity to the area of operations, in sharp contrast to the Russians, who had to transport supplies along the single-track Trans-Siberian railway. The war began with a Japanese surprise attack on the Russian fleet at Port Arthur, continued with some ferocious land battles in which the Japanese won with heavy casualties for both sides, and culminated in a great Japanese naval victory at Tsushima Strait. Contrary to what was believed in St. Petersburg, the Japanese were no mere 'short-tailed monkeys'.[112]

Another famous example of underestimation of the enemy was that of the Soviet Union by Hitler (and some of the generals of the German High Command) prior to the German invasion in 1941 (Operation Barbarossa). By this, we do not refer so much to the underestimation of the numerical strength and the technological condition of the Red Army; these were quite natural effects of the extreme secrecy maintained by the Soviet system, which made it difficult for the Germans to obtain accurate intelligence.[113] What we are really talking about is the belief, stemming consciously (in the case of Hitler) or subconsciously (in the case of some leading German generals) from racist attitudes, that the Russians were 'inferior' and thus no match for the German armies.

According to Hitler, Russia had been organised and developed by a Germanic elite, the native Slavs being 'subhuman' and thus unable to rule and develop their country. The Bolshevik revolution, however, had toppled that Germanic elite. Consequently, this led to internal rotten-ness and made the "colossal empire in the East ripe for dissolution". After the initial German victories, resistance was bound to collapse; as Hitler told Field-Marshal Gerd von Rundstedt: "you have only to kick in the door and the whole rotten structure will come crashing down." The hated Slavic 'sub humans' were incapable of withstanding the Aryan onslaught.[114]

There is no evidence that Colonel-General Franz Halder, Chief of the General Staff of the German Army, consciously subscribed to such views. However, even this supposedly detached professional soldier regarded the Russians as inferior. This was the very word (*minderw-ertig*) with which he described the Russian soldier in his estimates prior to the launch of 'Barbarossa'.[115]

The course of the war in the East showed how utterly nonsensical these views were, and little further comment is needed in this regard. Two things should be pointed out. First, that there were plenty of offic-ers within the German Army who had fought the Russians in the First World War and thus could testify to the great fighting valor of the Rus-sian soldier;[116] no excuses can be made for the underestimation of the enemy in this respect. Second, that the defective intelligence mentioned above is not to blame for Hitler's decision to invade the Soviet Union. Hitler later found it convenient to claim that had he known of the true Soviet strength he would never have launched the invasion,[117] but this was merely an *ex post facto* rationalization. Hitler did not launch 'Operation Barbarossa' because he had been misled by some intelligence estimates, but because of his belief in the racial inferiority of the Russians and his desire to create an empire in the East.[118]

There is a common thread running through these instances (Sicilian expedition, Russo-Japanese War, 'Operation Barbarossa'): the enemy, for one reason or another, is wishfully regarded as 'not up to standard'. The results were invariably disastrous. The question that now arises is whether future political leaders will heed Thucydides' warning and be objective in their assessment of their enemies, or follow Alcibiades' path and engage in fanciful and ultimately unfortunate designs.

With the supposedly increased current awareness about different cultures and understanding thereof, underestimating the enemy in a manner similar to the one described above should be rare. However, we contend that there are two areas where, in the future, one is still likely to underestimate an opponent, namely the morale of an armed force and/or a population and their determination to continue a given struggle.

Recent experience seems to confirm this view. The disastrous Soviet intervention in Afghanistan is a clear case in point. The Soviet political leadership was highly complacent as regards that intervention. For instance, a resolution of the Central Committee of the Communist Party of the Soviet Union dated 31 December 1979, that is only four days after the intervention, declared nonchalantly that "[t]he situation in the country becomes normal."[119] The Soviet leaders did not intend their troops to stay in Afghanistan for any length of time, and their main objective was to garrison the most important Afghan towns and the roads connecting them, believing that this would be enough to secure the country.[120] In other words, they severely underestimated the scale and the ferocity of the opposition–as well as overestimating the resolve of their own Afghan allies in Kabul.

Israel's intervention in Lebanon (1982–1985) also ended unsuccessfully, though less dramatically than the Soviet one in Afghanistan. This was not so much due to a failure in assessing enemy capabilities, although the Druze and certain elements of the Syrian armed forces did perform better than expected. Rather, the key seems to have been a persistent underestimation of enemy resolve (e.g. the resolve of PLO and Syrian forces to hang on to West Beirut), coupled with an arguable overestimation of the resolve of Israeli public opinion to continue the war, or even to embark upon it in the first place.[121]

Finally, the UN intervention in Somalia (1992–1995) did not fail because the military capabilities of the various local warlords had been misjudged. Instead, it failed because it had not been correctly appraised that those warlords were more determined than the intervening powers to go on with the struggle.[122]

To summarise: The vice of underestimating an enemy will not be eradicated in the future. On the other hand, considering enemies as inferior simply because they happen to live far away or belong to a different culture should be quite a rare occurrence. Nevertheless, there will still be difficulties in accurately estimating important imponderables such as the morale and the determination of the enemy. In fact, it might even be argued that each side will tend to view itself as the more determined or the one with the higher morale.[123]

EPILOGUE

This book set out to highlight Thucydides' contribution to the study of strategy. From the analysis that followed, Thucydides' text emerged as a classic. To start with, it contains the first detailed presentation of a theory of grand strategy. Furthermore, it graphically illustrates how grand strategies are formulated and put to the test. In addition, it provides us with a superb analysis of a great number of central concepts of modern strategic theory. To a great extent, contemporary analysts have made no significant contribution to Thucydides' treatment of these concepts. To paraphrase Gilpin, it is doubtful whether modern strategists know anything about strategy that was unknown to Thucydides. Without doubt, technology has been profoundly transformed since Thucydides' time. Nonetheless, "there is a certain logic of hostility, a dilemma about security that goes with interstate politics in a self-help system. Alliances, balances of power, and choices in policy between war and appeasement have remained similar over the millennia."[1] Thucydides was as well cognizant of this logic as any present-day analyst.

However, Thucydides has been somewhat neglected as a strategist. In all probability, this is due to his tremendous success as a historian and international relations analyst. Still, this is unfair. It is true that perceptive scholars and policy-makers have long since appreciated Thucydides' qualities as a strategist and his continued relevance to the field.[2] Thankfully, this appreciation is growing, but there is still a lot to be done. We hope that the present book has contributed to this direction.

APPENDIX

STRATEGIC CONCEPTS IN THUCYDIDES' *HISTORY*

We conclude by presenting a number of strategic concepts as they appear in Thucydides' text. Naturally, Thucydides did not use contemporary strategic jargon. Nevertheless, one cannot help being impressed by the remarkable clarity and dexterity with which he uses a multitude of supposedly modern concepts. Two things should be mentioned. First, it will become apparent that certain extracts can fall under various headings, since they contain more than one concept. Second, that the following selection does not claim to be exhaustive; indeed, given the richness of Thucydides' text it seems hardly possible to produce an exhaustive list of the various strategic concepts covered therein. This limitation notwithstanding, we hope that contemporary scholars might find some use in what follows.

Alliances: "In the past we have deliberately avoided all alliances [...] We used to think that our neutrality was a wise thing, since it prevented us being dragged into danger by other people's policies" (I 32).

"Perhaps the greatest advantage to you is that you can entirely depend on us because your enemies are the same as ours" (I 35).

"Identity of interest both among cities and among individuals is the surest of all guarantees" (I 124).

"In an alliance the only safe guarantee is an equality of mutual fear; for then the party that wants to break faith is deterred by the thought that the odds will not be on his side" (III 11).

"It was largely, or entirely, because of Thebes that the Spartans acted so mercilessly towards the Plateans; they considered that at this stage of the war the Thebans were useful to them" (III 68).

"In the future we are not making allies, as we have done in the past, of the kind of people that have to be helped by us in their misfortunes, but who can do nothing for us when we need help from them" (VI 13).

Appeasement: "Let none of you think that we shall be going to war for a trifle if we refuse to revoke the Megarian decree. [...] For you this trifle is both the assurance and the proof of your determination. If you give in, you will immediately be confronted with some greater demand, since they will think that you only gave way on this point through fear. But if you take a firm stand you will make it clear to them that they have to treat you properly as equals. [...] When one's equals, before resorting to arbitration, make claims on their neighbours and put those claims in the form of commands, it would still be slavish to give in to them, however big or however small such claims may be" (I 140–141).

Arms control: "[The Spartans] did not like the idea of Athens or any other city being fortified. [...] The Spartans proposed that not only should Athens refrain from building her own fortifications, but that she should join them in pulling down all the fortifications which still existed in cities outside the Peloponnese. In making this suggestion to the Athenians they concealed their real meaning and their real fears; the idea was, they said, that if there was another Persian invasion, the Persians would have no strong base from which to operate, such as they had in Thebes; and that the Peloponnese was capable of serving the needs of everyone, both as a place of refuge and as a place from which to attack" (I 90).

Balance of power: "The Athenians sent Phaeax out with the idea of persuading their allies on the spot and, if possible, the other Sicilians to make a combined military effort against Syracuse in view of her lust for power" (V 4).

"[The Argives] had been confident that, with Athens and Sparta at variance, supposing their treaty with Sparta came to an end, they could always fall back on the Athenian alliance" (V 40).

"It was better to have the two parties each in possession of its own separate sphere of influence, so that if the King had trouble with one of them, he would always be able to call in the other against it" (VIII 46).

"[Tissaphernes] was keeping the two sides evenly balanced, by not committing himself to either side and so giving it the advantage" (VIII 87).

Balancing, external: "We should be making our own preparations by winning over new allies both among Hellenes and among foreigners–from any quarter, in fact, where we can increase our naval and financial resources" (I 82).

"They [both sides] planned to send embassies to the King of Persia and to any other foreign Power from whom they hoped to obtain support, and they tried to ally themselves with other Hellenic states who were not yet committed to either side" (II 7).

Balancing, internal: "We must put our own affairs in order" (I 82).

"It will require money to carry out these projects, and we will contribute money" (I 121).

Bipolar international system: "The two sides were at the very height of their power and preparedness, and [...] the rest of the Hellenic world was committed to the one side or the other" (I 1).

"The Hellenes [...] split into two divisions, one group following Athens and the other Sparta" (I 18).

Border disputes: "At this time Megara also joined the Athenian alliance, abandoning her alliance with Sparta because the Corinthians were attacking her in a war concerning the frontier boundaries" (I 103).

"Going to the territory of Tegea, he began to divert the water from there into the territory of Mantinea. This water is a constant cause of fighting between the Tegeans and the Mantineans because of the harm it does to the country into which it flows" (V 65).

Coercive diplomacy: "You must think of their land [the Athenians'] as though it was a hostage in your possession, and all the more valuable the better it is looked after" (I 82).

"[Archidamus] expected that the Athenians would not face the idea of letting their land be devastated and would make some conciliatory gesture while it was still untouched" (II 18).

"I shall lay waste your land and try to bring you over by force" (IV 87).

Defense planning: "When dealing with an enemy it is not only his actions but his intentions that have to be watched, since if one does not act first, one will suffer first" (VI 38).

Deterrence: "One does not only defend oneself against a superior power when one is attacked; one takes measures in advance to prevent the attack materializing" (VI 18).

Domino theory: "If Syracuse falls, all Sicily falls with it, and Italy soon afterwards. It would not then be long before you were confronted with the dangers which I have just told you [Alcibiades to the Spartans] threatened you from the west" (VI 91).

Economics and strategy: "Some of them, on the strength of their new riches, built walls for their cities. The weaker, because of the general desire to make profits, were content to put up with being governed by the stronger, and those who won superior power by acquiring capital resources brought the smaller cities under their control" (I 8).

"[Pelops] brought great wealth with him, and, settling in a poor country, acquired such power that, though he was a foreigner, the whole land was called after him" (I 9).

"War is not so much a matter of armaments as of the money which makes armaments effective" (I 83).

"Wars are paid for by the possession of reserves rather than by a sudden increase in taxation" (I 141).

"Victory in war depended on a combination of intelligent resolution and financial resources" (II 13).

"The generals were willing to listen to the proposals [of the besieged Potidaeans] [...] considering also that Athens had already spent 2,000 talents on the siege" (II 70).

"A grand total of 250 [ships were] on active service in one summer. It was this, together with the campaign at Potidaea, which was the chief drain on the revenue" (III 17).

"The Athenians sent the fleet, ostensibly because of their kinship with the Leontinians, though their real aims were to prevent corn being brought in to the Peloponnese from the west" (III 86).

"They have the greatest quantities of gold and silver, which is what supports both war and everything else" (VI 34).

"Athens will immediately be deprived of her revenues from the silver mines at Laurium and from what she gets at present from the land and from the law-courts. Most important of all, she will lose her tribute from the allies, since they will pay it in much less regularly and will cease to be overawed by Athens herself once they see that you are now really making war seriously" (VI 91).

"Expenditure was not the same as it had been, but had grown bigger as the war grew bigger, while revenue was declining" (VII 28).

Expected utility as an incentive for war: "No one is forced into war by ignorance, nor, if he thinks he will gain from it, is he kept out of it by fear. The fact is that one side thinks that the profits to be won outweigh the risks to be incurred, and the other side is ready to face danger rather than accept an immediate loss" (IV 59).

"When one is being attacked and has to think about the safety of one's own country, one cannot go in for calculations about what is prudent. That is more the thing to be done by those whose own country is secure and who, in the desire to make further conquests, are deliberately attacking someone else" (IV 92).

Fear and national security policy: "Sparta is frightened of you and wants war" (I 33).

"Do not force the rest of us in despair to join a different alliance" (I 71).

"Fear of Persia was our chief motive, though afterwards we thought, too, of our own honour and our own interest" (I 75).

"Three very powerful motives prevent us [the Athenians] from doing so [giving up their empire]–security, honour and self-interest" (I 76).

"It was Brasidas, they [the Amphipolitans] considered, who had been their preserver, and at the same time, because of their fear of Athens, they were exceedingly anxious to have the Spartan alliance" (V 11).

"It is because of fear that we hold our empire in Hellas, and it is also because of fear that we have come here to settle matters for our own security" (VI 83).

Force-to-space ratio: "As for their numbers, there is no need to be too frightened. However many of them there are, they can only engage with small detachments at a time, because of their inability to bring the ships close in shore" (IV 10).

Friction, chance and unpredictability in war: "Think, too, of the great part that is played by the unpredictable in war: think of it now, before you are actually committed to war. The longer a war lasts, the more things tend to depend on accidents" (I 78).

125

"War is certainly not one of those things which follow a fixed pattern; instead it usually makes its own conditions in which one has to adapt oneself to changing situations" (I 122).

"In war opportunity waits for no man" (I 142).

"There is much that is unpredictable in war" (II 11).

"As for war, they [wise people] will know that its course is governed by the total chances in operation and can never be restricted in the conditions that one or other of the two sides would like to see permanently fixed" (IV 18).

"It was now [after the Spartan victory in Mantinea] thought that, though they [the Spartans] might have been cast down by fortune, they were still in their own selves the same as they always had been" (V 75).

"We know that in war fortune sometimes makes the odds more level than could be expected from the difference in numbers of the two sides" (V 102).

Geography: "The geographical situation of Corcyra gives its inhabitants a certain independence" (I 37).

"It was a fact that Corcyra lay very conveniently on the coastal route to Italy and Sicily" (I 44).

"Potidaea is the best possible base for any campaign in Thrace" (I 68).

Horizontal escalation: "Now that the Athenians were making their attacks on the Peloponnese, and particularly on the actual territory of Sparta, the Spartans thought that the best way of diverting these attacks would be to give Athens, too, the same kind of trouble by sending an army to her allies" (IV 80).

"Let us [the Syracusans] also send to Sparta and to Corinth urging them to send help to us here quickly and at the same time to go forward with the war in Hellas" (VI 34).

Hostile feelings–hostile intentions: "If ever there was a good time for making peace it is now, before some irremediable event overtakes us, something which would force us into an unending hatred of you, personal as well as political" (I 20).

Imperialism: "Now it is perfectly understandable that the Athenians should have these ambitions and should be making their plans accordingly. I am not blaming those who are resolved to rule, only those who show an even greater readiness to submit" (IV 61).

Legitimacy, domestic: "The city in which we live has always been free and always famous. 'Slow' and 'cautious' can equally well be 'wise' and 'sensible.' Certainly it is because we possess these qualities that we are the only people who do not become arrogant when they are successful, and who in times of stress are less likely to give in than others" (I 84).

"I declare that our city is an education to Greece. [...] This, then, is the kind of city for which these men, who could not bear the thought of losing her, nobly fought and nobly died" (II 41).

Legitimacy, international: "People's feelings were very much on the side of the Spartans, especially as they proclaimed that their aim was the liberation of Hellas. States and individuals alike were enthusiastic to support them in every possible way, both in speech and action" (II 8).

"Once you come forward in the role of liberators, you will find that your strength in the war is enormously increased" (III 13).

"In fact they [the Athenians] aimed at conquering the whole of it [Sicily], though they wanted at the same time to make it look as though they were sending help to their own kinsmen and to their newly acquired allies there" (VI 6).

Logistics: "There was nothing at Pylos itself–indeed not even in summer could they supply the place adequately" (IV 27).

"They divided the fleet into three parts and allotted one part to each general. This was so that they should not have to sail all together, which would mean difficulties with regard to water and harbourage and supplies whenever they landed" (VI 42).

Loss-of-strength gradient: "There have certainly not been many great expeditions, either Hellenic or foreign, which have been successful when sent far from home. They cannot come in greater numbers than the inhabitants of the country and their neighbours, all of whom will unite together through fear; and if things go wrong with them because of lack of supplies in a foreign country, even though they themselves are chiefly responsible for their failure, they nevertheless leave the honours of war to those against whom their plots were made" (VI 33).

Military discipline: "The best and safest thing of all is when a large force is so well disciplined that it seems to be acting like one man" (II 11).

"When it comes to action, put your trust in discipline and in silence" (II 89).

Military initiative: "The enemy has as many or more ships than we have, and keeps us in the constant expectation of having to face an attack. We can see them at their maneuvres, and the initiative is in their hands" (VII 12).

Military necessity: "It was reasonable to suppose that even the gods would look indulgently on any action done under the stress of war and danger" (IV 98).

Military tactics: "The two armies met, the Argives and their allies advancing with great violence and fury, while the Spartans came on slowly and to the music of many flute-players in their ranks. This custom of theirs has nothing to do with religion; it is designed to make them keep in step and move forward steadily without breaking their ranks, as large armies often do when they are just about to join battle" (V 70).

"It is true of all armies that, when they are moving into action, the right wing tends to get unduly extended and each side overlaps the enemy's left with its own right. This is because fear makes every man want to do his best to find protection for his unarmed side in the shield of the man next to him on the right, thinking that the more closely the shields are locked together, the safer he will be" (V 71).

Military training: "The long discipline of action is a more effective safeguard than hurried speeches, however well they may be delivered" (V 69).

Misperceptions: "Our resources are the same as ever; we simply miscalculated them, and this is a mistake that may be made by everyone" (IV 18).

Morale: "At the beginning of an undertaking the enthusiasm is always greatest" (II 8).

"When things happen suddenly, unexpectedly, and against all calculation, it takes the heart out of a man" (II 61).

"Beaten men never have quite the same resolution as they had before when they come up against the same danger for the second time" (II 89).

"In all probability, since they have only just taken the city, we shall find that their precautions have been greatly relaxed" (III 30).

"I do not want any of you in our present awkward position to try to show off his intelligence by making a precise calculation of the dangers which surmount us; instead we must simply make straight at the enemy, and not pause to discuss the matter, confident in our hearts that these dangers, too, can be surmounted" (IV 10).

"How impossible it is to force a landing if the defenders stand firm and do not give way through fear of the surf or the frightening appearance of the ships as they sail in" (IV 10).

"Not wanting the army to get depressed by being constantly in the same position, he broke up his camp and moved forward" (V 7).

"When a second force appears later on the scene it causes more terror among the enemy than the force with which he is actually fighting at the time" (V 9).

"It is at the beginning [...] that every army inspires most fear; but if time is allowed to pass before it shows itself, men's spirits revive and, when they actually do see it, they are less impressed than they would have been" (VI 49).

"The idea of Syracusans daring so unexpectedly to stand up to the Athenian navy would [...] have such a disturbing effect on the enemy that it would amply make up for anything they might lose owing to Athenian skill and their own inexperience" (VII 21).

"In going into action it is generally the case that where hopes are highest hearts are stoutest" (VII 67).

National character: "[The Athenians] are by nature incapable of either living a quiet life themselves or of allowing anyone else to do so" (I 70).

"After the Spartans, the Chians are the only people I know of who have kept their heads in prosperity and who, as their city increased in power, increased also their own measures for its security" (VIII 24).

"On this occasion, as on many others, the Spartans proved to be quite the most remarkably helpful enemies that the Athenians could have had. For Athens, particularly as a naval power, was enormously helped by the very great difference in the national characters–her speed as against their slowness, her enterprise as against their lack of initiative. This was shown by the Syracusans, who were most like the Athenians in character and fought best against them" (VIII 96).

National interest: "We must [...] convince you first that by giving us this help you will be acting in your own interests, or certainly not against your own interests" (I 32).

"When tremendous dangers are involved no one can be blamed for looking to his own interest" (I 75).

"After calculating your own interest, you are beginning to talk in terms of right and wrong. Considerations of this kind have never yet turned people aside from the opportunities of aggrandisement offered by superior strength" (I 76).

"If [...] whatever the rights or wrongs of it may be, you propose to hold power all the same, then your interest demands that these too [the Mytilenian rebels], rightly or wrongly, must be punished" (III 40).

"If we are sensible people, we shall see that the question is not so much whether they are guilty as whether we are making the right decision for ourselves. [...] This is not a law-court, where we have to consider what is fit and just; it is a political assembly, and the question is how Mytilene can be most useful to Athens" (III 44).

"As for Hagnon, being at war with Athens, they [the people of Amphipolis] could no longer honour him with the same profit as before, or with the same goodwill" (V 11).

"Of all the people we know the Spartans are most conspicuous for believing that what they like doing is honourable and what suits their interests is just" (V 105).

"If one follows one's self-interest one wants to be safe, whereas the path of justice and honour involves one in danger" (V 107).

"It is for our own security that we are in Sicily, and we see that here your interests are the same as ours" (VI 83).

"When the Syracusan representative says that it is illogical for us to enslave Chalcidians in Hellas and liberate them in Sicily, he should remember that it is in our interest that in Hellas they should be unarmed and should merely contribute money, but here in Sicily we should like to see both the people of Leontini and all our other friends as independent as possible. When a man or a city exercises absolute power the logical course is the course of self-interest, and ties of blood exist only when they can be relied upon; one must choose one's friends and enemies according to the circumstances on each particular occasion" (VI 84–85).

Naval power: "Your aim, no doubt, should be, if it were possible, to prevent anyone else having a navy at all: the next best thing is to have on your side the strongest navy that there is" (I 35).

"There are three considerable naval powers in Hellas–Athens, Corcyra and Corinth. If Corinth gets control of us first and you allow our navy to be united with hers, you will have to fight against the combined fleets of Corcyra and the Peloponnese. But if you receive us into your alliance, you will enter upon the war with our ships as well as your own" (I 36).

"If we can neither defeat them at sea, nor take away from them the resources on which their navy depends, we shall do ourselves more harm than good" (I 81).

"Seamanship, just like anything else, is an art. It is not something that can be picked up and studied in one's spare time; indeed it allows one no spare time for anything else" (I 142).

"Sea-power is of enormous importance" (I 143).

"The world before our eyes can be divided in two parts, the land and the sea, each of which is valuable and useful to man. Of the whole of one of these parts you are in control–not only of the area at present in your power, but elsewhere too, if you want to go further. With your navy as it is today there is no power on earth–not the King of Persia nor any people under the sun–which can stop you from sailing where you wish" (II 62).

Neutrality: "Argos was very well off in every direction, having taken no part in the Attic war, indeed having profited greatly from her position of neutrality" (V 28).

Numerical superiority: "Perhaps there is ground for confidence in the superiority which we have in heavy infantry and in actual numbers" (I 81).

"We are superior in numbers and in military experience" (I 121).

"We must not [...] join battle with the greatly superior forces of the Peloponnesians" (I 143).

"As a rule the side that wins is the side with the numbers and the equipment" (II 87).

"The fighting broke out again and the democrats, who had the advantage of better positions and superior numbers, were victorious" (III 74).

"We are Ionians and the Peloponnesians are Dorians; they are more numerous than we are and they live close to us" (VI 82).

Overextension: "In going to Sicily you are leaving many enemies behind you, and you apparently want to make new ones there and have them also on your hands" (VI 10).

"But what chiefly encouraged the Spartans to act with energy was their belief that Athens, with two wars on her hands—one against them and one against the Sicilians—would be now easier to crush" (VII 18).

"What wore them down more than anything else was the fact that they had two wars on their hands at once" (VII 28).

Power: "We have no right [...] to judge cities by their appearances rather than by their actual power" (I 10).

"It has always been a rule that the weak should be subject to the strong" (I 76).

"The strong do what they have the power to do and the weak accept what they have to accept" (V 89).

"This is no fair fight, with honour on the one side and shame on the other. It is rather a question of saving your lives and not resisting those who are far too strong for you" (V 101).

"It is a general and necessary law of nature to rule whatever one can" (V 105).

"Goodwill shown by the party that is asking for help does not mean security for the prospective ally. What is looked for is a positive preponderance of power in action" (V 109).

"This is the safe rule—to stand up to one's equals, to behave with deference towards one's superiors, and to treat one's inferiors with moderation" (V 111).

"They had no more right to give us orders than we had to give orders to them, except that at the time they were stronger" (VI 82).

Prestige: "The Spartans have sent us here [...] to try to come to an arrangement with you which will do you good and bring to us, in our present plight, as much honour as can be expected in the circumstances" (IV 17).

"This event [the Spartan surrender at Sphacteria] caused much more surprise among the Hellenes than anything else that happened in the war. The general impression had been that Spartans would never surrender their arms whether because of hunger or any other form of compulsion; instead they would keep them to the last and die fighting as best they could" (IV 40).

"The reputation of Sparta had sunk very low indeed and she was despised for the losses she had suffered" (V 28).

"By this one action [the Spartan victory at Mantinea] they did away with all the reproaches that had been levelled against them by the Hellenes at this time, whether for cowardice, because of the disaster in the island, or for incompetence and lack of resolution on other occasions" (V 75).

"There was a time when the Hellenes imagined that our city had been ruined by the war, but they came to consider it even greater than it really is, because of the splendid show I made as its representative at the Olympic games" (VI 16).

Preventive war: "Finally the point was reached when Athenian strength attained a peak plain for all to see and the Athenians began to encroach upon Sparta's allies. It was at this point that Sparta felt the position to be no longer tolerable and decided by starting this present war to employ all her energies in attacking and, if possible, destroying the power of Athens" (I 118).

"The Thessalians, who were the dominant power in the area and whose territory was threatened by the new foundation, were frightened of having a powerful state on their frontiers, and so were constantly doing damage and making war on the new settlers until they wore them down to a state of insignificance" (III 93).

"The Spartans, hearing of the building of the walls, marched against Argos [...] They captured and demolished the walls that were being built" (V 83).

"If Syracuse, after driving out the people of Leontini, were allowed to escape scot-free, and to go on destroying the remaining allies of Athens until she acquired complete control of Sicily, the danger would then have to be faced that at some time or other the Syracusans, who were Dorians themselves, would come with a large force to the aid of their Dorian kinsmen and would join the Peloponnesians, who had originally sent them out as colonists, in the work of utterly destroying the power of Athens. It would be a wise thing, therefore, for Athens to make use of the allies she still had and to put a check on Syracuse" (VI 6).

Principle of concentration of force: "They were afraid that, if they divided their force in two, the Poteidaeans and their allies would attack them" (I 64).

"Because of the length of the voyage it will be difficult for this force to keep its order, but easy for us to attack it as it comes up slowly and in detachments" (VI 34).

Principle of unity of command: "They have no central deliberative authority to produce quick decisive action" (I 141).

"As for choosing the generals, they should be few in number and they should have unrestricted power; the people should swear an oath to them guaranteeing that they would be allowed to carry out their responsibilities exactly as they saw fit" (VI 72).

Reputation as a strategic asset: "This event [the Spartan surrender at Sphacteria] caused much more surprise among the Hellenes than any-thing else that happened in the war. The general impression had been that Spartans would never surrender their arms whether because of hunger or any other form of compulsion; instead they would keep them to the last and die fighting as best they could" (IV 40).

Security dilemma: "There came a time when we were surrounded by enemies; [...] at this point it was clearly no longer safe for us to risk letting our empire go" (I 75).

"We say that in Hellas we rule in order not to be ruled; in Sicily we come as liberators in order not to be harmed by the Sicilians; we are forced to intervene in many directions simply because we have to be on our guard in many directions" (VI 87).

Surprise: "The Thebans were anxious to get control of Plataea first [...] while it was still peace time and war had not yet actually broken out" (II 2).

"The Acarnanians from the ambush set upon them from the rear and broke them at the first attack so completely that no one stood his ground to put up any resistance. Indeed, the panic into which they were thrown spread to most of the rest of the army" (III 108).

"The enemy [...] could thus attack him unexpectedly at any point they chose, since the initiative would be in their hands" (IV 29).

"The landing had taken them by surprise, since they thought that the ships were only sailing as usual to their stations for the night" (IV 32).

"About 600 of the Athenians had fallen, and only seven on the other side. This was the result of there having been no set battle, but only the unforeseen panic-ridden affair that I have described" (V 11).

Terrain: "His own army, in spite of its size, might get cut to pieces without knowing what was happening, since the lack of visibility would prevent one detachment from helping the other as it should. These calculations of his were largely based on the Aetolian disaster, which had been, to some extent, caused by the forests" (IV 30).

"This force was divided into companies of roughly 200 men [...] who occupied the highest points of ground, with the object of causing the enemy the greatest possible embarrassment" (IV 32).

Unequal growth: "What made war inevitable was the growth of the Athenian power and the fear which this caused in Sparta" (I 23).

"The Spartans voted that the treaty had been broken and that war should be declared not so much because they were influenced by the speeches of their allies as because they were afraid of the further growth of Athenian power, seeing, as they did, that already the greater part of Hellas was under the control of Athens" (I 88).

NOTES

PREFACE

1. The Peloponnesian War has been inextricably linked with Thucydides. Since, however, he did not finish his work and consequently one who wishes to have a complete picture of that war is forced to rely on other ancient historians as well, chiefly Xenophon (Xenophon, *Hellenica*), an obvious injustice is done. Although duly acknowledging that the present book perpetuates this injustice, we also wish to cite two mitigating factors. First, that none of the other ancient historians dealing with the Peloponnesian War remotely approaches Thucydides' analytical depth; Xenophon gives a fairly reliable, 'factual' presentation, but nothing more. Second, the contribution of other ancient historians notwithstanding, the overwhelming majority of the material in the present book comes from Thucydides. Hence, we feel that we are not too wrong to talk about 'Thucydides' analysis' even when dealing with events actually mentioned by somebody else.

2. Louis J. Halle, *The Elements of International Strategy* (Lanham, MD: University Press of America, 1984), p. 15.

3. See, among others, Bruce Russett, "A Post-Thucydides, Post-Cold-War World," *Occasional Research Papers*, Athens: Institute of International Relations, Panteion University, 1992.

4. See, among others, John Mueller, *Quiet Cataclysm: Reflections on the Recent Transformation of World Politics* (New York: Harper Collins, 1995), and Edward Morse, *Modernization and Transformation of International Relations* (New York: Free Press, 1976).

5. Robert Gilpin, *War and Change in World Politics* (Cambridge: Cambridge University Press, 1981), p. 7.

6. Athanassios Platias, "Thucydides On Grand Strategy: Periclean Grand Strategy During The Peloponnesian War," in *Thucydides: The Classical Theorist of International Relations, Études Helléniques/Hellenic Studies*, vol. 6, no. 2 (Autumn 1998), pp. 53–103.

7. See previous footnote, as well as Athanassios Platias and Constantinos Koliopoulos, "Thucydides on Grand Strategy II: Spartan Grand Strategy During the Peloponnesian War," *Études Helléniques/Hellenic Studies*,

vol. 8, no. 1 (Spring 2000), pp. 23–70, and Athanassios G. Platias and Constantinos Koliopoulos, "Grand Strategies Clashing: Athenian and Spartan Strategies in Thucydides' 'History of the Peloponnesian War'", *Comparative Strategy*, vol. 21, no. 5, October-December 2002, pp. 377–399.

1. GRAND STRATEGY: A FRAMEWORK FOR ANALYSIS

1. Michael I. Handel, *Masters of War: Classical Strategic Thought* (London: Frank Cass, 1992), p. 1; Sun Tzu, *The Art of War* (trans. by Samuel B. Griffith) (Oxford: Oxford University Press, 1963); Carl von Clausewitz, *On War* (edited and translated by Michael Howard and Peter Paret) (Princeton, NJ: Princeton University Press, 1989).
2. Thucydides, *History of the Peloponnesian War* (trans. Rex Warner) (London: Penguin, 1972).
3. Robert Gilpin, *War and Change in World Politics* (Cambridge: Cambridge University Press, 1981), p. 227.
4. Colin Gray has declared that 'the strategist's toolkit' is Clausewitz' *On War*; Colin S. Gray, *Modern Strategy* (Oxford: Oxford University Press, 1999), ch. 3. We do not dispute that, but want to point out that Thucydides' *History* may legitimately aspire to at least equal status.
5. Gray, *Modern Strategy*, p. 1, emphasis in text.
6. Definition by the German war theorist Heinrich Dietrich von Bülow, early 19th century. See Peter Paret, "Clausewitz," in Peter Paret (ed.), *Makers of Modern Strategy from Machiavelli to the Nuclear Age* (Princeton, NJ: Princeton University Press, 1986), p. 190.
7. Definition by the Swiss General and strategist Antoine Henry de Jomini (1779–1869); Henry de Jomini, *Summary of the Art of War* (abridged edn. by Brig. Gen. J.D. Hittle) reproduced in *Roots of Strategy*, Book 2 (Harrisburg, PA: Stackpole Books, 1987), p. 460.
8. See B. H. Liddell Hart, *Strategy* (2nd revised edn.) (London: Meridian, 1991), p. 321.
9. See André Beaufre, *Introduction to Strategy* (London: Faber and Faber, 1965), p. 22.
10. Clausewitz, *On War*, bk. 1, ch. 1, p. 75.
11. For the 'horizontal dimension' of strategy, see Edward N. Luttwak, *Strategy: The Logic of War and Peace* (Cambridge, MA: The Belknap Press of Harvard University Press, 1987), p. 70.
12. For an analysis of the paradoxical logic of strategy, not free from overstatement, see Luttwak, *Strategy*.
13. Daniel J. Hughes (ed.), *Moltke on the Art of War: Selected Writings* (trans. Daniel J. Hughes and Harry Bell) (Novato, CA: Presidio, 1995), p. 45.
14. See Gunther E. Rothenberg, "Moltke, Schlieffen, and the Doctrine of Strategic Envelopment," Paret, *Makers of Modern Strategy*, pp. 296–325, as

well as the famous analysis of Gerhard Ritter, *The Schlieffen Plan* (London: Wolff, 1958).

15. Bernard Brodie, *Strategy in the Missile Age* (Princeton, NJ: Princeton University Press, 1959), p. 43. See also S.E. Finer, *The Man on Horseback* (Middlesex: Penguin Books, 1975).

16. Athanassios Platias, *High Politics in Small Countries* (Ph.D. Diss., Cornell University, 1986), pp. 3–4.

17. Alfred Thayer Mahan, *The Influence of Sea Power Upon History, 1660–1783* (London: Sampson Low, Marston, 1892), p. 8.

18. See Jomini, *Summary of the Art of War*, reproduced in *Roots of Strategy, Book 2*, p. 460; Clausewitz, *On War*, bk. 2, ch. 1, p. 129; Helmuth von Moltke, *Moltkes Kriegslehren*, extract reproduced in Lawrence Freedman (ed.), *War* (Oxford: Oxford University Press, 1994), p. 221.

19. Colin S. Gray, *War, Peace, and Victory: Strategy and Statecraft for the Next Century* (New York: Simon and Schuster, 1990), p. 35.

20. See Luttwak, *Strategy*, p. 70.

21. Stalin ruled the Soviet Union from the beginning of the 1920s until the eve of the German invasion of 1941 by merely holding the party office of General Secretary, while Deng during the last years of his life was officially nothing more than Chairman of the Chinese Bridge Federation.

22. On this issue, see Bernard Brodie, *War and Politics* (London: Cassell, 1973).

23. Barton Whaley, *Stratagem: Deception and Surprise in War* (Cambridge, MA: MIT, 1969) (mimeo), p. 245.

24. See Edward N. Luttwak, *The Grand Strategy of the Roman Empire from the First Century A.D. to the Third* (Baltimore, MD: Johns Hopkins University Press, 1976); Edward N. Luttwak, *The Grand Strategy of the Soviet Union* (London: Weidenfeld and Nicolson, 1983); Luttwak, *Strategy*; Paul Kennedy, "Grand Strategies in War and Peace: Toward a Broader Definition," in Paul Kennedy (ed.), *Grand Strategies in War and Peace* (New Haven, CT: Yale University Press, 1991), pp. 1–7. The French General André Beaufre uses the term 'total strategy'; see Beaufre, *Introduction to Strategy*.

25. See Gray, *War, Peace, and Victory*, pp. 38–41. In that text Gray uses the term 'theory of war', but we believe that 'theory of victory' is a better term, as in fact used by Gray himself in "Nuclear Strategy: The Case for a Theory of Victory," *International Security*, vol. 4, no. 1 (Summer 1979), pp. 54–87.

26. Clausewitz, *On War*, bk. 8, ch. 9, pp. 627–628.

27. Lenin openly favoured both Russia's defeat in the war and a subsequent civil war that would enable him to establish the dictatorship of the proletariat. The German assistance to Lenin was not confined to helping him reach Russia in 1917, but also extended to granting financial support to the Bolsheviks. For these two points, see Dmitri Volkogonov, *Lenin: Life and Legacy* (London: Harper Collins, 1995), pp. 79–81, 109–128.

28. During the initial stages of 'Operation Barbarossa' the Germans were often welcomed as liberators by the Soviet population; see Heinz Guderian, *Panzer Leader* (New York: Da Capo, 1996), pp. 159, 193–194; J.F.C. Fuller, *The Conduct of War, 1789–1961* (London: Methuen, 1972), pp. 262–264. For the amazing results of the friendly policy towards the conquered population, followed–on his own initiative–by the German Field-Marshal Ewald von Kleist, see Samuel W. Mitcham, Jr., "Kleist," in Correlli Barnett (ed.) *Hitler's Generals* (London: Weidenfeld and Nicolson, 1990), pp. 256–257.

29. There is no reason why the concepts of the operational and tactical level cannot be applied on the other components of grand strategy as well.

30. For an analysis of the concept of military strategy, see Barry Posen, *The Sources of Military Doctrine* (Ithaca, NY: Cornell University Press, 1984), ch. 1. It must be mentioned here that Posen uses the term 'military doctrine' in order to describe both military strategy and what we will later call 'operational doctrine.'

31. The spread of chemical (and to a lesser extent biological) weapons makes it preferable to talk about 'mass destruction forces' instead of 'nuclear forces', although the destructive capacity of chemical and biological weapons cannot be compared to that of nuclear ones.

32. Barry Posen distinguishes only the first three categories; see Posen, *The Sources of Military Doctrine*, p. 14. Robert Art distinguishes four purposes of force: defensive, deterrent, compellent, and swaggering (*viz.* the display of military force in order to enhance prestige); Robert J. Art, "To What Ends Military Power," *International Security*, vol. 4, no. 4 (Spring 1980), pp. 4–35.

33. For a further discussion of offensive and defensive military strategies, with special emphasis on the various forms of defense, see Platias, *High Politics in Small Countries*, pp. 31–58.

34. For a discussion, see Platias, *High Politics in Small Countries*, pp. 32–34.

35. Alfred Vagts, *Defense and Diplomacy: The Soldier and the Conduct of Foreign Relations* (New York: King's Crown Press, 1956), ch. 8.

36. Thomas C. Schelling, *The Strategy of Conflict* (Cambridge, MA: Harvard University Press, 1960), part 4.

37. For a moral argument concerning the distinction between preventive and pre-emptive war, see Michael Walzer, *Just and Unjust Wars: A Moral Argument with Historical Illustrations* (2nd. edn.) (New York: Basic Books, 1992), ch. 5.

38. The bibliography on deterrence is immense. For two classic analyses, see Glenn H. Snyder, *Deterrence and Defense* (Princeton, NJ: Princeton University Press, 1961) and Thomas C. Schelling, *Arms and Influence* (New Haven, CT: Yale University Press, 1966). For a recent treatise, see Lawrence Freedman, *Deterrence* (Cambridge: Polity Press, 2004).

39. See the excellent analysis of Robert Art, "The Influence of Foreign Policy on Seapower," *Sage Professional Papers in International Studies*, 2,

02–019 (Beverly Hills, CA and London: Sage Publications, 1973). See also Constantinos Koliopoulos, *Understanding Strategic Surprise* (Ph.D. Diss., Lancaster University, 1996), ch. 7.

40. Art, "To What Ends Military Power."
41. André Beaufre prefers to view procurement as operational strategy in peacetime; see Beaufre, *Introduction to Strategy*. For the importance of procurement strategies, see Ariel Levite and Athanassios Platias, "Evaluating Small States' Dependence on Arms Imports: An Alternative Perspective," *Peace Studies Program Occasional Paper No. 16* (Ithaca, NY: Cornell University, 1983).
42. One should note that the lower levels of strategy appear solely in wartime. Cf. the dissenting view of Beaufre, mentioned above.
43. The concept of the operational level entered Western strategic thought only in the 1980s. Characteristically, Constantine Fitzgibbon, the translator of the German General Guderian's book in English is somewhat at a loss when encountering this term (the book was translated in 1952). See Guderian, *Panzer Leader*, p. 22, fn. 1. Sir Basil Liddell Hart immediately after the Second World War made an unsuccessful attempt to bring back the usage of the pre-Napoleonic term 'grand tactics' which, in any case, was less broad than the "operational level". For a presentation of the pre-Napoleonic terminology, see Jomini, *Summary of the Art of War*, reproduced in *Roots of Strategy*, Book 2, p. 460 and Whaley, *Stratagem*, pp. 245–246.
44. The German Field-Marshal Erich von Manstein makes it clear that, as far as the Germans were concerned, the Crimean theatre was autonomous to such a degree, that there was no interference even from the High Command itself; see Erich von Manstein, *Lost Victories* (Novato, CA: Presidio, 1994), pp. 204, 285.
45. Luttwak, *Strategy*, p. 92.
46. Luttwak, *Strategy*. The concept of operational method is closely connected with that of military doctrine. Military doctrine is a particular range of ideas that explains how an armed force will fight; see Gray, *War, Peace, and Victory*, p. 41. Obviously, the concept of military doctrine can be employed at all levels of military strategy, depending on the range of forces it covers. When a military doctrine governs all or most branches of the armed forces (e.g. the German Blitzkrieg in Operation Barbarossa), it then becomes part of military strategy. At the same time, there are smaller-range doctrines, which usually represent the way each service prefers to accomplish its mission. These can be called operational doctrines or operational methods. For instance, aerial bombardment can be conducted through the operational methods of deep interdiction, area bombing or precision bombing and each of these operational methods can in turn be implemented through various tactical methods; see *Luttwak, Strategy*, p. 108. Of course, this is not the only contemporary use of the term 'military doctrine'; we have already encountered a different use by Barry Posen

(see above, n. 30). In Soviet strategic thought, the concept of military doctrine had a far broader meaning. For the Soviets, military doctrine had two dimensions: political-military and military-technical. The first specifically stated the requisite criteria for a Soviet decision to wage war, whereas the second concerned all aspects of military practice, from military strategy to tactics (as defined above); see Todd Clark, "Soviet Military Doctrine in the Gorbachev Years: Doctrinal Revolution and Counter-Revolution, 1985–1991," *Bailrigg Paper 24* (Lancaster: CDISS, Lancaster University, 1996), pp. 7–8.

47. Some analysts discern yet a lower level, namely the technical one (military technology); see Luttwak, *Strategy*. We contend that technology would be better viewed as one of the structural factors influencing strategy, such as geography. For a treatise following this approach, see Martin van Creveld, *Technology and War* (New York: Free Press, 1989).

48. Immediately after that, he defined strategy as "the use of engagements for the object of the war"; see Clausewitz, *On War*, bk. 2, ch. 1, p. 128. It has been argued that Clausewitz had also discerned what was later to be defined as operational level; see Wallace P. Franz, "Two Letters on Strategy: Clausewitz' Contribution to the Operational Level of War," in Michael I. Handel (ed.), *Clausewitz and Modern Strategy* (London: Frank Cass, 1986), pp. 171–194.

49. Cf. the increased importance Clausewitz assigned to the availability of reserves at the tactical level, while at the same time claiming that reserves have no place on strategy, which must make use of all available forces; Clausewitz, *On War*, bk. 3, chs. 12–13.

50. This does not mean that senior commanders should not be brave, but only that personal bravery is not the primary thing to ask from them. The French Field-Marshal Bazaine, despite his unsurpassed bravery, proved disastrous as commander-in-chief of the French Army during the Franco-Prussian War of 1870–1871. In fact, there were instances where his very bravery was a disadvantage, since he insisted on being on the front line and thus was in no position to exercise overall command; see Michael Howard, *The Franco-Prussian War* (London: Routledge, 1988), p. 155.

51. For a comparative assessment of the effectiveness of the main belligerents in the Second World War at various levels of strategy, see Allan R. Millett and Williamson Murray (eds.), *Military Effectiveness, Volume III: The Second World War* (Boston, MA: Unwin Hyman, 1988).

52. For competing views on the soundness of the American grand strategy and the prospects for Iraq, see among others Wesley K. Clark, *Winning Modern Wars: Iraq, Terrorism and the American Empire* (New York: Public Affairs, 2003); John Lewis Gaddis, *Surprise, Security, and the American Experience* (Massachusetts: Harvard University Press, 2004); Toby Dodge, "Iraq's Future," *Adelphi Paper 372* (London: International Institute for Strategic Studies, 2005); Daniel Byman, "Five Bad Options for Iraq," *Survival*, vol. 47 no. 1 (Spring 2005), pp. 7–32; Yahia Said, "Iraq in the

Shadow of Civil War," *Survival*, vol. 47, no. 4 (Winter 2005–06), pp. 85–92; Christopher J. Fettweis, "On the Consequences of Failure in Iraq," *Survival*, vol. 49, no. 4 (Winter 2007–08), pp. 83–98.

53. See Williamson Murray and Major General Robert H. Scales, Jr., *The Iraq War* (Cambridge, MA: The Belknap Press of Harvard University Press, 2003).

54. This refers chiefly to the inspired leadership of Generals Petraeus and Odierno; see Frederick W. Kagan and Kimberly Kagan, "The Patton of Counterinsurgency: With a sequence of brilliant offensives, Raymond Odierno adapted the Petraeus doctrine into a successful operational art", *The Weekly Standard*, vol. 13, no. 25 (March 10, 2008).

55. See John Erickson, *The Road to Stalingrad* (London: Weidenfeld and Nicolson, 1993), ch. 8.

56. The classic description of Xerxes' campaign can be found in Herodotus, bks. VII-IX. For the battles of Salamis and Plataea, see VIII 84–89 and IX 60–65. For a modern analysis, see J.F.C. Fuller, *The Decisive Battles of the Western World* (London: Eyre & Spottiswoode, 1954), ch. 1. For a less satisfactory analysis, attributing the Persian failure to the psychological need of every Persian king to achieve conquests, which in turn made him prone to committing the sin of overextension, see Barry S. Strauss and Josiah Ober, *The Anatomy of Error: Ancient Military Disasters and Their Lessons for Modern Strategists* (New York: St. Martin's Press, 1990), ch. 1. The psychological need for making conquests and the concomitant danger of overextension certainly existed, but if the Persians had not given battle at Salamis and had not committed that tactical blunder at Plataea, it is difficult to see how they would have lost the war. Many of the points highlighted in our analysis have been touched upon by the late Professor Olmstead, an eminent historian of the Persian Empire. However, he also made the completely unsubstantiated claim that even after Plataea the Persians were still capable of "throwing fresh troops upon the battle-weary allies and sweeping them rapidly to the southernmost tip of the Peloponnese"; A.T. Olmstead, *History of the Persian Empire* (Chicago, IL: The University of Chicago Press, 1948), p. 259. In fact, not only were the Persians unable to do anything of the sort but, as will be seen in the next chapter, immediately after Plataea the Greeks were able to mount offensive operations against the Persians in Asia.

57. This section draws heavily on Posen, *The Sources of Military Doctrine*, p. 13.

58. For a more elaborate analysis of the concept of security, based on the distinction between strong and weak states, see Barry Buzan, *People, States and Fear* (2nd edn.) (London: Harvester Wheatsheaf, 1991), ch. 2.

59. According to Paul Kennedy, the idea that grand strategy functions in peacetime as well as in wartime was Liddell Hart's (and, to a lesser degree, Edward Mead Earle's) own contribution to the study of the concept; in

other words, this is a comparatively recent idea; see Paul Kennedy, "Grand Strategies in War and Peace."
60. Liddell Hart, *Strategy*, p. 322.
61. See also Michael Howard, "The Forgotten Dimensions of Strategy," in Michael Howard, *The Causes of War* (London: Temple Smith, 1983), pp. 101–109.
62. See for instance Stephen M. Walt, *The Origins of Alliances* (Ithaca, NY: Cornell University Press, 1987), chs. 1, 2, 8.
63. See Henry Kissinger, *A World Restored: Metternich, Castlereagh and the Problems of Peace 1812–1822* (Boston, MA: Houghton Mifflin, 1973).
64. See David A. Baldwin, *Economic Statecraft* (Princeton, NJ: Princeton University Press, 1985); Paul Kennedy, *The Rise and Fall of the Great Powers: Economic Change and Military Conflict from 1500 to 2000* (New York: Random House, 1987).
65. The classic analysis on this subject is Alfred Thayer Mahan, *The Influence of Sea Power Upon the French Revolution and Empire, 1793–1812* (2 vols.) (London: Sampson Low, Marston, 1893).
66. For this concept, see Joseph S. Nye, Jr., *Soft Power: The Means to Success in World Politics* (New York: Public Affairs, 2004).
67. See Haralambos Papasotiriou, *Byzantine Grand Strategy* (Ph.D. Diss., Stanford University, 1991).
68. Hans Delbrück, *History of the Art of War* (4 vols.) (Lincoln, NE: University of Nebraska Press, 1975–1985). See also Gordon A. Craig, "Delbrück: The Military Historian," in Paret, *Makers of Modern Strategy*, pp. 326–353.
69. As Lawrence Freedman points out, wars are rarely confined to pitched battles that lead to the decisive victory of one combatant. This, however, does not negate the utility of the ideal type of the strategy of annihilation as a tool of strategic planning and analysis. See Lawrence Freedman, "The Changing Forms of Military Conflict," *Survival* 40, 4 (Winter 1998–99), p. 40.
70. The term 'grand strategy of exhaustion' roughly coincides with what André Beaufre terms 'indirect strategy'; see Beaufre, *Introduction to Strategy*. Though he does distinguish between 'indirect strategy' and 'indirect approach', we feel that the confusion between these two terms cannot be altogether avoided, hence the term 'grand strategy of exhaustion' serves the analyst better.
71. The bibliography on Napoleon is immense. See among others Fuller, *The Conduct of War*, pp. 42–58; Peter Paret, "Napoleon and the Revolution in War," in Paret, *Makers of Modern Strategy*, pp. 123–142; David G. Chandler, *The Military Maxims of Napoleon* (New York: Macmillan, 1997). For a critical view, see Correlli Barnett, *Bonaparte* (Ware: Wordsworth, 1997).
72. See B. H. Liddell Hart, *The British Way in Warfare* (London: Faber, 1932). For a critical presentation of the "British way of warfare," see Colin Gray,

"History for Strategists," in Geoffrey Till (ed.), *Seapower: Theory and Practice* (Ilford: Frank Cass, 1994), pp. 23–25.

73. On Clausewitz, see Clausewitz, *On War* and Michael Howard, *Clausewitz* (Oxford: Oxford University Press, 1983). For the association of Napoleon and Clausewitz with the strategy of annihilation, see Edward N. Luttwak, "Toward Post-Heroic Warfare," *Foreign Affairs* 74, 3 (May/June 1995), pp. 109–122 and Azar Gat, *The Development of Military Thought: the Nineteenth Century* (Oxford: Clarendon Press, 1992), pp. 1–45.

74. For the strategic thought of Liddell Hart, see Liddell Hart, *Strategy* and Brian Bond, *Liddell Hart: A Study of his Military Thought* (London: Cassell, 1977).

75. For the early incarnations of the concept of indirect approach in Liddell Hart's strategic thought, as well as the fluidity of the concept, see John J. Mearsheimer, *Liddell Hart and the Weight of History* (Ithaca, NY: Cornell University Press 1988), pp. 89–93.

76. See, among others, Kennedy, "Grand Strategies in War and Peace"; Papasotiriou, *Byzantine Grand Strategy*.

77. See the analysis in Papasotiriou, *Byzantine Grand Strategy*, pp. 34–37; also, Haralambos Papasotiriou, *Byzantine Grand Strategy*, 6th-11th century (Athens: Poiotita, 2000) (text in Greek), pp. 33–34.

78. Platias, *High Politics in Small Countries*, ch. 2, and Michael I. Handel, *Weak States in the International System* (London: Frank Cass, 1981).

79. For a classic analysis, see Kennedy, *The Rise and Fall of the Great Powers*.

80. See Platias, *High Politics in Small Countries*, ch. 5; Ariel Levite, *Offense and Defense in Israeli Military Doctrine* (Boulder, CO: Westview, 1989).

2. ATHENS AND SPARTA: POWER STRUCTURES, EARLY CONFLICT AND THE CAUSES OF WAR

1. See Thucydides, I 89–117.

2. For these events, namely the crises of Corcyra and Potidaea, see Thucydides, I 24–68.

3. Thucydides, I 23.

4. In the same vein, the assassination of the Austrian Archduke Francis Ferdinand in 1914 obviously influenced the timing of the outbreak of the First World War. Still, it was a trivial thing compared to the deep structural causes of that war, the primary one being the rise of the power of Germany and the concomitant German attempt to change the status quo. For two excellent structural analyses of the European interstate system prior to the outbreak of the First World War, see Paul Kennedy, "The First World War and the International Power System," *International Security* 9, 1 (1984), pp. 7–40 and Michael Mandelbaum, *The Fate of Nations* (Cambridge: Cambridge University Press, 1988), pp. 31–56.

5. For the concept of strategic culture, see Ken Booth, *Strategy and Ethnocentricism* (London: Croom Helm, 1979); Colin Gray, *Nuclear Strategy and National Style* (London: Hamilton Press, 1986); Yitzhak Klein, "A Theory of Strategic Culture," *Comparative Strategy* vol. 10, no. 1 (January-March 1991) pp. 3–23; Thomas U. Berger, "Norms, Identity and National Security in Germany and Japan," in Peter J. Katzenstein (ed.), *The Culture of National Security* (New York: Columbia University Press, 1996), pp. 317–356.

6. For an ancient description of the Athenian polity, see Aristotle, *Athenaion Politeia*. For modern accounts, see Anton Powell, *Athens and Sparta: Constructing Greek Political and Social History from 478 B.C.* (London: Routledge, 1988) and Donald Kagan, *Pericles of Athens and the Birth of Democracy* (London: Guild, 1990).

7. Herodotus was the first to point out the beneficial impact of the democratic regime as far as Athenian power was concerned; see Herodotus, V 78. See also Michael W. Doyle, *Empires* (Ithaca, NY: Cornell University Press, 1986), pp. 66–67.

8. For detailed analyses of the Spartan polity, see K.M.T. Chrimes, *Ancient Sparta: A Re-examination of the Evidence* (Manchester: Manchester University Press, 1949); Humphrey Michell, *Sparta* (Cambridge: Cambridge University Press, 1952); George L. Huxley, *Early Sparta* (London: Faber, 1962); A.H.M. Jones, *Sparta* (Oxford: Blackwell & Mott, 1967); W.G. Forrest, *A History of Sparta, 950–192 B.C.* (New York: Norton, 1968); G.E.M. de Ste. Croix, *The Origins of the Peloponnesian War* (London: Duckworth, 1972); M.I. Finley, "Sparta", in M.I. Finley, *The Use and Abuse of History* (London: Penguin, 1990), pp. 161–177; Powell, *Athens and Sparta*. For the Spartan legal system, see D.M. MacDowell, *Spartan Law* (Edinburgh: Scottish Academic Press, 1986).

9. For the original Spartan text, the so-called *Rhetra*, which describes Spartan polity as it was supposedly created by the lawmaker Lycurgus, see Plutarch, *Lycurgus*, 6.1–2, 7–8. For the name of the Spartan citizen assembly which, contrary to what many people nowadays think, seems to have been *Ecclesia* and not *Apella*, see Ste. Croix, *The Origins of the Peloponnesian War*, pp. 346–347.

10. The exact procedure of the *ephors'* election is not known. See P.A. Rahe, "The Selection of Ephors at Sparta," *Historia* 29 (1980), 385–401; P.J. Rhodes, "The Selection of Ephors at Sparta," *Historia* 30 (1981), 498–502; H.D. Westlake, "Reelection to the ephorate?" *Greek, Roman and Byzantine Studies* 17 (1976), 343–52.

11. In fact, things were not so simple. Austerity did not dominate Spartan life until some time in the sixth century B.C. Moreover, the huge inequalities of wealth within Sparta were a source of continuous division. For a treatise that connects the onset of austerity with the rise of the power of the commoners in Sparta, see L.F. Fitzhardinge, *The Spartans* (London: Thames and Hudson, 1980). However, Fitzhardinge is completely wrong

in claiming that the aristocratic families and the *Gerousia* lost their power in the process. The *Gerousia* and the nobles behind it were in firm control of the destinies of Sparta throughout the city's independent existence.

12. This was unanimously acknowledged in Ancient Greece. See Herodotus, VII 104, VII 204, IX 62, IX 71; Thucydides, I 141, V 72, V 75; Xenophon, *Lacedaimonion Politeia*, 13. For the Spartan military organization, see Chrimes, *Ancient Sparta*, pp. 356–396; Michell, *Sparta*, pp. 233–280 (pp. 274–280 deal with the Spartan navy); J.F. Lazenby, *The Spartan Army* (Warminster: Aris & Phillips, 1985).

13. Thucydides states that in Sparta the ratio of slaves to freemen was greater than in any other city; Thucydides, VIII 40. The ratio has been estimated between seven to one and ten to one; see respectively Paul Cartledge, *Sparta and Laconia: A Regional History*, 1300–362 B.C. (London: Routledge & Kegan Paul, 1979), p. 175, and G.B. Grundy, quoted in Donald Kagan, *The Outbreak of the Peloponnesian War* (Ithaca, NY: Cornell University Press, 1969/1994), p. 26.

14. In fact, each year upon entering office the *ephors* formally declared war against the helots; Plutarch, *Lycurgus*, 28. Consequently, a Spartan could kill a helot without legally committing a homicide. In practice, however, although the Spartans could be extremely harsh on occasion, their treatment of the helots is believed to have been tolerably good. Furthermore, there was always a distinction between Laconian helots, who were normally loyal to Sparta, and Messenian helots, who were Sparta's greatest enemies; see Michell, *Sparta*, pp. 75–84.

15. See Thucydides, I 101, IV 41, IV 80.

16. Plutarch, *Lycurgus*, 24.

17. Thucydides, I 70–all quotations from Thucydides are from the Rex Warner translation (London: Penguin, 1972), which still remains the most powerful–though of course not perfect–English translation of Thucydides. The valuable Strassler edition of Thucydides [Robert B. Strassler (ed.), The Landmark Thucydides: A Comprehensive Guide to the Peloponnesian War (New York: Free Press, 1996)] uses a less satisfactory translation based on an older one by Richard Crawley.

18. Thucydides makes much of the difference between Athenian and Spartan national character; see Thucydides, I 69, I 84, I 118, IV 55, V 54–55, VIII 24. See also Victor Davis Hanson, *A War like no Other: How the Athenians and the Spartans Fought the Peloponnesian War* (New York: Random House, 2005), pp. 8–9, and W. Daniel Garst, "Thucydides and the Domestic Sources of International Politics," in Lowell S. Gustafson (ed.), *Thucydides' Theory of International Relations: A Lasting Possession* (Baton Rouge, LA: Louisiana University Press, 2000), pp. 67–97.

19. Spartan foreign policy did fluctuate violently on occasion, but there was an amazing overall consistency in maintaining a high military capability and striving after hegemony first in the Peloponnese and then in the whole of Greece.

20. Thucydides, I 89–117. See also below.

21. This is a very interesting illustration of what is nowadays called a security dilemma, namely the situation that arises when the measures that increase the security of a state decrease the security of others. Thus, the Persian threat prompted the Athenians to establish their empire ("fear of Persia was our chief motive"; Thucydides, I 75). The empire provided security to Athens, but soon proved to be a threat to Sparta and its allies. For an analysis of the security dilemma, see Robert Jervis, "Cooperation Under the Security Dilemma," *World Politics* 30, 2 (January 1978), pp. 167–214. For the Athenian Empire, see Russell Meiggs, *The Athenian Empire* (Oxford: Clarendon Press, 1972).

22. Thucydides, I 99. Similarly, Pericles stated that the strength of Athens derived by allied payments; Thucydides, II 13. The British East India Company used a similar scheme: the Company forced the native Indian states to contribute money which it then used to raise sepoy troops, thus perpetuating both the financial drain of its opponents and its military supremacy in the Indian subcontinent; see Bruce P. Lenman, "The Transition to European Military Ascendancy in India, 1600–1800," pp. 100–130 in John A. Lynn (ed.), *Tools of War: Instruments, Ideas and Institutions of Warfare, 1445–1871* (Urbana, IL and Chicago, IL: University of Illinois Press, 1990).

23. For the dynamics behind the growth of Athenian power, see Robert Gilpin, "The Theory of Hegemonic War," in R.I. Rotberg and T.K. Rabb (eds.) *The Origin and Prevention of Major Wars* (Cambridge: Cambridge University Press, 1988), pp. 21–23, and Doyle, *Empires*. Michael Doyle states that "slave agriculture, imperial tribute and imperial mines produced monetary supremacy, which again produced commercial superiority, which in turn, through a stimulation of shipping, produced naval superiority, which in turn sustained the empire. And the empire generated the slaves, the tribute and the mines"; *Empires*, p. 63. This passage shows remarkably well the dynamic inherent in the elements of Athenian power. Still, one must point out that it overvalues the role of slave agriculture as a source of Athenian power. Furthermore, naval superiority was the generator rather than the outcome of the acquisition of the Empire and its concomitant wealth.

24. Thucydides, I 19. Some of Sparta's Peloponnesian allies like Elis and Mantineia were democracies and retained their preferred regime as long as they remained loyal to Sparta. Incidentally, this means that one should not exaggerate the importance of the supposedly antagonistic nature of the Spartan and Athenian socio-political systems; this is done in, among others, Justin Rosenberg, *The Empire of Civil Society: A Critique of the Realist Theory of International Relations* (London: Verso, 1994). For the Peloponnesian League, see Kagan, *The Outbreak of the Peloponnesian War*, pp. 9–30 and especially Ste. Croix, *The Origins of the Peloponnesian War*, pp. 96–124, 333–342.

25. Kagan characteristically states that the allies were bound together by distrust of Argos and their common interest in the preservation of oligarchy; Kagan, *The Outbreak of the Peloponnesian War*, p. 13.
26. This was precisely what the great Greek historian and statesman Polybius argued a few centuries later. According to him, although Sparta's political organization was enough to ensure its dominant position in the Peloponnese, its limited economic power, which was a result of that very political organization, did not allow Sparta to extend its influence further. The message was clear: Sparta had to either change its political organization or confine itself to the Peloponnese. See Polybius, I 6. 49–50.
27. The rapid decline of the Spartan population during the fifth and fourth centuries B.C. astonished the rest of the Ancient Greeks; see Aristotle, *Politics* II 9, 1270a 33–34; cf. Xenophon, *Lacedaimonion Politeia*, 1. The subject has received detailed treatment from modern scholars; see among others Forrest, *A History of Sparta*, pp. 134–137; Ste. Croix, *The Origins of the Peloponnesian War*, pp. 331–332; Cartledge, *Sparta and Laconia*, pp. 307–318. For a less satisfactory account that tries to minimise the importance of the decline, see Chrimes, *Ancient Sparta*, pp. 348–356.
28. Doyle, *Empires*, pp. 54–81.
29. In other words, this particular grand strategic design did not fit with Sparta's domestic political environment and thus failed the criterion of external fit.
30. For the idea of the creation of a Spartan Empire and the disastrous consequences this scheme brought about, see Forrest, *A History of Sparta*, pp. 123–126; Donald Kagan, *The Fall of the Athenian Empire* (Ithaca, NY: Cornell University Press, 1987), pp. 13, 27, 306, 328, 397–426; Barry S. Strauss and Josiah Ober, *The Anatomy of Error: Ancient Military Disasters and Their Lessons for Modern Strategists* (New York: St. Martin's Press, 1990); Doyle, *Empires*, p. 73. Strauss and Ober, drawing from Aristotle, claim that Sparta was in no position to conduct an imperialist policy because the strict military-oriented education of the Spartans made them overestimate the role of military power and consequently rendered them unable to conduct successful diplomacy and reach compromise; see Strauss and Ober, *The Anatomy of Error*, ch. 3. Despite Aristotle's authority, this claim must be rejected. Sparta had been successfully playing the diplomatic game for centuries and can hardly be called incapable of conducting diplomacy. Moreover, the Athenians (and later the Romans and so many others) did not acquire their empire through rhetorical and diplomatic skill, but basically through successful application of military power. Sparta's problem was not excessive emphasis on military power, but lack of adequate military power.
31. Thucydides, I 71.
32. Herodotus, IX 96–106.
33. Herodotus, IX 104; Thucydides, I 94.

34. For the reluctance of the Spartans to go on with the war see Herodotus, IX 114. For Pausanias' conduct and the transfer of the leadership to Athens, see Thucydides, I 95–96.
35. Thucydides, I 90.
36. Thucydides, I 90–91. For an important critique of the concept of arms control, see Colin S. Gray, *House of Cards: Why Arms Control Must Fail* (Ithaca, NY: Cornell University Press, 1992).
37. For Cimon's successes, see Thucydides, I 98–100 and Plutarch, *Cimon*. For a modern account of the battle of Eurymedon, see Meiggs, *The Athenian Empire*, pp. 74–82, 454–455.
38. Thucydides, I 104.
39. Thucydides, I 103.
40. See Herodotus, IX 35; Isocrates, *Archidamus*, 99; Pausanias, *Laconica*, 11.7; Jones, *Sparta*, 61; Kagan, *The Outbreak of the Peloponnesian War*, pp. 54–55. It is a pity we do not know more about these battles and their surrounding circumstances.
41. Thucydides, I 101–103.
42. For the First Peloponnesian War, see Thucydides, I 105–108, I 111–115. For modern accounts, see Kagan, *The Outbreak of the Peloponnesian War*, pp. 77–130 and Ste. Croix, *The Origins of the Peloponnesian War*, pp. 187–200, 293–294.
43. See Thucydides, I 107–108.
44. If the Athenians had won and the Peloponnesian expeditionary force had been annihilated, *then* Tanagra would have been a strategic turning point.
45. Thucydides, I 108.
46. Thucydides, I 108.
47. Thucydides, I 109–110.
48. See Meiggs, *The Athenian Empire*, pp. 109–128.
49. Thucydides, I 112. In the same year Sparta concluded a Thirty Years' Peace with Argos; see Thucydides, V 14. The relationship between the Athenian-Spartan and the Argive-Spartan treaty is not known.
50. For the Cyprus campaign, see Thucydides, I 112. The historicity of the Peace of Callias has often been denied, especially since Thucydides does not mention it. However, there are compelling arguments for accepting that peace as genuine. For a summary of the relevant debate, see Meiggs, *The Athenian Empire*, pp. 129–151, 487–495.
51. See Meiggs, *The Athenian Empire*, pp. 129–151, 487–495 and Ste. Croix, *The Origins of the Peloponnesian War*, pp. 310–314.
52. It is unclear whether the Athenian fleet was similarly forbidden to sail east of those limits. Also, it is unlikely that the Persian king would have relinquished his right to exact tribute from the Greek cities, although he would be unable to exercise that right in practice; see Ste. Croix, *The Origins of the Peloponnesian War*, p. 313.
53. Thucydides, I 113–114.

54. If the revolts in Boeotia, Euboea and Megara and the Peloponnesian invasion were pre-planned to coincide with the expiration of the Five Years'
Treaty, then the Spartan political leaders must be regarded as first-class
strategists. If, on the other hand, the invasion was not part of a previously
devised plan but came as an immediate response to the opening of a 'window of opportunity' by the Megarian revolt, the Spartans must still receive
credit for their rapid exploitation of that opportunity. For a more detailed
treatment of the Spartan tendency to exploit windows of opportunity, see
Powell, *Athens and Sparta*, pp. 118–128.
55. Thucydides, I 114.
56. Thucydides, II 21.
57. Thucydides, I 115; see also Ste. Croix, *The Origins of the Peloponnesian
War*, pp. 293–294.
58. See Thucydides, I 24–44.
59. For these concepts, see A.F.K. Organski, "The Power Transition," in James
N. Rosenau (ed.), *International Politics and Foreign Policy: A Reader in
Research and Theory* (New York: The Free Press of Glencoe, 1961),
pp. 367–375; A.F.K. Organski and Jacek Kugler, *The War Ledger* (Chicago, IL: The University of Chicago Press, 1980); Robert Gilpin, *War and
Change in World Politics* (Cambridge: Cambridge University Press, 1981).
For a discussion of Thucydides' impact thereon, see Despina A. Taxiarchi,
"The Impact of Thucydides in Post War Realist Thinking and Its Critique," in *Thucydides: The Classical Theorist of International Relations,
Études Helléniques/Hellenic Studies*, vol. 6, no. 2 (Autumn 1998),
pp. 132–139.
60. Gilpin, "The Theory of Hegemonic War," p. 15.
61. Thomas Hobbes, *Leviathan or the Matter, Forme and Power of a Com-
monwealth* (Oxford: Blackwell, edn. 1946); *Hegel's Philosophy of Right*
(trans. T. M. Knox) (Oxford: Clarendon Press, 1952); Karl Marx, *Capital*
(trans. Samuel Moore and Edward Aveling) (3 vols.) (Chicago, IL: Charles
H. Kerr, 1909–1910).
62. Kenneth N. Waltz, *Man, the State, and War* (New York: Columbia University Press, 1959); Kenneth N. Waltz, *Theory of International Politics*
(Reading, MA: Addison-Wesley, 1979); Gilpin, *War and Change in World
Politics*.
63. It is interesting that two of the most prominent advocates of that school,
namely Donald Kagan and Richard Ned Lebow, accept the validity of the
classical Thucydidean explanation regarding the causes of the First Peloponnesian War; see Kagan, *The Outbreak of the Peloponnesian War*,
pp. 77–130, and Richard Ned Lebow, "Thucydides, Power Transition
Theory and the Causes of War," in Richard Ned Lebow and Barry S.
Strauss (eds.), *Hegemonic Rivalry from Thucydides to the Nuclear Age*
(Boulder, CO: Westview, 1991) pp. 125–165.
64. Richard Ned Lebow, *Between Peace and War: The Nature of International
Crisis* (Baltimore, MD: Johns Hopkins University Press, 1987).

65. As John Mearsheimer puts it, "France backed down, because it knew the United Kingdom would win the ensuing war, and because France did not want to pick a fight with the United Kingdom when it was more worried about the emerging German threat on its eastern border"; John J. Mearsheimer, *The Tragedy of Great Power Politics* (New York: W.W. Norton, 2001), p. 153.
66. See Bruce Bueno de Mesquita, *The War Trap* (New Haven, CT: Yale University Press, 1981).
67. Thucydides, IV 59.
68. Thucydides, II 8. Cf. Martin van Creveld, *The Transformation of War* (New York: Free Press, 1991), where he argues that the main cause of war is simply that men like war. Here it must be pointed out that, though Thucydides does regard human nature as a cause of war, he never abandons the systemic 'big picture'.

3. PERICLEAN GRAND STRATEGY

1. See, for instance, J.F.C. Fuller, *The Decisive Battles of the Western World* (London: Eyre & Spottiswoode, 1954); Colin Gray, *The Leverage of Sea Power: The Strategic Advantage of Navies in War* (New York: Free Press, 1992); Chester G. Starr, *The Influence of Sea Power on Ancient History* (New York: Oxford University Press, 1995).
2. Among others, J.F.C. Fuller has stated that "Pericles relied upon the strategy of exhaustion"; J.F.C. Fuller, *A Military History of the Western World, Vol. 1: From the Earliest Times to the Battle of Lepanto* (New York: Da Capo, 1954), p. 57. As will be seen at a later point in this book, the Athenians were eventually to depart from the strategy devised by Pericles. For an analysis of the various strategies that the city of Athens adopted during the Peloponnesian War, see Donald Kagan, "Athenian strategy in the Peloponnesian War," pp. 24–55 in Williamson Murray, MacGregor Knox, and Alvin Bernstein (eds.), *The Making of Strategy: Rulers, States, and War* (Cambridge: Cambridge University Press, 1994).
3. In fact, the term 'city-state system' is not totally accurate, since both city-states and bigger entities, such as the various kingdoms of Epirus and Macedonia, comprised Ancient Greece. For an analysis of the politics in the Greek city-state system, see Raphael Sealey, *A History of the Greek City States, 700–338 B.C.* (Berkeley, CA: University of California Press, 1976).
4. See, for example, Peter J. Fliess, *Thucydides and the Politics of Bipolarity* (Baton Rouge, LA: Louisiana State University Press, 1966).
5. One might be tempted to find other additional poles of the system, such as the powerful Odrysian state, situated in Thrace and described with admiration by Thucydides. See Thucydides, II 95–101.
6. W.R. Connor, "Polarization in Thucydides," in Richard Ned Lebow and Barry S. Strauss (eds.), *Hegemonic Rivalry from Thucydides to the Nuclear Age* (Boulder, CO: Westview, 1991), pp. 54–57.

7. See the discussion in Carlo M. Santoro, "Bipolarity and War: What Makes the Difference?" in Lebow and Strauss, *Hegemonic Rivalry from Thucy-dides to the Nuclear Age*, pp. 71–86. Thucydides' narrative suggests several historical parallels to the current reader. On the utility and pitfalls of historical comparisons, see Ernest R. May, *The Lessons of the Past: The Use and Misuse of History in American Foreign Policy* (New York: Oxford University Press, 1973); Richard E. Meastand and Ernest R. May, *Thinking in Time: The Uses of History for Decision Makers* (New York: Free Press, 1986). See also Michael Howard, *The Lessons of History* (New Haven, CT: Yale University Press, 1991), pp. 6–20.

8. Thucydides, I 23.

9. Thucydides describes Pericles' account as follows: "Apart from all other sources of revenue, the average yearly contribution from the allies to Athens amounted to 600 talents, then there still remained in the Acropolis a sum of 6,000 talents of coined silver. This reserve fund, at its maximum, had been 9,700 talents. It had been drawn on to pay for the Propylea and other public buildings, and for Potidea. In addition to this, there was the uncoined gold and silver in offerings made either by individuals or by the state; there were the sacred vessels and furniture used in the processions and in the games; there were the spoils taken from the Persians, and other resources of one kind or another, all of which would amount to no less than 500 talents. To this he [Pericles] added the money in the other temples which might be used and which came to a considerable sum, and said that, if they were ever really reduced to absolute extremities, they could even use the gold on the statue of Athene herself. There was, he informed them, a weight of forty talents of pure gold on this statue, all of which was removable. [...] Thus he reassured them about their financial position"; Thucydides, II 13.

10. This truth is captured by the statement of the Spartan king Archidamus that "war is not so much a matter of armaments as of the money which makes armaments effective"; Thucydides, I 83.

11. Donald Kagan, *The Outbreak of the Peloponnesian War* (Ithaca, NY: Cornell University Press, 1969/1994), pp. 345–374. The same view is advanced in A.H.M. Jones, *Sparta* (Oxford: Blackwell & Mott, 1967), pp. 68–69. Richard Ned Lebow has taken a more moderate position, arguing that "Athens had increased its power under Pericles and had largely recovered from the disasters of the 440s, but in 433 its power and reputation were still not what they had been in 450;" Richard Ned Lebow, "Thucydides, Power Transition Theory and the Causes of War," in Lebow and Strauss, *Hegemonic Rivalry*, pp. 158–159.

12. Economic performance that determines a state's power and military success is always to be measured on a relative and not on an absolute basis. The crucial factor that seems to elude Kagan and his followers is to be doing better, even if only a little better, than one's rivals. In the long run, this asymmetry is reflected in the balance of power. This insight is utilised

in, among others, Paul Kennedy, *The Rise and Fall of the Great Powers Economic Change and Military Conflict from 1500 to 2000* (New York: Random House, 1987), and John J. Mearsheimer, *The Tragedy of Great Power Politics* (New York: W.W. Norton, 2001), esp. ch. 3.

13. Thucydides, I 19. A similar case is that of the British Empire after the War of American Independence (1775–1783). Although the loss of the American colonies was a serious blow, British economic power kept growing at a fast pace, securing the global supremacy of Great Britain.

14. See, among others, Lisa Kallet-Marx, *Money, Expense and Naval Power in Thucydides' History 1–5.24* (Berkeley, CA: University of California Press, 1993).

15. See, among others, Robert Gilpin, *The Political Economy of International Relations* (Princeton, NJ: Princeton University Press, 1987); Edward Mead Earle, "Adam Smith, Alexander Hamilton, Friedrich List: The Economic Foundations of Military Power," in Peter Paret (ed.), *Makers of Modern Strategy from Machiavelli to the Nuclear Age* (Princeton, NJ: Princeton University Press, 1986), pp. 217–261; Alfred Thayer Mahan, *The Influence of Sea Power Upon History, 1660–1783* (London: Sampson Low, Marston, 1892); Alfred Thayer Mahan, *The Influence of Sea Power Upon the French Revolution and Empire, 1793–1812*, (2 vols.) (London: Sampson Low, Marston, 1893); E.H. Carr, *The 20 Years' Crisis, 1919–1939* (2nd edn.) (London: Papermac, 1946/1995); Robert G. Gilpin, "The Richness of the Tradition of Political Realism," in Robert O. Keohane (ed.), *Neorealism and its Critics* (New York: Columbia University Press, 1986), pp. 308–313. In light of this perceptive Realist analysis of the importance of economic factors, dating back to the days of Thucydides, it is amazing that Political Realism has been accused of having ignored the economic dimensions of international relations. See Gilpin, "The Richness of the Tradition of Political Realism," pp. 308–313.

16. Thucydides, I 141–143.

17. Thucydides, I 144.

18. Thucydides, I 80–81.

19. Jingoism was the sentiment of vulgar chauvinism that appeared in late nineteenth century Great Britain in response to the German challenge; see Paul Kennedy, *The Rise of the Anglo-German Antagonism 1860–1914* (London: Allen and Unwin, 1980).

20. Kagan, "Athenian strategy in the Peloponnesian War," p. 30.

21. Thucydides, I 141–142, II 13. For an analysis of the law of uneven growth, see Robert Gilpin, *War and Change in World Politics* (Cambridge: Cambridge University Press, 1981), and Robert Gilpin, "The Theory of Hegemonic War," in R.I. Rotberg and T.K. Rabb (eds.) *The Origin and Prevention of Major Wars* (Cambridge: Cambridge University Press, 1988), pp. 15–37.

22. Thucydides, I 139.

23. Bernard Brodie, *War and Politics* (London: Cassell, 1973), p. 1.

24. According to Doyne Dawson: "The most original contribution of the Greeks to military thought was their self-conscious development of the concept of *raison d' état*: They perceived warfare as a rational and utilitarian instrument of politics ..."; Doyne Dawson, *The Origins of Western Warfare: Militarism and Morality in the Ancient World* (Boulder, CO: Westview, 1996), p. 79.
25. See Hans Delbrück, *History of the Art of War*, vol. 1 (Lincoln, NE: University of Nebraska Press, 1975), pp. 135–143.
26. B. H. Liddell Hart, *Strategy* (2nd revised edn.) (London: Meridian, 1991), p. 355.
27. According to tradition, the ancient Chinese general Sun Tzu lived during the late sixth and the early fifth century B.C. However, it has been persuasively argued that the text of the famous treatise *The Art of War* attributed to Sun Tzu has been written sometime in the fourth century B.C. This would mean that Sun Tzu, if he was indeed a historical personage and the author of the *Art of War*, lived later than Thucydides or was at best a younger contemporary of his. For a summary of the literature regarding the identity of the author and the date of writing of *The Art of War*, see Sun Tzu, *The Art of War* (trans. by Samuel B. Griffith) (Oxford: Oxford University Press, 1963), pp. 1–12, and Sun Tzu, *Art of War* (trans. Ralph D. Sawyer) (Boulder, CO: Westview, 1994), pp. 151–162.
28. Sun Tzu, *The Art of War* (trans. by Samuel B. Griffith), ch. 3, par. 3, p. 13.
29. Thucydides, I 139. See also the extensive analysis in G.E.M. de Ste. Croix, *The Origins of the Peloponnesian War* (London: Duckworth, 1972), pp. 225–289, 381–393, 396–399. Ste. Croix argues fairly convincingly that the Megarian Decree was a religious nuisance for individual Megarians rather than a full-scale economic embargo against Megara. The Megarians were deemed sacrilegious, hence they could not themselves appear at the ports of the Athenian Alliance and the marketplace of Athens. However, they could always appear at nearby places and transact their business through representatives.
30. Thucydides, I 140–141.
31. Thucydides, I 144. For an interesting analysis of *xenelasia*, see Anton Powell, *Athens and Sparta: Constructing Greek Political and Social History from 478 B.C.* (London: Routledge, 1988), pp. 228–229.
32. Hitler said to his commander-in-chief shortly before the Polish campaign: "Our enemies are little worms; I saw them at Munich;" Chester Wilmot, *The Struggle for Europe* (New York: Carol and Graf, 1952), p. 21. This statement demonstrates how decision-makers use past behavior to predict future irresolution. For an analysis of this point, see Glenn H. Snyder and Paul Diesing, *Conflict Among Nations: Bargaining, Decision Making, and System Structure in International Crisis* (Princeton, NJ: Princeton University Press, 1977), p. 187. Also, Fred Charles Iklé, *How Nations Negotiate* (New York: Harper and Row, 1964), p. 82.

33. See Haralambos Papasotiriou, *Byzantine Grand Strategy* (Ph.D. Diss., Stanford University, 1991). For other instances of successful use of appeasement, see Peter Karsten, "Response to Threat Perception: Accommodation as a Special Case," in Klaus Knorr (ed.), *Historical Dimensions of National Security Problems* (Lawrence, KA: University Press of Kansas, 1976), pp. 120–163.

34. In all probability, it was for the same reasons that the US rejected appeasement as a strategy towards the Soviet Union after the Second World War. See also the discussion in Chapter Five.

35. Thucydides, I 144, II 65.

36. Kennedy, *The Rise and Fall of the Great Powers*. The experience of the First Peloponnesian War, where Athens had clearly overextended (viz. Egyptian campaign and Boeotian conquest) and had dearly paid for it, must have been all too vivid in Pericles' mind.

37. See Kenneth N. Waltz, *Theory of International Politics* (Reading, MA: Addison-Wesley, 1979), p. 168.

38. There is also a second dimension of external balancing, which is essentially to manipulate the international balance of power. A common ploy in this manipulation is to follow the saying "the enemy of the enemy is a friend." The Athenians had repeatedly resorted to this ploy in their dealings with Argos. Unfortunately for Pericles, he lacked the alternative of a continental strategy in order to apply peripheral pressure on Sparta, since the Thirty Years' Treaty of 451 B.C. between Argos and Sparta prohibited Argos from coming into play before 421 B.C. Following that though, Athens could once again play the 'Argive card'. For the conflict between Sparta and Argos that erupted in the Peloponnese after the expiration of the Thirty Years' Treaty, and the Athenian role therein, see Thucydides, V 42–82, as well as the discussion in the next chapter. The Athenian relation with Argos is strongly reminiscent of the American relation with China during the Cold War.

39. Thucydides, II 8, where he gives a detailed description of the allies of both Sparta and Athens, plus the status of the various Athenian allies, i.e. free or tributary states.

40. Thucydides, II 25.

41. Thucydides, II 9.

42. Thucydides, I 143.

43. Thucydides, II 24.

44. See Kallet-Marx, *Money, Expense and Naval Power*, pp. 110–111.

45. Thucydides, I 142–143.

46. For a similar approach adopted by Great Britain in the first part of the twentieth century, see Michael Howard, *Grand Strategy: Official History of the Second World War*, vol. 4 (London: HMSO, 1973), p. 1.

47. Josiah Ober, "National Ideology and Strategic Defense of the Population, from Athens to Star Wars," in Lebow and Strauss, *Hegemonic Rivalry*, p. 254. One may discern here a similarity between the Athenian fortifica-

tions and the Strategic Defense Initiative (SDI), which was intended to neutralise the Soviet strength. The similarity is even more striking if one considers that the Soviets reacted in the same way as the Spartans had done, i.e. coming up with arms control proposals.
48. Thucydides, I 143.
49. For a description of the qualities of the trireme, the standard warship in the Mediterranean at that time, see Chester G. Starr, "The Athenian Century," in Robert Cowley (ed.), *Experience of War* (New York–London: Norton, 1992), p. 4.
50. Thucydides, II 62. The Athenians could indeed 'sail where they wished', but Pericles never claimed that they could seize and retain any overseas territory they wished. This fine point was lost to them when they undertook the Sicilian expedition.
51. For the classic analysis of the maritime grand strategy of Great Britain, see Mahan, *The Influence of Sea Power Upon History, 1660–1783* and Mahan, *The Influence of Sea Power Upon the French Revolution and Empire, 1793–1812*. Also, B. H. Liddell Hart, *The British Way in Warfare* (London: Faber, 1932). For a modern scholar drawing the same comparison between Athens and Great Britain, see Starr, *The Influence of Sea Power on Ancient History*, pp. 40–41.
52. Paul Kennedy, *The Rise and Fall of British Naval Mastery* (London: Fontana, 1991), p. 11.
53. Donald Kagan puts the estimate at 2,000 talents a year–an enormous sum by Greek standards; see Kagan, *The Archidamian War* (Ithaca, NY: Cornell University Press, 1974/1990), pp. 36–40.
54. This term refers to the strategy adopted by Fabius, dictator of Rome, against Hannibal after the latter's victory at Lake Trasimene in 218 B.C. This strategy entailed avoidance of battle and the wearing down of the Carthaginian strength by 'military pin pricks', see Liddell Hart, *Strategy*, pp. 26–27. Liddell Hart correctly perceived that both the Periclean and the Fabian strategies were actually designs at the grand strategic level: "The Periclean plan was a grand strategy with the aim of gradually draining the enemy's endurance in order to convince him that he could not gain a decision;" *Strategy*, p. 10.
55. Thucydides, I 143.
56. Thucydides, I 141.
57. Thucydides, I 143.
58. See Thomas C. Schelling, *Arms and Influence* (New Haven, CT: Yale University Press, 1966), pp. 1–34. Also, Glenn H. Snyder, *Deterrence and Defense* (Princeton, NJ: Princeton University Press, 1961).
59. Cf. Victor Davis Hanson, *The Western Way of War* (New York: Alfred A. Knopf, 1989), p. 32.
60. For the long war assumption in Periclean strategy, see Thucydides, I 141. For the Spartans' view that the war would be completed successfully within a few years cf. Thucydides, V 14.

61. Cf. Pericles' statement to his compatriots: "And if I thought I could persuade you to do it, I would urge you to go out and lay waste your property with your own hands and show the Peloponnesians that it is not for the sake of this that you are likely to give in to them;" Thucydides, I 143. The fact that he could not persuade them to actually do it should not be taken as an indication of the failure of his strategy, as some analysts have thought; cf. Donald Kagan, *On the Origins of War and the Preservation of Peace* (New York: Doubleday, 1995) p. 65. Pericles' statement was a rhetorical scheme, intended to show to the Athenians that the decision they had actually taken, namely to abandon their land to the mercy of the enemy, was a necessary one.

62. Liddell Hart, *Strategy*, p. 355.

63. "This overseas deployment marked a first for the Athenians: For the first time in history, their *hippeis* and mounts sailed on horse transports;" Leslie J. Worley, *Hippeis: The Cavalry of Ancient Greece* (Boulder, CO: Westview, 1994), pp. 87–88. This is an extremely interesting development, since the Athenian force comprising navy, horse transports and mounted archers, essentially marks the origins of the combined arms operation. After the Athenian seizure of Cythera, an island located just south of Laconia, in 424 B.C., the Spartans were forced to raise a unit of 400 mounted archers; Thucydides, IV 55. See also Oliver Lyman Spaulding and Hoffman Nickerson, *Ancient and Medieval Warfare* (New York: Barnes and Noble Books, 1993), p. 57.

64. Thucydides, II 56.

65. This view is advanced by Donald Kagan; "Athenian strategy in the Peloponnesian War," pp. 41–47.

66. Thucydides, I 142.

67. For an alternative view, see Donald Kagan; "Athenian strategy in the Peloponnesian War," pp. 46–47.

68. Cf. David A. Baldwin, *Economic Statecraft* (Princeton, NJ: Princeton University Press, 1985).

69. Thucydides, I 141–142, II 13. This might be conceived as a distant ancestor of the economic and technological denial that the West resorted to in order to isolate and weaken the Soviets during the Cold War.

70. The Melian Dialogue took place during the 16th year of the war (416 B.C.) and is covered in Thucydides, V 84–113. To the question of the Melians: "So you would not agree to our being neutral, friends instead of enemies, but allies of neither side?", the Athenians gave the characteristic reply: "No, because it is not so much your hostility that injures us; it is rather the case that, if we were on friendly terms with you, our subjects would regard that as a sign of weakness in us, whereas your hatred is evidence of our power"; Thucydides, V 94–95.

71. Thucydides, I 141–142.

72. Thucydides, V 16–17.

73. See Benjamin Schwarz, "Strategic Interdependence: Learning to Behave like a Great Power," in Norman Levin (ed.), *Prisms and Policy: U.S. Secu-*

rity Strategy After the Cold War (Santa Monica, CA: RAND, 1994), pp. 79–98. Also, Paul Bracken, "Strategic Planning for National Security: Lessons from Business Experience," *RAND Note*, N-3005–DAG/USDP, February 1990, pp. 12–17.

74. Delbrück, *History of the Art of War*, vol. 1, p. 137.

75. Thucydides, II 21. The problem of the Periclean grand strategy was that it depended on loyalty to the city-state taking precedence over individual household and family loyalties; see Lin Foxhall, "Farming and Fighting in Ancient Greece," in John Rich and Graham Shipley (eds.), *War and Society in the Greek World*, (London: Routledge, 1993), p. 142.

76. Thucydides, II 21, II 65.

77. See next chapter. Pericles died two years and six months after the start of the war; Thucydides, II 65. In 430 B.C., under the influence of the plague (see below), the Athenians flinched for a while and sent a peace embassy to Sparta. However, nothing came of it, and Thucydides makes it clear that this was merely a temporary whim of the Athenian *Ecclesia* (Thucydides, II 59, II 65)–see also next chapter.

78. Thucydides, II 35–46. A characteristic part of the speech reads as follows: "I declare that our city is an education to Greece, and I declare that in my opinion each single one of our citizens, in all the manifold aspect of life, is able to show himself the rightful lord and owner of his own person, and do this, moreover, with exceptional grace and exceptional versatility. And to show that this is no empty boasting for the present occasion, but real tangible fact, you have only to consider the power which our city possesses and which has been won by those very qualities which I have mentioned. Athens, alone of the states we know, comes to her testing time in a greatness that surpasses what was imagined of her. [...] Future ages will wonder at us, as the present age wonders at us now. [...] This, then, is the kind of city for which these men, who could not bear the thought of losing her, nobly fought and nobly died"; Thucydides, II 41. It is interesting to note that during the First World War placecards on London buses displayed extracts from Pericles' *Epitaph*, intended to remind the British public of the values for which they were fighting; see Paul Millett, "Warfare, economy and democracy in classical Athens," in Rich and Shipley, *War and Society in the Greek World*, p. 179.

79. Thucydides, II 25. The Athenian capture of Pylos was even more helpful in this respect; see Thucydides, IV 3, IV 41. See also Josiah Ober, "Classical Greek Times," in Michael Howard, George J. Andreopoulos, and Mark R. Shulman (eds.), *The Laws of War: Constraints on Warfare in the Western World* (New Haven, CT: Yale University Press, 1994), p. 22. From the above analysis it can be surmised that a theory of victory against Sparta ought to contain two permanent elements, i.e. enlisting Argive alliance and fomenting a helot revolt. One must also point out that there is an interesting parallel between the assistance that Athens offered to the helots and the huge campaign of psychological operations that the West launched towards the nations of Eastern Europe during the Cold War.

80. See Kenneth N. Waltz, *Man, the State, and War* (New York: Columbia University Press, 1959).

81. Thucydides, I 75.

82. Thucydides, II 63. However, it must be noted that there was another side of the coin as well. The subjects of the Athenian Empire stood to gain from the Athenian commercial activities, and the empire provided a number of collective goods such as integration in a huge market, suppression of piracy, etc. Consequently, international legitimacy was not completely absent from the Athenian Empire; see Michael W. Doyle, *Empires* (Ithaca, NY: Cornell University Press, 1986), p. 57 and the sources cited therein. See also next chapter.

83. Thucydides, II 8. See next chapter.

84. Kagan, "Athenian strategy in the Peloponnesian War," p. 54.

85. Barry S. Strauss and Josiah Ober, *The Anatomy of Error: Ancient Military Disasters and Their Lessons for Modern Strategists* (New York: St. Martin's Press, 1990), p. 47.

86. For the various repercussions of offensive strategies, see Stephen Van Evera, *Causes of War: Power and the Roots of Conflict* (Ithaca, NY and London: Cornell University Press, 1999).

87. Kallet-Marx, *Money, Expense and Naval Power*, p. 203.

88. See, among others, Steven Forde, *The Ambition to Rule: Alcibiades and the Politics of Imperialism in Thucydides* (Ithaca, NY: Cornell University Press, 1989).

89. See Alcibiades' account of the Athenian war aims in Thucydides, VI 90, reproduced in the next chapter. See also the discussion in Chapter Five.

90. Thucydides, II 65.

91. Kagan, "Athenian strategy in the Peloponnesian War," p. 38.

92. Thucydides, II 47–54, III 87.

93. Arther Ferrill, *The Origins of War from the Stone Age to Alexander the Great* (London: Thames and Hudson, 1985), p. 127.

94. See Thucydides, IV 22.

95. Ferrill, *The Origins of War from the Stone Age to Alexander the Great*, p. 128.

96. For these two battles, see respectively Thucydides, IV 89–101 and V 6–11. For the Brasidas expedition, see also next chapter.

97. As Starr has put it: "... the Spartans acquiesced in a peace treaty that led to massive discontent and defection of their allies, whose grounds of complaint against Athens were almost ignored in the treaty. Athens had done as well, or better, than could have been expected. The Aegean Empire was intact; in western waters its power had risen; the Peloponnesian League had been shaken"; Starr, *The Influence of Sea Power on Ancient History*, p. 43.

98. See among others Kagan, *The Archidamian War*; Strauss and Ober, *The Anatomy of Error*; Angelos Vlahos, *Commentary on Thucydides*, vol. I: Books I–IV (Athens: Estia, 1992) (text in Greek).

99. For a critical discussion of Pericles' decision, see Lebow, "Thucydides, Power Transition Theory and the Causes of War," in Lebow and Strauss, *Hegemonic Rivalry*, pp. 147–156. Also, Barry S. Strauss, "Of Balances, Bandwagons and Ancient Greeks," in Lebow and Strauss, *Hegemonic Rivalry*, pp. 203–204.

100. Baldwin, *Economic Statecraft*, p. 154.

101. Kagan, *On the Origins of War*, p. 64.

102. Thucydides, I 81.

103. For exponents of the 'feebleness' theory, see Vlahos, *Commentary on Thucydides*, pp. 401–405, as well as the sources cited in Kagan, *The Archidamian War*, pp. 28–29.

104. See Schelling, *Arms and Influence*.

105. See Schelling, *Arms and Influence*; also, Stephen Cimbala: *Military Persuasion: Deterence and Provocation in Crisis and War* (University Park, PA: Pennsylvania State University Press, 1994).

106. Thucydides, I 143.

107. This also explains why Pericles refrained from creating a fort on Spartan territory; this measure was reserved for the future. It also shows the fallacy of Donald Kagan's statement that "we may therefore disregard the construction of a fortress on the Peloponnese as part of the offensive element of the Periclean strategy"; *The Archidamian War*, p. 28.

108. See Alexander L. George, *Some Thoughts on Graduated Escalation* RM-4844–IR (Santa Monica, CA: RAND Corporation, 1965).

109. Kagan, *The Archidamian War*, p. 41. For an excellent response to the critique of feebleness similar to that of the present book, see Delbrück, *History of the Art of War*, vol. 1, p. 140.

110. See Kagan, *On the Origins of War*, p. 65.

111. See W. Robert Connor, *Thucydides* (Princeton, NJ: Princeton University Press, 1984), p. 50.

112. See Bracken, "Strategic Planning for National Security," pp. 14–15.

113. Thucydides, II 65.

114. Gray, *The Leverage of Sea Power*, p. 7.

115. Thucydides, I 144.

4. SPARTAN GRAND STRATEGY

1. For an analysis of the Spartan grand strategy during the initial phase of the war, see P.A. Brunt, "Spartan Policy and Strategy in the Archidamian War," in P.A. Brunt, *Studies in Greek History and Thought* (Oxford: Clarendon Press, 1993), pp. 84–111.

2. Thucydides repeatedly makes this point; see I 67–68, I 71, I 86, I 118.

3. Thucydides, I 82. Archidamus' clear reference to an alliance with the Persians (foreigners) is an interesting predecessor of a number of cases where *Realpolitik* brought irreconcilable enemies together. The alliance of France with the Ottomans against Spain during the Renaissance is the first such

example in modern history, whereas the alliance of Catholic Cardinal Richelieu with the Protestant states of Europe against the Catholic Holy Roman Empire is another case in point. In the twentieth century, the Molotov-Ribbentrop Pact and Nixon's rapprochement with China constitute similar cases. For a comparison of the Spartan-Persian alliance with the modern diplomatic surprises mentioned above, see Strauss and Ober, *The Anatomy of Error: Ancient Military Disasters and Their Lessons for Modern Strategists* (New York: St. Martin's Press, 1990), p. 75. For Richelieu's partnership with the Protestants, see J.H. Elliott, *Richelieu and Olivares* (Cambridge: Cambridge University Press, 1984/1991) pp. 113–142 and Henry Kissinger, *Diplomacy*, (New York: Simon & Schuster, 1994), ch. 3. For the concept of diplomatic surprise and an analysis of some modern instances of diplomatic surprise, see Michael I. Handel, *The Diplomacy of Surprise: Hitler, Nixon, Sadat* (Cambridge, MA: Harvard Center for International Studies, 1981) and Constantinos Koliopoulos, *Understanding Strategic Surprise* (Ph.D. Diss., Lancaster University, 1996), pp. 208–216.
4. Thucydides, I 86.
5. Cf. Thucydides, IV 18, IV 21, IV 85, V 14. An impossible theory has been put forward by Gregory Crane, namely that Sthenelaidas stressed "the fundamental bonds that bind human beings together", grasping that "Sparta's personalised relationships with its allies are its strength"; see Gregory Crane, *Thucydides and the Ancient Simplicity: The Limits of Political Realism* (Berkeley, CA: University of California Press, 1998), pp. 212–221. Interstate alliances are not built on moral bonds and this was perhaps least of all the case with the Peloponnesian League. Alliances are vehicles through which the states try to enhance their security. As already pointed out, for Sparta the Peloponnesian League was a means of extending its influence and increasing its military strength, whereas for the allies it was a means of warding off external threats and (as far as the ruling classes were concerned) perpetuating oligarchic rule at home. If the League could not fulfill this purpose, the parties would be inclined to leave it, moral bonds among them notwithstanding. Actually, although Sparta did go to war and suffered some major defeats in the process, its allies had no scruples about defecting the League en masse once the Peace of Nicias showed that Sparta was not strong enough to guarantee their security. Thus, Sthenelaidas did not appeal to moral bonds, but simply misjudged the balance of power.
6. Thucydides, IV 85, V 14. Thucydides states that nobody in Greece expected that Athens would hold its position for more than three years if the Spartans invaded Attica; Thucydides, VII 28. In view of this, the statement of Barry Strauss and Josiah Ober that "at the start of the Peloponnesian War in 431, few people expected Athens to suffer a crushing defeat" (Strauss and Ober, *The Anatomy of Error*, pp. 47–48), is incomprehensible.
7. For analyses of the balance of power between Athens and Sparta after Sicily, see Thucydides, VIII 1, VIII 48, VIII 53. For a presentation of Spartan relations with the Persians, see David M. Lewis, *Sparta and Persia* (Leiden: E.J. Brill, 1977).

8. Thucydides, VIII 53. Tissaphernes was the powerful Persian satrap of
   Sardis in Asia Minor.
9. Donald Kagan holds a different view regarding the origins of the Peloponnesian War (the recurring issue of underlying *vs.* proximate causes of war).
   Having doubted the growth of the Athenian power prior to the war (see
   previous chapter), the American historian claims that the Spartans were
   reluctant to start a war with Athens but were dragged into it by their allies
   and their own bellicose *ephors*. See Donald Kagan, *The Outbreak of the
   Peloponnesian War* (Ithaca, NY: Cornell University Press, 1969/1994),
   esp. pp. 286–316. Actually, there is no evidence whatsoever to support the
   view that Spartan citizens wanted peace in contrast to their *ephors* who
   wanted war. In addition, Kagan claims that the *ephors* must have initially
   been supporters of peace, but changed their minds after the incidents of
   Corcyra and Potidaea (Kagan, *The Outbreak of the Peloponnesian War*,
   p. 307, fn. 46). If this was the case, one may well enquire why it was only
   the *ephors* that changed their minds while the majority of the Spartans
   continued to favour peace. This does not make sense and consequently
   renders Kagan's argument groundless. For analyses that, like the present
   one, endorse the Thucydidean view that Sparta began the war willingly in
   order to check Athenian power, see G.E.M. de Ste. Croix, *The Origins of
   the Peloponnesian War* (London: Duckworth, 1972) and Anton Powell,
   *Athens and Sparta: Constructing Greek Political and Social History from
   478 B.C.* (London: Routledge, 1988), pp. 118–128. For an analysis of the
   debate in the Spartan Assembly regarding the issue of war against Athens,
   see A.W. Gomme, *A Historical Commentary on Thucydides*, vol. 1 (Oxford:
   Clarendon Press, 1998) (reprint), pp. 252–256.
10. A number of scholars have claimed that since the end of the Persian Wars
    there existed in Sparta a group which they have called the 'peace party' or
    the 'doves', in contrast to the 'war party' or 'the hawks'. The only evi-
    dence one can find for this is that in two sessions of the Assembly sepa-
    rated by about half a century (475 and 432 B.C. respectively), one part
    favoured war with Athens while the other one disagreed. The effort to
    explain the whole of Spartan security policy in the meantime as a struggle
    between these two parties is based on pure conjecture. It is highly interest-
    ing, however, that the exponents of this theory have depicted Archidamus
    as the leader of the 'peace party' [Brunt, "Spartan Policy and Strategy in
    the Archidamian War," p. 111; A.H.M. Jones, *Sparta* (Oxford: Blackwell
    & Mott, 1967), pp. 63–71; Kagan, *The Outbreak of the Peloponnesian
    War*, pp. 87, 300–304] or the 'doves' (Ste. Croix, *The Origins of the Pelo-
    ponnesian War*, pp. 142–143). However, his speech at the Spartan Assem-
    bly should leave no doubt that in principle he was not at all averse to the
    idea of a war with Athens. If coercive diplomacy failed, Archidamus was
    ready to go to war on completion of the relevant preparations. In this war,
    he believed that Sparta ought to follow a grand strategy of annihilation.
    A.H.M. Jones attempts to get round Archidamus' clear advocacy of an

eventual preventive war by claiming that the Spartan king "evidently real-
ised that it was hopeless to urge peace, and he therefore pressed for
delay"; Jones, *Sparta*, p. 67. This is an unacceptable distortion of what
Archidamus said in the Assembly. For a treatise that points out that there
exists no evidence for considering Archidamus a 'dove', see Lewis, *Sparta
and Persia*, pp. 46–48.

11. Sparta's Corinthian allies must have shared this belief as well; see the
    strategy they outlined in their speech in Thucydides, I 120–122. Although
    that strategy was basically sound and included many of the elements of
    the grand strategy Sparta actually followed (e.g. naval balancing, creation
    of a fort in Attica), the balance of power was so adverse to the Pelopon-
    nesians, that this strategy could not be implemented. Most importantly,
    the strategy outlined by the Corinthians lacked the crucial dimension of
    external balancing through an alliance with the Persians. The successful
    balancing of the Athenian naval power with Persian help was the decisive
    factor which gave victory to Sparta.

12. The same point is made by Brunt; "Spartan Policy and Strategy in the
    Archidamian War," p. 88.

13. See Alcibiades' speech at Sparta in Thucydides, VI 90. Some scholars do
    not accept Alcibiades' account at face value, in the supposition that he
    was exaggerating so as to alarm the Spartans; see, for instance, Donald
    Kagan, *The Peace of Nicias and the Sicilian Expedition* (Ithaca, NY: Cor-
    nell University Press, 1981/1992), pp. 254–257. Still, the Athenians had
    obviously embarked upon the conquest of Sicily. This by itself constituted
    pursuit of unlimited objectives. For an enthusiastic approval of Alcibiades'
    grand scheme as genuine and viable, see Jacqueline de Romilly, *Alcibiades*
    (Greek trans., 2nd. edn.) (Athens: Asty, 1995), pp. 103–104.

14. Thucydides, I 82; see also II 18–20. For the classic analysis of coercion in
    international relations, see Thomas C. Schelling, *Arms and Influence*,
    (New Haven, CT: Yale University Press, 1966). For a general theory of
    coercive diplomacy, see Alexander L. George, David K. Hall, and William
    E. Simons, *The Limits of Coercive Diplomacy* (Boston, MA: Little, Brown,
    1971) and Alexander George, *Forceful Persuasion: Coercive Diplomacy
    as Alternative to War* (Washington, D.C.: United States Institute of Peace,
    1991).

15. Thucydides, I 114–115. See also Raphael Sealey, *A History of the Greek
    City States, 700–338 B.C.* (Berkeley, CA: University of California Press,
    1976), p. 321.

16. See Schelling, *Arms and Influence*. Also, James Alt, Randall Calvert, Brian
    Humes, "Reputation and Hegemonic Stability: A Game Theoretical
    Analysis," *American Political Science Review* 92 (June 1988), pp. 445–
    466; John D. Orne, *Deterrence, Reputation and the Prevention of Cold-
    War Cycles* (London: Macmillan, 1992). For an interesting discussion of
    this topic see Daryl G. Press, *Calculating Credibility: How Leaders Assess
    Military Threats* (Ithaca, NY and London: Cornell University Press, 2005),
    pp. 8–41.

17. For an analysis of this point, see John J. Mearsheimer, *The Tragedy of Great Power Politics* (New York: W.W. Norton, 2001), pp. 162–164. See also Chapters Three and Five of the present book.

18. See Kagan, *The Outbreak of the Peloponnesian War*, pp. 123–126, as well as the discussion in Chapter Two of the present book.

19. Humphrey Michell points out that the Spartan monetary and financial system was "primitive and absurd" and that the fiscal methods were "impossible"; Humphrey Michell, *Sparta* (Cambridge: Cambridge University Press, 1952), p. 334. However, he also states that although the Peloponnesian League lacked a system of war finance and was based on an ad hoc arrangement, nevertheless that arrangement "worked all right"; Michell, *Sparta*, p. 313. We argue that it did not. The League was desperately short of money, as became evident by their acute dependence on Persian funds.

20. This had been the constant nightmare of British policy-makers in the last three centuries, and their motivation for preserving the balance of power in Europe. See Paul Kennedy, *The Rise and Fall of British Naval Mastery* (London: Fontana, 1991).

21. Thucydides, II 7.

22. Cf. Thucydides, VI 34.

23. Thucydides, IV 50. The Persian satrap Pissuthnes had been backing anti–Athenian elements in the east Aegean tributaries of the Athenian Empire since 440 B.C.; see Thucydides, I 115, III 34. It has been pointed out that "whether external support for internal political strife is aggression is one of the hardest diplomatic problems in all periods down to our own day" and thus it is not clear whether Pissuthnes' undoubtedly hostile actions constituted a technical breach of the Peace of Callias; Lewis, *Sparta and Persia*, p. 61.

24. For this treaty between Athens and Persia, also known as the 'Treaty of Epilycus' from the name of an Athenian negotiator, see A.T. Olmstead, *History of the Persian Empire* (Chicago, IL: The University of Chicago Press, 1948), p. 357; Russell Meiggs, *The Athenian Empire* (Oxford: Clarendon Press, 1972), pp. 134–135, 330; Ste. Croix, *The Origins of the Peloponnesian War*, p. 310; Lewis, *Sparta and Persia*, pp. 76–77; Donald Kagan, *The Fall of the Athenian Empire* (Ithaca, NY: Cornell University Press, 1987), pp. 19–22.

25. Thucydides, IV 75.

26. Plutarch has made the startling claim that, since the military training relaxed during wartime, the Spartans viewed war as a respite! See Plutarch, *Lycurgus*, 22.

27. See Thucydides, I 121. However, the Peloponnesian citizen armies could not easily campaign during the harvest period; cf. Thucydides, III 15.

28. See also Lin Foxhall, "Farming and Fighting in Ancient Greece," in John Rich and Graham Shipley (eds.), *War and Society in the Greek World*, (London: Routledge, 1993), pp. 142–143.

29. Thucydides, I 58, I 97.
30. Thucydides, III 16.
31. Thucydides, III 26–33.
32. For Brasidas' campaign, see Thucydides, IV 70, IV 78–88, IV 102–117, IV 120–134, V 2–3, V 6–13. This campaign has many similarities with the 'southern strategy' proposed to Hitler by Admiral Raeder, namely a massive German move to North Africa with a view to dismantling the British Empire in the Middle East. One might be tempted to pursue this analogy further still, by pointing out the similarities between Brasidas and another daring commander, Erwin Rommel. However, there are at least two important differences. First, that Brasidas had also to exercise considerable diplomatic skill apart from operational dexterity. Second, that Brasidas' campaign did conform to a grand strategic design, whereas Rommel's exploits did not, for Hitler had decided to concentrate against the Soviet Union instead of the British Empire. For critical views of Rommel's conduct, see Martin van Creveld, *Supplying War* (Cambridge: Cambridge University Press, 1976), pp. 181–201 and Edward N. Luttwak, *Strategy: The Logic of War and Peace* (Cambridge, MA: The Belknap Press of Harvard University Press, 1987), pp. 210–221. For an analysis of Brasidas' campaign, see Simon Hornblower, *A Commentary on Thucydides*, vol. II (Oxford: Clarendon Press, 1996), pp. 38–61.
33. See Thucydides, III 100, III 114.
34. Thucydides, VII 27–28.
35. As recorded in Thucydides, VI 91. For a modern treatise that adopts this view, see Romilly, *Alcibiades*, pp. 140–143.
36. Angelos Vlahos, *Commentary on Thucydides*, vol. I: Books I–IV (Athens: Estia, 1992), pp. 401–408 (text in Greek). Cf. also the comment of A.H.M. Jones that "neither side [Sparta and Athens] showed much intelligence and initiative in their operations"; Jones, *Sparta*, p. 70. It must be obvious that we are in total disagreement with these views.
37. Thucydides, I 122, V 17. Alcibiades might have played a role in the selection of Decelea as the locus for the establishment of the fort. However, even this may not have been the case, since the Spartans had from time immemorial been well acquainted with Decelea. According to Herodotus, because of an incident dating from the days of the Trojan War, the Spartans had always held the inhabitants of Decelea in high esteem and granted them special honors. Moreover, Herodotus goes on to say that in the Peloponnesian War the Spartans spared the lands of the Deceleans; Herodotus, IX 73. In other words, the Spartans did not need Alcibiades to inform them about the merits of that place.
38. For the problems associated with the creation of a permanent fort in Athens, see also Donald Kagan, *The Archidamian War* (Ithaca, NY: Cornell University Press, 1974/1990), pp. 350–351.
39. Thucydides, VI 93, VII 1–7. Some scholars have attributed this Spartan action to Alcibiades; see Romilly, *Alcibiades*, pp. 138–140. In fact, the

same measure had been suggested to the Spartans by the Corinthian and Syracusan ambassadors (Thucydides, VI 88) and it is difficult to believe that Alcibiades' words carried greater weight with the Spartans. Moreover, the aid that was finally sent was much smaller than the one urged by Alcibiades. In general, one should not overestimate the contribution of Alcibiades to Spartan grand strategy. The Athenian exile always remained a controversial figure in the eyes of the Spartans and his influence was therefore limited. See also Kagan, *The Peace of Nicias and the Sicilian Expedition*, pp. 257–259.

40. Cf. Thucydides, VII 18, VII 28. The doctrine of 'two-and-a-half wars' had been suggested as the core military strategy of the United States during the Cold War. According to this, the US ought to be prepared to simultaneously conduct a major war in Europe, another one in Asia and retain some additional military capability for dealing with regional conflicts in the Western hemisphere. This doctrine was never implemented. For an analysis of this doctrine in the post Cold War security environment, see Paul K. Davis and Richard L. Kuger, "New Principles for Force Sizing," in Zalmay M. Khalilzad and David Ochmanek (eds.), *Strategy and Force Planning for the 21st Century* (Santa Monica, CA: RAND Corporation, 1997), pp. 95–140.

41. Thucydides, VIII 2.

42. Thucydides, VIII 3, VIII 26.

43. See Thucydides, Book VIII. Tissaphernes followed the strategy of '*divide et impera*,' by providing inadequate help to the Spartans with a view to exhausting both belligerents. See especially Thucydides, VIII 46, VIII 87. Pharnabazus, on the other hand, helped the Spartans as much as he could, but the resources at his disposal were limited compared with those of Tissaphernes; see Xenophon, *Hellenica* A I 25; Lewis, *Sparta and Persia*, pp. 51–53, 86, 127; Donald Kagan, *The Fall of the Athenian Empire*, pp. 34, 247.

44. Xenophon, *Hellenica*, A IV 1–4, A V 1–7; Plutarch, *Lysander*, 4.

45. In the beginning of 406 B.C. a personal feud between Cyrus and the Spartan admiral Callicratidas led to the cessation of Persian payments. However, the two men quickly came to terms and the payments were resumed; Xenophon, *Hellenica*, A VI 6–7, A VI 10–11, A VI 18; Plutarch, *Lysander*, 6. For Cyrus' tremendous financial help to the Spartans after their defeat at Arginousae the same year, see Xenophon, *Hellenica*, B I 11–14; Plutarch, *Lysander*, 9.

46. Thucydides, VIII 1.

47. Thucydides, VIII 48–56; Xenophon, *Hellenica*, A IV 5–7. On the other hand, in 413–412 B.C. the Athenians also supported the Persian Amorges–an illegitimate son of Pissuthnes–who had staged a revolt against the Great King in south-west Asia Minor; see Thucydides, VIII 54. This was hardly conducive to earning King Darius' sympathy, but may have been an act of despair on Athens' part; see Kagan, *The Fall of the Athenian Empire*, pp. 31–32.

48. Thucydides, II 7, IV 50.
49. Herodotus, III 46–56, V 63–65, V 92; Thucydides, I 122, VI 53; Plutarch, *Moralia*, 859d. See also W.G. Forrest, *A History of Sparta, 950–192 B.C.* (New York: Norton, 1968), pp. 79–83.
50. Thucydides, II 8. See also III 13, III 31. On the other hand, it has already been demonstrated that Sparta did not receive much help of substance until after the Athenian disaster in Sicily.
51. Thucydides, IV 81; see also IV 85–89, IV 106–108.
52. See also Foxhall, "Farming and Fighting in Ancient Greece," in Rich and Shipley, *War and Society in the Greek World*, p. 143.
53. Thucydides, II 20, emphasis added. However, the Acharnians continued to be ardent advocates of the continuation of the war even after the devastation of their land; see Kagan, *The Archidamian War*, pp. 51–52.
54. Thucydides, II 59.
55. The Athenians did offer battle outside their walls in 410 B.C. Interestingly enough, the Peloponnesians declined; Xenophon, *Hellenica*, A I 33–34.
56. Thucydides, V 16–17.
57. See Thucydides, III 70–86. The existence in most cities of a democratic faction that was looking to Athens for support was a factor that increased the international legitimacy of the Athenian grand strategy.
58. The regime and customs of Sparta enjoyed high legitimacy among Spartan citizens, at least until the middle of the fourth century B.C. Thucydides was one of many Ancient Greek writers who praised the Spartan polity; see Thucydides, I 18, VIII 24. For praise of the Spartan customs and national character from Archidamus, who countered the accusations of the Corinthians presented in Chapter Two, see Thucydides, I 84. See also Xenophon, *Lacedaimonion Politeia* and Plutarch, *Lycurgus*. However, it must be pointed out that Xenophon's and especially Plutarch's accounts present a highly idealised picture of Sparta.
59. For the oligarchic coup and subsequent developments, see Thucydides, VIII 47–98. For the negotiations of the oligarchs with the Spartans and the alleged conspiracy, see VIII 70–71, VIII 86, VIII 90–96. This oligarchic 'fifth column' can be regarded as a predecessor of the fascist fifth column that was reputedly in action during the siege of Madrid by Franco's troops in 1939.
60. Thucydides, II 65.
61. P.A. Brunt claims that the Spartans had to adopt a strategy of attrition; Brunt, "Spartan Policy and Strategy in the Archidamian War," p. 94. However, only the cost-raising aspects of Spartan grand strategy can really be given this name. Annihilation was what the Spartans were chiefly aiming at. Even the annual devastation of Attica primarily aimed at bringing about a decisive land battle. See above, as well as Victor Davis Hanson, *Warfare and Agriculture in Classical Greece* (revised edn.) (Berkeley, CA: University of California Press, 1998), pp. 131–173.

62. For the issue of moral justification of preventive war, see Michael Walzer, *Just and Unjust Wars: A Moral Argument with Historical Illustrations* (2nd. edn.) (New York: Basic Books, 1992), pp. 74–80. Two U.S. Presidents, Franklin Roosevelt and John Kennedy had rejected possible American strikes against Japan (prior to Pearl Harbor) and the Soviet Union (during the Cuban Missile Crisis) as incompatible with the United States' moral standing; see respectively Gordon Prange quoted in Ariel Levite, *Intelligence and Strategic Surprises* (New York: Columbia University Press, 1987), p. 154 and Robert Kennedy, *Thirteen Days: A Memoir of the Cuban Missile Crisis* (New York: Norton, 1971), pp. 9, 15–17, 27.
63. Interestingly enough, moral qualms started troubling the Spartans *after* preventive war had failed to deliver the goods; see Thucydides, VII 18.
64. That the Spartans had been thinking the war would be decided swiftly by their invasions of Attica and thus had not felt the need to take these measures, is obvious in Brasidas' speech cited in Thucydides, IV 85.
65. See the analysis in the previous chapter.
66. Sir Basil Liddell Hart has stated that "the scales were definitely turned against Athens" by Brasidas' expedition; B. H. Liddell Hart, *Strategy* (2nd revised edn.) (London: Meridian, 1991), p. 13. We consider this to be wrong: Athens could still obtain an advantageous peace after Brasidas' expedition.
67. Thucydides, V 28.
68. Thucydides, V 75. For Sparta's strategy against the resurgent Argos, culminating in the Battle of Mantinea, see Thucydides, V 57–76.
69. See the now classic analysis of Victor Davis Hanson, *The Western Way of War* (New York: Alfred A. Knopf, 1989).
70. This was the chief objection raised against such battles by two of the greatest 18th-century generals, namely Marshal Maurice de Saxe and King Frederick the Great. See their treatises reproduced in Thomas R. Phillips (ed.), *Roots of Strategy: A Collection of Military Classics* (London: John Lane the Bodley Head, 1943), chs. 3, 4.
71. Cf. the discussion of the battle of Plataea in Chapter One.
72. For the decisive effects of a timely Athenian and Elean intervention in Mantinea, see Kagan, *The Peace of Nicias and the Sicilian Expedition*, p. 134. Of course, other things could have happened as well: the Spartans could have achieved a crushing victory over the Argives some months earlier (Thucydides, V 59–60) or their Corinthian and Boeotian allies could in turn have intervened in Mantinea. All this clearly shows that Alcibiades was right to boast that with his policy (Athens' alliance with Argos) he forced the Spartans to "risk their all on the issue of one day's fighting at Mantinea" (Thucydides, VI 16). This was something that happened to the Spartans from time to time. For two earlier instances when they were forced to risk (and won) their hegemony in the Peloponnese with decisive battles in Tegea and Dipaieis during the 470s and 460s, see Chapter Two.

73. Thucydides, VII 18.
74. Gradually the Spartans adopted the view that they should succeed the Athenians in creating an empire of their own in Greece. As was mentioned in Chapter Two, this undertaking was contrary to the Spartan political organization and led to catastrophe.
75. Thucydides, VIII 84. G.E.M. de Ste. Croix speculates that perhaps the Spartans had prepared a subtle diplomatic trap for the Persians: as soon as the war ended, the Spartans, based on the wording of their treaty with the Persians, would claim that they had agreed to hand over to the Persians only the country surrounding the Greek cities of Asia Minor, but not the cities themselves; see Ste. Croix, *The Origins of the Peloponnesian War*, pp. 313–314. David Lewis, on the other hand, believes that the Spartans managed to find a successful solution to the problem: a formula must have been reached, probably in 408–407 (the so-called Treaty of Boiotios) where the Greek cities would remain autonomous and merely pay tribute to the Persians; Lewis, *Sparta and Persia*, ch. 5. Although such an arrangement would not be a 'sell-out' of the Asia Minor Greeks, it would not be liberation either.
76. For these battles, see Xenophon, *Hellenica*, A I 16–18, A VI 28–35.
77. Thucydides, VIII 1.
78. Xenophon, *Hellenica*, A VI 31.
79. See respectively Diodorus, XIII 52–53 and Aristotle, *Athenaion Politeia*, 34. 1.
80. For ancient accounts of this battle, see Xenophon, *Hellenica*, B I 22–30, Diodorus, XIII 105–106 and Plutarch, *Lysander*, 10–11. Diodorus' account seems to be the most accurate one; cf. Christopher Ehrhardt, "Xenophon and Diodorus on Aegospotami" *Phoenix* 24, 3 (1970), pp. 225–228. For an excellent modern analysis collating various ancient sources, see Donald Kagan, *The Fall of the Athenian Empire*, pp. 386–393.
81. See Xenophon, *Hellenica*, B II 19–23. It would be wrong to attribute the Spartan decision to sentiment, as David Lewis does; Lewis, *Sparta and Persia*, p. 112. Sentiment did not prevent the Spartans in 427 B.C. from wiping off the face of the earth that most brave city, Plataea, which had been far more politically innocuous than Athens. For the Plataean affair, see Thucydides, III 52–68.

5. THUCYDIDES AND STRATEGY IN PERSPECTIVE

1. Thucydides, II 65.
2. See, for instance, John J. Mearsheimer, *The Tragedy of Great Power Politics* (New York: W.W. Norton, 2001), p. 58.
3. See, André Corvisier and John Childs, "Planning/Plans," in André Corvisier (ed.), *A Dictionary of Military History* (London: Blackwell, 1994), p. 654 and Doyne Dawson, *The Origins of Western Warfare* (Boulder, CO: Westview, 1996).

NOTES — pp. [82–85]

4. Hans Delbrück, *History of the Art of War*, vol. 1 (Lincoln, NE: University of Nebraska Press, 1975), p. 137. For different assessments of Pericles and his grand strategy, see the discussion in Chapter Three.

5. A.H.M. Jones calls him "a patriotic, able and courageous king"; A.H.M. Jones, *Sparta* (Oxford: Blackwell & Mott, 1967), p. 71. W.G. Forrest, on the other hand, merely says that Archidamus conducted the invasions of Attica "without alacrity but without obvious incompetence"; W.G. Forrest, *A History of Sparta, 950–192 B.C.* (New York: Norton, 1968), p. 112.

6. See B.H. Liddell Hart, *Strategy* (2nd revised edn.) (London: Meridian, 1991).

7. See, for instance, John J. Mearsheimer, *Liddell Hart and the Weight of History* (Ithaca, NY: Cornell University Press 1988).

8. Liddell Hart, *Strategy*, p. 13.

9. For the battle of Aegospotami, see the sources cited in Chapter Four, n. 80.

10. For a similar approach, see Stephen Van Evera, *Causes of War: Power and the Roots of Conflict* (Ithaca, NY and London: Cornell University Press, 1999).

11. See the relevant extracts in the Appendix. Modern realist scholars have used these factors in order to explain the strategic behavior of states with regard to alignment; see Stephen M. Walt, *The Origins of Alliances* (Ithaca, NY: Cornell University Press, 1987), and Athanassios Platias, *High Politics in Small Countries* (Ph.D. Diss., Cornell University, 1986), pp. 82–97.

12. An early exposition of the impact that both the existing balance and future trends in the distribution of power have on states' grand strategies can be found in Kautilya, *Arthasastra* (trans. R. Shamasastry, 2nd. edn) (Mysore: Wesleyan Mission Press, 1923), pp. 312–320. For an excellent treatise on the impact of trends in the distribution of power, see A.F.K. Organski and Jacek Kugler, *The War Ledger* (Chicago, IL: The University of Chicago Press, 1980).

13. Conceivably, there is also a third possibility, namely that the balance of power between a state and its strategic opponent may not alter significantly in the long run. This possibility has independent significance only when the two opponents are roughly equal in power in the first place (otherwise, we have a clear case of stronger *vs.* weaker state, with both of them acting accordingly). However, we know of no such instance in history; for better or for worse, two strategic opponents are unlikely to remain equal in power for very long.

14. See, among others, Joseph De Rivera, *The Psychological Dimension of Foreign Policy* (Columbus, OH: Charles E. Merrill, 1968); Robert Jervis, "Hypotheses on Misperception," *World Politics*, vol. 20, no. 2 (1968), pp. 454–479; Robert Jervis, *Perception and Misperception in International Politics* (Princeton, NJ: Princeton University Press, 1976).

171

15. Bernard Brodie, *Strategy in the Missile Age* (Princeton, NJ: Princeton University Press, 1959), p. 378. The technological and geographical environment may at times accentuate this capability-oriented perception of threat. Thus, whenever technology and/or geography are believed to favour the adoption of offensive military strategies, the political leadership of a state will tend to focus on the offensive capabilities of their state's strategic opponent and the concomitant 'window of vulnerability' these capabilities open. See George Quester, *Offense and Defense in the International System* (New York: Wiley, 1977), and Stephen Van Evera, "The Cult of the Offensive and the Origins of the First World War," *International Security*, vol. 9, no. 1 (Summer 1984), pp. 58–107.
16. See the excellent article of Raymond L. Garthoff, "On Estimating and Imputing Intentions," *International Security*, vol. 2, no. 3 (Winter 1977–78), pp. 22–32.
17. See H.H. Scullard, *A History of the Roman World, 753–146 B.C.* (4th edn.) (London and New York: Routledge, 1980/1995), pp. 308–317.
18. On threat perception, see Klaus Knorr, "Threat Perception," in Klaus Knorr, (ed.), *Historical Dimensions of National Security Problems* (Lawrence, KA: Kansas University Press, 1976) pp. 78–119, and Raymond Cohen, "Threat Perception in International Crisis," *Political Science Quarterly*, vol. 93, no. 1 (1978), pp. 93–107. For detailed analyses of the role of threat perception in matters of strategic surprise, see Ariel Levite, *Intelligence and Strategic Surprises* (New York: Columbia University Press, 1987) and Constantinos Koliopoulos, *Understanding Strategic Surprise* (Ph.D. Diss., Lancaster University, 1996).
19. See Jervis, "Hypotheses on Misperception." Still, it has been pointed out that, even after such changes of threat perception, it is not easy to reverse extremist policies (i.e. overly competitive or overly cooperative) that had been previously adopted in accordance with the threat perception prevalent at the time; see Charles A. Kupchan, *The Vulnerability of Empire* (Ithaca, NY: Cornell University Press, 1994).
20. For definitions of 'great' and 'small' powers, see Platias, *High Politics in Small Countries*, pp. 483–492, and Mearsheimer, *The Tragedy of Great Power Politics*, p. 5.
21. See Robert Gilpin, *War and Change in World Politics* (Cambridge: Cambridge University Press, 1981). For the different forms of imperialism, namely military, economic and cultural, see Hans J. Morgenthau, *Politics Among Nations*, (5th edn.) (New York: Alfred A. Knopf, 1985). For the belief that there are no status quo states in the international system, save the occasional hegemon, see Mearsheimer, *The Tragedy of Great Power Politics*.
22. Of course, throughout history, states have continued their quest for expansion long after reaching the point of diminishing returns. For a treatise pointing out that the roots of overextension are often to be found in the domestic structures of states, see Jack Snyder, *Myths of Empire: Domestic*

Politics and International Ambition (Ithaca, NY: Cornell University Press, 1991).

23. John Mearsheimer depicts four strategies for a state that is, or would like to be, on the rise: war (use of force); blackmail (threat of force); bait and bleed (weaken one's rivals by provoking a long and costly war between them); and bloodletting (taking measures to ensure that any war in which an adversary is involved is protracted and deadly); Mearsheimer, *The Tragedy of Great Power Politics*, pp. 138–139, 147–155. Thus, it transpires that 'war' and 'blackmail' are means to expansion, whereas 'bait and bleed' and 'bloodletting' are normally preludes to expansion.

24. Mearsheimer, *The Tragedy of Great Power Politics*, pp. 139, 157–162.

25. Haralambos Papasotiriou, *Byzantine Grand Strategy* (Ph.D. Diss., Stanford University, 1991), p. 9; Mearsheimer, *The Tragedy of Great Power Politics*, pp. 162–164. One can point out a difference between tactical and strategic appeasement. Tactical appeasement refers to concessions that are made as a temporary measure in order to gain time for a more assertive response later on. Strategic appeasement, on the other hand, is a longer-term course. Here we will deal with strategic appeasement only.

26. Morgenthau, *Politics Among Nations*.

27. For the issue of interstate cooperation, see Joseph M. Grieco, *Cooperation Among Nations* (Ithaca, NY: Cornell University Press, 1990), pp. 40–49; Joseph M. Grieco, "Anarchy and the Limits of Cooperation," in David Baldwin (ed.), *Neorealism and Neoliberalism: The Contemporary Debate* (New York: Columbia University Press, 1993), pp. 116–140; Arthur A. Stein, *Why Nations Cooperate* (Ithaca, NY and London: Cornell University Press, 1990).

28. See Thucydides, V 84–113.

29. Herodotus, VIII 115.

30. See Barry S. Strauss and Josiah Ober, *The Anatomy of Error: Ancient Military Disasters and Their Lessons for Modern Strategists* (New York: St. Martin's Press, 1990), ch. 1.

31. Thucydides, I 98–100.

32. Thucydides, I 105–108, I 111–115.

33. Thucydides, I 113–115.

34. Thucydides, I 139–141, I 144.

35. Thucydides, IV 3–5, IV 8–23, IV 26–38.

36. Thucydides, IV 89–101, V 6–20.

37. Thucydides, V 27–33.

38. Thucydides, V 57–76.

39. Thucydides, VI-VII.

40. Actually, one cannot be sure whether the Persian political leadership perceived Athens as posing a high or a low threat. We assume the latter, since the western coast of Asia Minor, and the Greek world in general, was but a peripheral concern for the Persian Empire until the advent of Alexander the Great; cf. A.T. Olmstead, *History of the Persian Empire* (Chicago, IL:

The University of Chicago Press, 1948). On the other hand, the Persian court may have regarded the loss of that area to the Athenian intruders as a heavy blow to its prestige, the Athenian support to the rebel Amorges adding insult to injury. Hence, the Persian political leadership could possibly perceive Athens as highly threatening, and the recovery of the western Asia Minor coast as a very important matter indeed; cf. David M. Lewis, *Sparta and Persia* (Leiden: E.J. Brill, 1977), pp. 25–26.

41. Thucydides, VIII 17–18, VIII 36–37, VIII 55–58.
42. Thucydides, VIII 1.
43. Thucydides, VIII 48–56.
44. Correlli Barnett attributes this change to a 'moral revolution' in Great Britain that supposedly began in late eighteenth century and was completed in the first half of the nineteenth; see Correlli Barnett, *The Collapse of British Power* (Phoenix Mill: Allan Sutton, 1984). Barnett's analysis is highly impressive. However, he himself acknowledges the role initially played by the elimination of the high threats of previous eras; see Barnett, *The Collapse of British Power*, pp. 20–21.
45. It remains to be seen how American threat perceptions will be influenced by Russia's assertive stance against Georgia (rising-power behavior?) as exemplified in the August 2008 war and its aftermath.
46. Mearsheimer, *The Tragedy of Great Power Politics*, ch. 7.
47. The French, for their own part, proved benevolent hegemons, going as far as to cede French territory in America to Spain, so that the latter could make good its territorial losses to Great Britain; see Martin Wight, *Power Politics* (edited by Hedley Bull and Carsten Holbraad) (London: Leicester University Press, 1978), pp. 127–130.
48. See John Gooch, "The weary titan: Strategy and policy in Great Britain, 1890–1918," in Williamson Murray, MacGregor Knox, and Alvin Bernstein (eds.), *The Making of Strategy: Rulers, States, and War* (Cambridge: Cambridge University Press, 1994), pp. 289–290; also, Mearsheimer, *The Tragedy of Great Power Politics*, pp. 238–252.
49. Correlli Barnett makes much of the previously mentioned belief in Anglo-American racial brotherhood, and is highly critical of the British decision to appease the United States; see Barnett, *The Collapse of British Power*, pp. 255–263. Paul Kennedy and John Gooch, on the other hand, point out that Great Britain had to face a difficult strategic situation indeed, and had to make some hard choices. Concentrating on Germany was easily the lesser evil; see Paul Kennedy, *The Realities Behind Diplomacy: Background Influences on British External Policy, 1865–1980* (London: Fontana, 1981), pp. 107–108, 118–120 and Gooch, "The weary titan," pp. 289–290.
50. The United States was, strictly speaking, not an ally of the Entente Powers in the First World War, but an 'associated power'. Still, American power obviously augmented French power.
51. Similar arguments can be made with regard to Great Britain's balancing behavior prior to the First World War.

52. According to Correlli Barnett, there was no way out of the predicament and British independence was bound to be lost, since Great Britain had become totally dependent on American industry and technology in order to wage war, and would simply go bankrupt in the process; see Barnett, *The Collapse of British Power*, pp. 12–15.

53. For Churchill's famous comment that "if Hitler invaded Hell I would make at least a favourable reference to the Devil in the House of Commons," see Winston S. Churchill, *The Second World War, Vol. III: The Grand Alliance* (London: Guild, 1985), p. 331.

54. British grand strategy was successful in the sense that it preserved the survival and the independence of Great Britain. On the other hand, it has been criticised for failing to take care of the preservation of the balance of power in Europe, thus resulting in an all-powerful Soviet Union. For a critique of the British and American grand strategies on these grounds, see J.F.C. Fuller, *The Conduct of War, 1789–1961* (London: Methuen, 1972), ch. 13.

55. For the strategic relationship between Austria and Prussia at that time, see Dennis Showalter, *The Wars of Frederick the Great* (London: Longman, 1996).

56. This incident created a long-lived impression; see Jonathan Steinberg, "The Copenhagen Complex," *Journal of Contemporary History*, vol. 1, no. 3 (1966), pp. 23–46.

57. Although Gorbachev's attempt to save his state met with failure, this most probably shows that the Soviet Union was beyond salvation. It should not be construed to prove that external appeasement was the wrong course of action.

58. For recent sources on the rise of China and China's relations with other powers, especially the United States, see Lanxin Xiang, "Washington's Misguided China Policy," *Survival*, vol. 43, no. 3 (Autumn 2001), pp. 7–23; David Shambaugh, "China or America: Which is the Revisionist Power?" *Survival*, vol. 43, no. 3 (Autumn 2001), pp. 25–30; G. John Ikenberry and Michael Mastanduno (eds.), *International Relations Theory and the Asia-Pacific* (New York: Columbia University Press, 2003); Denny Roy, "China's Reaction to American Predominance," *Survival*, vol. 45, no. 3 (Autumn 2003), pp. 57–78; Avery Goldstein, *Rising to the Challenge: China's Grand Strategy and International Security* (Stanford, CA: Stanford University Press, 2005); "China in Africa: A more responsive approach?" *Strategic Comments*, vol. 13, no. 05 (June 2007); "The Beijing Olympics: A focus for Chinese diplomacy," *Strategic Comments*, vol. 14, no. 2 (March 2008).

59. For an article that argues forcefully that "the Middle Kingdom is a middle power", see Gerald Segal, "Does China Matter?" *Foreign Affairs*, vol. 78, no. 5 (September/October 1999), pp. 24–36. However, Segal definitely overstates his case.

60. Erica Strecker Downs and Philip C. Saunders, "Legitimacy and the Limits of Nationalism: China and the Diaoyu Islands," *International Security*, vol. 23, no. 3 (Winter 1998/99), pp. 114–146.
61. Roy, "China's Reaction to American Predominance."
62. You Ji, *The Armed Forces of China* (London–New York: I.B. Tauris, 1999), ch. 6; cf. also "The Pentagon eyes China's military: Back to threat-based planning?" *Strategic Comments*, vol. 11, no. 5 (July 2005).
63. For the American Civil War, see among others Fuller, *The Conduct of War*, pp. 95–112 and Russell F. Weigley, "Military Strategy and Civilian Leadership," in Knorr, *Historical Dimensions of National Security Problems*, pp. 38–77. For an analysis of the influence of Grant's strategy on American strategic thought, see Russell F. Weigley, "American Strategy from its Beginnings through the First World War," in Peter Paret (ed.), *Makers of Modern Strategy from Machiavelli to the Nuclear Age* (Princeton, NJ: Princeton University Press, 1986), pp. 408–443.
64. For the Prussian/German General Staff, see Walter Goerlitz, *History of the German General Staff, 1657–1945* (New York: Praeger, 1959), and T.N. Dupuy, *A Genius for War: The German Army and General Staff, 1807–1945* (Falls Church, VA: NOVA, 1984).
65. For the Austro-Prussian War, see Geoffrey Wawro, *The Austro-Prussian War: Austria's War with Prussia and Italy in 1866* (Cambridge: Cambridge University Press, 1996). For the Franco-Prussian War, see Michael Howard, *The Franco-Prussian War* (London: Routledge, 1988). The relationship between the Prussian political and military leaderships was not untroubled. For the rivalry between Bismarck and Moltke, see Howard, *The Franco-Prussian War*, esp. pp. 350–359.
66. Liddell Hart proclaimed the term 'battle' obsolete and argued that nowadays the key idea is the 'strategic operation'; Liddell Hart, *Strategy*, p. 352. Today this has become conventional wisdom.
67. For this development, see Fuller, *The Conduct of War*. For the transformation of the 'war of annihilation' to 'total war' as seen through the eyes of one of its leading practitioners, see Erich Ludendorff, *The Nation at War* (London: Hutchinson, 1938).
68. It goes without saying, that the manipulation of the threat to resort to nuclear war is used as an instrument of policy (i.e. nuclear deterrence, compellence).
69. In theory, however, it is still possible to achieve a swift decisive victory in a conventional war and, therefore, avoid the huge damage associated with a protracted conventional war; see John J. Mearsheimer, *Conventional Deterrence* (Ithaca, NY: Cornell University Press, 1983), pp. 1–66.
70. For the durability of war as a phenomenon and its likely survival both at present and in the future, see Martin van Creveld, *The Transformation of War* (New York: Free Press, 1991). For an analysis suggesting that war between great powers is obsolete, without however claiming that war in general tends to disappear, see Michael Mandelbaum, "Is Major War Obsolete?" *Survival*, vol. 40, no. 4 (Winter 1998–99), pp. 20–38.

71. See Hans Delbrück, *History of the Art of War* (4 vols.) (Lincoln, NE: University of Nebraska Press, 1975–1985). We have seen that the Spartans caused economic damage to Athens by devastating Attica. These actions, however, were not aimed primarily at this kind of damage, but were chiefly a means of forcing the Athenians to give battle outside their walls. Actually, the extent of crop devastation was relatively limited. See Victor Davis Hanson, *Warfare and Agriculture in Classical Greece* (revised edn.) (Berkeley, CA: University of California Press, 1998), pp. 131–173.

72. See Athanassios Platias, "Post-Heroic Warfare: Lessons from the Periclean Grand Strategy," paper delivered at the International Conference on "War in a Changing World" organised by the Jaffee Center for Strategic Studies, Tel Aviv University, 5–7 November 1996. For the American strategy during the Cold War, see among others John Lewis Gaddis, *Strategies of Containment* (New York: Oxford University Press, 1982), and John Lewis Gaddis, *The Long Peace* (New York: Oxford University Press, 1987). See also Diane Kunz, *Butter and Guns: America's Cold War Economic Diplomacy* (New York: Free Press, 1997).

73. For an analysis of the relevant bibliography, see among others Lawrence Freedman, "The Revolution in Strategic Affairs," *Adelphi Paper* 318 (London: IISS, 1998), and Thomas Keany and Eliot Cohen, *Revolution in Warfare?* (Annapolis, MD: Naval Institute Press, 1995). For healthy correctives of the fairly widespread current obsession with military technology, see Colin S. Gray, *Weapons Don't Make War: Policy, Strategy, and Military Technology* (Lawrence, KA: University Press of Kansas, 1993), and Colin S. Gray, *Strategy for Chaos: Revolutions in Military Affairs and the Evidence of History* (London: Frank Cass, 2002).

74. Edward N. Luttwak, "Toward Post-Heroic Warfare," *Foreign Affairs*, vol. 74, no. 3 (May/June 1995), pp. 109–122.

75. It must be pointed out that some analysts have disputed the view that public opinion in Western countries is as sensitive to war casualties as conventional wisdom has it; see Bruce W. Jentleson, "Normative Dilemmas and Political Myths: The Contemporary Political Context of the Use of Military Force," paper presented at the international conference "Employing Air and Space Power at the Turn of the Millennium: Lessons and Implications," Fisher Institute for Air and Space Strategic Studies, Tel Aviv, December 1999. However, even if Jentleson is correct, it is undeniable that the agenda of perceived interests warranting military action involving heavy casualties has shrunk considerably since the end of the Second World War.

76. What follows is confined to the conventional military strategic aspects of these conflicts and does not delve on their broader strategic and political contexts.

77. For the Kuwait War, see among others Norman Friedman, *Desert Victory: The War for Kuwait* (Annapolis, MD: Naval Institute Press, 1991); Joseph S. Nye, Jr. and Roger K. Smith (eds.), *After the Storm: Lessons from the*

Gulf War (Lanham, MD: Madison Books, 1992); Lawrence Freedman and Ephraim Karsh, *The Gulf Conflict, 1990–1991: Diplomacy and War in the New World Order* (Princeton, NJ: Princeton University Press, 1993). The land operations of the Allies are a remarkable instance of a crushing blow against enemy armed forces with minimal friendly casualties (147 dead).

78. Achievement of the strategic objective is the acid test of strategic effectiveness, and there is no doubt that NATO forces passed it with flying colors. On the other hand, the operational results of the campaign were less clearcut. The power structure of the Serbian political leadership did sustain tremendous damage. In contrast, Serbian armed forces managed, for a substantial part of the campaign, to avoid extensive destruction. Having quickly defeated the KLA, they could afford to remain concealed and dispersed, thus limiting the damage suffered from aerial bombardment. This situation changed at the later stages of the campaign, when the re-emergence of the KLA forced the concentration of the Serbian forces, thus making them targetable by the NATO bombing. It seems that this development played a crucial role in the Serbian leadership's decision to come to terms. For strategic analyses of the Kosovo War, see Benjamin Lambeth, *NATO's Air War for Kosovo: A Strategic and Operational Assessment* (Santa Monica, CA: RAND Corporation, 2001), and Harry Papasotiriou, "The Kosovo War: Kosovar Insurrection, Serbian Retribution and NATO Intervention," *Journal of Strategic Studies*, vol. 25, no. 1 (March 2002), pp. 39–62.

79. The first American casualty caused by the enemy took place in January 2002, about three months after the beginning of hostilities; friendly fire had earlier taken its toll.

80. For an analysis on the war on terror via Thucydides' text, see Victor Davis Hanson, "A Voice from the Past: General Thucydides Speaks about the War," in *National Review Online*, 27 November 2001, reproduced in Victor Davis Hanson, *An Autumn of War: What America Learned from September 11 and the War on Terrorism* (New York: Anchor Books, 2002). For prescient analyses by a veteran strategic analyst, see Michael Howard, "A Long War?" *Survival*, vol. 48, no. 4 (Winter 2006–07), pp. 7–14, and Michael Howard, "Are we at war?" *Survival*, vol. 50, no. 4 (August-September 2008), pp. 247–256.

81. It has been reported that the elite Iraqi armored divisions lost almost 90 per cent of their tanks due to aerial bombardment. For an analysis, see Williamson Murray and Major General Robert H. Scales, Jr., *The Iraq War* (Cambridge, MA: The Belknap Press of Harvard University Press, 2003).

82. For the new military technologies, see among others, *Technology for National Security* (Washington, D.C.: The Pentagon, October 1989); Kostas Tsipis, *New Technologies, Defence Policy and Arms Control* (New York: Harper and Row, 1989); Vincent Kiernan, "Weird Weapons: Con-

quering without Killing," *New Scientist*, 11 December 1993, pp. 14–17; Eliot A. Cohen, "A Revolution in Warfare," *Foreign Affairs*, vol. 75, no. 2 (March/April 1996), pp. 37–55; "C4ISR challenges the cream of US defence," *Jane's Defence Weekly*, 4 September 1996, pp. 61–62; John Arquilla and David Ronfeld, *In Athena's Camp: Preparing for Conflict in the Information Age* (Santa Monica, CA: RAND, 1997).

83. The increased concern for minimizing casualties is a new element in the 'American way of war.' From Grant's era until the Vietnam War, American strategy was not much concerned with casualties.

84. Thucydides, II 65.

85. For a detailed account, see Donald Kagan, *The Peace of Nicias and the Sicilian Expedition* (Ithaca, NY: Cornell University Press, 1981/1992).

86. Thucydides repeatedly makes this point; see Thucydides, VI 1, VI 20, VII 55. However, one cannot help pointing out that the great historian has contradicted himself in this respect, by stating that in the case of the Sicilian expedition "the mistake was not so much an error of judgment with regard to the opposition to be expected as a failure on the part of those who were at home to give proper support to their forces overseas"; Thucydides, II 65. This was obviously not the case, since Thucydides himself points out that the Athenians lavished a vast amount of resources both on the initial expedition and the subsequent reinforcements; see Thucydides, VI 31, VI 43–44, VII 16, VII 42.

87. Thucydides, VI 17.

88. The classic analysis of the religious and civic institutions of Ancient Greece and Rome is Numa Denis Fustel de Coulanges, *The Ancient City: A Study on the Religion, Laws, and Institutions of Greece and Rome* (trans. Willard Small) (Garden City, NY: Doubleday Anchor Books, n.d.). The French original was published in 1864 and the Small English translation dates from 1873.

89. Cf. Thucydides, VI 1.

90. Thucydides, VI 18.

91. Even Thucydides himself seems to have found it difficult to escape from Alcibiades' spell. Thus, although in II 65 he criticises Alcibiades for deviating from the Periclean grand strategy, it is in the very same section that (contradicting himself, as we mentioned above) he states that the Sicilian expedition was not an error of judgment with regard to the opposition to be expected. Thucydides has additionally praised Alcibiades by stating that "in a public capacity his conduct of the war was excellent"; Thucydides, VI 15. We have already pointed out that Alcibiades indeed deserves credit for forging Athens' alliance with Argos; see Chapter Four, n. 72.

92. See Herodotus, VII 153–167.

93. The expulsion of the inhabitants of the city of Leontini from their homeland by the Syracusans was one of the reasons put forward for the Athenian intervention.

94. Thucydides, VI 20.

95. Thucydides, VII 55.
96. Thucydides, VII 57–58.
97. For the initial qualitative disparity between Syracusan and Athenian troops, see Thucydides, VI 69, VI 72, VII 3. For the first Syracusan victory on land, see Thucydides, VII 6.
98. The Syracusan cavalry, that Alcibiades had not condescended to mention at all in his speech at the *Ecclesia*, was a major factor in the war in Sicily. It was continually harassing the Athenians (Thucydides, VI 52, VI 64, VII 5), prevented them from pursuing the defeated Syracusan infantry (Thucydides, VI 70–71) and played a central role in the first Syracusan victory on land (Thucydides, VII 6).
99. Thucydides, VI 93, VII 1–7. Characteristically, Nicias failed to take any precautions against Gylippus' arrival until it was too late; Thucydides, VI 104, VII 1.
100. Thucydides, VII 23.
101. For the ingenuity of the Syracusans, see Thucydides, VII 36, VII 65.
102. For the initial Athenian defeat of the Syracusan navy, see Thucydides, VII 23. For the three Syracusan naval victories, see Thucydides, VII 41, VII 52, VII 69–71.
103. After the first Syracusan victory at sea the Athenians were about to depart, but Nicias postponed the departure because of an eclipse of the moon; see Thucydides, VII 50.
104. Thucydides' narrative of the retreat and the final destruction of the Athenian force is not for the faint-hearted; see Thucydides, VII 72–87.
105. See Thucydides, VI 33–34.
106. See Thucydides, V 76–83.
107. Thucydides, V 11.
108. Liddell Hart seems at a loss as to how to evaluate the Sicilian expedition. Although quick to dissociate it from a 'proper' indirect approach, he would obviously prefer to see it succeeding: "As a grand strategy of indirect approach it had the defect of striking, not at the enemy's actual partners, but rather at his business associates. Thereby, instead of distracting the enemy's forces, it drew fresh forces into opposition. Nevertheless, the moral and economic results of success might well have changed the whole balance of the war if there had not been an almost unparalleled chain of blunders in execution. [...] The best-founded hopes of a recovery [from the alleged turning of the scales against Athens by Brasidas' expedition] came from Alcibiades' indirect approach–on the plane of grand strategy–to Sparta's economic root in Sicily;" Liddell Hart, *Strategy*, pp. 12–13.
109. For a brief sketch of a number of cases, see Van Evera, *Causes of War*, pp. 16–34.
110. See Paul Kennedy, *The Rise and Fall of the Great Powers: Economic Change and Military Conflict from 1500 to 2000* (New York: Random House, 1987), pp. 232–241.

111. See Richard Ned Lebow, *Between Peace and War: The Nature of International Crisis* (Baltimore, MD: Johns Hopkins University Press, 1987), pp. 245–249, and Bruce W. Menning, *Bayonets before Bullets: The Imperial Russian Army, 1861–1914* (Bloomington, IN: Indiana University Press, 1992), ch. 5.
112. For the diplomatic aspects of the war, see A.J.P. Taylor, *The Struggle for Mastery in Europe, 1848–1918* (Oxford: Oxford University Press, 1971), pp. 417–420, 422–427, 432–433. For the Japanese strategic surprise, see Patrick M. Morgan, "Examples of Strategic Surprise in the Far East," in Klaus Knorr and Patrick M. Morgan (eds.), *Strategic Military Surprise: Incentives and Opportunities* (New Brunswick, NJ: Transaction Books, 1983), pp. 43–76. For further references, see Paul Dukes, *A History of Russia: Medieval, Modern, Contemporary* (2nd edn.) (Houndmills: Macmillan, 1990), p. 188, and Mearsheimer, *The Tragedy of Great Power Politics*, p. 466.
113. For the German intelligence estimates of the Red Army and German intelligence on the Soviet Union in general, see Heinz Guderian, *Panzer Leader* (New York: Da Capo, 1996), p. 143; B. H. Liddell Hart, *The Other Side of the Hill* (London: Papermac, 1993), pp. 257–262; William L. Shirer, *The Rise and Fall of the Third Reich*, (London: Mandarin, 1991), pp. 797–799, 822; Kenneth Strong, *Men of Intelligence* (London: Giniger-Cassell, 1970), pp. 88–95; Michael I. Handel, *War, Strategy and Intelligence* (London: Frank Cass, 1989), p. 326.
114. See Hitler, *Mein Kampf*, quoted in Fuller, *The Conduct of War*, pp. 231–232; Albert Speer, *Inside the Third Reich* (London: Phoenix, 1995), p. 250; Alan Clark, *Barbarossa* (London: Phoenix, 1996), p. 43; John Erickson, *The Road to Stalingrad* (London: Weidenfeld, 1993), p. 232; John G. Stoessinger, *Why Nations Go to War* (2nd. edn.) (New York: St. Martin's Press, 1978), ch. 2; Alan Bullock, *Hitler and Stalin: Parallel Lives* (London: Fontana, 1993), pp. 748–751. It is indicative of Hitler's irrationality that prior to the launch of Operation Barbarossa he had also expressed the opposite view, namely that the inhabitants of European Russia and Siberia were in the long run biologically superior to the Germans! See Speer, *Inside the Third Reich*, pp. 150, 265.
115. Erickson, *The Road to Stalingrad*, pp. 46–47.
116. See Günther Blumentritt, "Moscow," in William Richardson and Seymour Freidin (eds.), *The Fatal Decisions* (London: Michael Joseph, 1956), pp. 37–39. The soldier-like narrative of General Blumentritt makes a strong impression.
117. See Strong, *Men of Intelligence*, p. 94.
118. For a similar argument, see Albert Seaton, *The Russo-German War 1941–45* (London: Arthur Barker, 1971), p. 49.
119. Reproduced in John Cooley, *Unholy Wars: Afghanistan, America and International Terrorism* (3rd edn.) (London–Sterling, VA: Pluto Press, 2002), pp. 245–249.

120. Robert S. Litwak, "The Soviet Union in Afghanistan", in Ariel E. Levite, Bruce W. Jentleson, and Larry Berman (eds.), *Foreign Military Intervention: The Dynamics of Protracted Conflict* (New York: Columbia University Press, 1992), pp. 65–94.

121. See Shai Feldman, "Israel's Involvement in Lebanon: 1975–1985", in Levite, Jentleson, and Berman (eds.), *Foreign Military Intervention*, pp. 129–161.

122. As was pointed out in Chapter One, instability and conflict might be perpetuated in Iraq as well. However, we contend that this does not have much to do with American underestimation of enemy capability and will to resist the invasion, though the Iraqi armed forces did offer tougher resistance than anticipated; conflict in Iraq would have erupted even if Saddam Hussein had surrendered without a fight. One might plausibly argue that the Americans misjudged the impact of regime change in Iraq, but this is something different from underestimating an enemy.

123. Cf. Charles A. Kupchan, "Getting In: The Initial Stage of Military Intervention", in Levite, Jentleson, and Berman (eds.), *Foreign Military Intervention*, pp. 256–259; see also Van Evera, *Causes of War*, pp. 25–28.

EPILOGUE

1. Joseph S. Nye, *Understanding International Conflicts: An Introduction to Theory and History* (New York: Harper Collins, 1993), p. 1.

2. Consider the insertion of Thucydides' *History* in the syllabus of the United States Naval War College by Admiral Stansfield Turner in August 1972. "For many students, that was an unknown book about an apparently irrelevant war by an author with an unpronounceable name. Yet to Turner it was the essence of his approach, 'the best example of how you could use historical case studies to teach contemporary or strategic problems'"; Harry Summers, *On Strategy II: A Critical Analysis of the Gulf War* (New York: Dell, 1992), pp. 78–79. Professor Karl Walling has brought to our attention that this tradition is still alive at the U.S. Naval War College.

SELECT BIBLIOGRAPHY

Art, Robert J., "To What Ends Military Power", *International Security*, vol. 4, no. 4 (Spring 1980), pp. 4–35.

Baldwin, David A., *Economic Statecraft* (Princeton, NJ: Princeton University Press, 1985).

Barnett, Correlli, *The Collapse of British Power* (Phoenix Mill: Allan Sutton, 1984).

Beaufre, André, *Introduction to Strategy* (London: Faber and Faber, 1965).

Bond, Brian, *Liddell Hart: A Study of his Military Thought* (London: Cassell, 1977).

Booth, Ken, *Strategy and Ethnocentricism* (London: Croom Helm, 1979).

Bracken, Paul, "Strategic Planning for National Security: Lessons from Business Experience", *RAND Note*, N-3005–DAG/USDP, February 1990.

Brodie, Bernard, *War and Politics* (London: Cassell, 1973).

Brunt, P.A., "Spartan Policy and Strategy in the Archidamian War", in P.A. Brunt, *Studies in Greek History and Thought* (Oxford: Clarendon Press, 1993), pp. 84–111.

Cartledge, Paul, *Sparta and Laconia: a regional history, 1300–362 B.C.* (London: Routledge & Kegan Paul, 1979).

Chandler, David G., *The Military Maxims of Napoleon* (New York: Macmillan, 1997).

Chrimes, K.M.T., *Ancient Sparta: A Re-examination of the Evidence* (Manchester: Manchester University Press, 1949).

Cimbala, Stephen, *Military Persuasion: Deterrence and Provocation in Crisis and War* (University Park, PA: Pennsylvania State University Press, 1994).

Clausewitz, Carl von, *On War* (edited and translated by Michael Howard and Peter Paret) (Princeton, NJ: Princeton University Press, 1989).

Cohen, Raymond, "Threat Perception in International Crisis", *Political Science Quarterly* 93, 1 (1978), pp. 93–107.

Connor, W. Robert, *Thucydides* (Princeton, NJ: Princeton University Press, 1984).

Craig, Gordon A., "Delbrück: The Military Historian", in Peter Paret (ed.), *Makers of Modern Strategy from Machiavelli to the Nuclear Age* (Princeton, NJ: Princeton University Press, 1986), pp. 326–353.

Crane, Gregory, *Thucydides and the Ancient Simplicity: The Limits of Political Realism* (Berkeley, CA: University of California Press, 1998).

Dawson, Doyne, *The Origins of Western Warfare: Militarism and Morality in the Ancient World* (Boulder, CO: Westview, 1996).

Delbrück, Hans, *History of the Art of War* (4 vols.) (Lincoln, NE: University of Nebraska Press, 1975–1985).

Doyle, Michael W., *Empires* (Ithaca, NY: Cornell University Press, 1986).

Fliess, Peter J., *Thucydides and the Politics of Bipolarity* (Baton Rouge, LA: Louisiana State University Press, 1966).

Forde, Steven, *The Ambition to Rule: Alcibiades and the Politics of Imperialism in Thucydides* (Ithaca, NY: Cornell University Press, 1989).

Forrest, W.G., *A History of Sparta, 950–192 B.C.* (New York: Norton, 1968).

Freedman, Lawrence, *Deterrence* (Cambridge: Polity Press, 2004).

Fuller, J.F.C., *The Decisive Battles of the Western World* (London: Eyre & Spottiswoode, 1954).

Garst, W. Daniel, "Thucydides and the Domestic Sources of International Politics", in Lowell S. Gustafson (ed.), *Thucydides' Theory of International Relations: A Lasting Possession* (Baton Rouge, LA: Louisiana University Press, 2000), pp. 67–97.

George, Alexander L., *Some Thoughts on Graduated Escalation* RM-4844–IR (Santa Monica, CA: RAND Corporation, 1965).

—— Hall, David K., and Simons, William E., *The Limits of Coercive Diplomacy* (Boston, MA: Little, Brown, 1971).

—— *Forceful Persuasion: Coercive Diplomacy as Alternative to War* (Washington, D.C.: United States Institute of Peace, 1991).

Gilpin, Robert, *War and Change in World Politics* (Cambridge: Cambridge University Press, 1981).

Gilpin, Robert G., "The Richness of the Tradition of Political Realism", in Robert O. Keohane (ed.), *Neorealism and its Critics* (New York: Columbia University Press, 1986), pp. 308–313.

Gilpin, Robert, "The Theory of Hegemonic War", in R.I. Rotberg and T.K. Rabb (eds.) *The Origin and Prevention of Major Wars* (Cambridge: Cambridge University Press, 1988), pp. 15–37.

Gomme, A.W., *A Historical Commentary on Thucydides* (5 vols.) (Oxford: Clarendon Press, 1998) (reprint).

Gray, Colin S., *Nuclear Strategy and National Style* (London: Hamilton Press, 1986).

—— *War, Peace, and Victory: Strategy and Statecraft for the Next Century* (New York: Simon and Schuster, 1990).

—— *The Leverage of Sea Power: The Strategic Advantage of Navies in War* (New York: Free Press, 1992).

—— *Modern Strategy* (Oxford: Oxford University Press, 1999).

Grieco, Joseph M., *Cooperation Among Nations* (Ithaca, NY: Cornell University Press, 1990).

184

—— "Anarchy and the Limits of Cooperation", in David Baldwin (ed.), *Neorealism and Neoliberalism: The Contemporary Debate* (New York: Columbia University Press, 1993), pp. 116–140.

Handel, Michael I., *Masters of War: Classical Strategic Thought* (London: Frank Cass, 1992).

Hanson, Victor Davis, *The Western Way of War* (New York: Alfred A. Knopf, 1989).

—— *Warfare and Agriculture in Classical Greece* (revised edn.) (Berkeley, CA: University of California Press, 1998).

—— *A War like no Other: How the Athenians and the Spartans Fought the Peloponnesian War* (New York: Random House, 2005).

Hornblower, Simon, *A Commentary on Thucydides*, (2 vols.) (Oxford: Clarendon Press, 1990–1996).

Howard, Michael, *The Causes of War* (London: Temple Smith, 1983).

—— *Clausewitz* (Oxford: Oxford University Press, 1983).

—— *The Lessons of History* (New Haven, CT: Yale University Press, 1991).

Jervis, Robert, "Hypotheses on Misperception", *World Politics* 20, 2 (1968), pp. 454–479.

—— *Perception and Misperception in International Politics* (Princeton, NJ: Princeton University Press, 1976).

—— "Cooperation Under The Security Dilemma", *World Politics* 30, 2 (January 1978), pp. 167–214.

Jomini, Henry de, *Summary of the Art of War* (abridged edn. by Brig. Gen. J.D. Hittle) reproduced in *Roots of Strategy, Book 2* (Harrisburg, PA: Stackpole Books, 1987).

Jones, A.H.M., *Sparta* (Oxford: Blackwell & Mott, 1967).

Kagan, Donald, *The Outbreak of the Peloponnesian War* (Ithaca, NY: Cornell University Press, 1969/1994).

—— *The Archidamian War* (Ithaca, NY: Cornell University Press, 1974/1990).

—— *The Peace of Nicias and the Sicilian Expedition* (Ithaca, NY: Cornell University Press, 1981/1992).

—— *The Fall of the Athenian Empire* (Ithaca, NY: Cornell University Press, 1987).

—— "Athenian strategy in the Peloponnesian War", pp. 24–55 in Williamson Murray, MacGregor Knox, and Alvin Bernstein (eds.), *The Making of Strategy: Rulers, States, and War* (Cambridge: Cambridge University Press, 1994).

—— *On the Origins of War and the Preservation of Peace* (New York: Doubleday, 1995).

Kallet-Marx, Lisa, *Money, Expense and Naval Power in Thucydides' History 1–5.24* (Berkeley, CA: University of California Press, 1993).

Kautilya, *Arthasastra* (trans. R. Shamasastry, 2nd edn.) (Mysore: Wesleyan Mission Press, 1923).

SELECT BIBLIOGRAPHY

Kennedy, Paul, "The First World War and the International Power System", *International Security* 9, 1 (1984), pp. 7–40.

—— *The Rise and Fall of the Great Powers: Economic Change and Military Conflict from 1500 to 2000* (New York: Random House, 1987).

—— "Grand Strategies in War and Peace: Toward a Broader Definition", in Paul Kennedy (ed.), *Grand Strategies in War and Peace* (New Haven, CT: Yale University Press, 1991), pp. 1–7.

Klein, Yitzhak, "A Theory of Strategic Culture", *Comparative Strategy* vol. 10, no. 1 (January-March 1991), pp. 3–23.

Knorr, Klaus, "Threat Perception", in Klaus Knorr, (ed.), *Historical Dimensions of National Security Problems* (Lawrence, KA: Kansas University Press, 1976), pp. 78–119.

Lebow, Richard Ned, *Between Peace and War: The Nature of International Crisis* (Baltimore, MD: Johns Hopkins University Press, 1987).

—— and Strauss, Barry S. (eds.), *Hegemonic Rivalry from Thucydides to the Nuclear Age* (Boulder, CO: Westview, 1991).

—— "Thucydides, Power Transition Theory and the Causes of War", in Richard Ned Lebow and Barry S. Strauss (eds.), *Hegemonic Rivalry from Thucydides to the Nuclear Age* (Boulder, CO: Westview, 1991), pp. 125–165.

Levite, Ariel, *Intelligence and Strategic Surprises* (New York: Columbia University Press, 1987).

—— *Offense and Defense in Israeli Military Doctrine* (Boulder, CO: Westview, 1989).

—— and Platias, Athanassios, "Evaluating Small States' Dependence on Arms Imports: An Alternative Perspective", *Peace Studies Program Occasional Paper No. 10* (Ithaca, NY: Cornell University, 1983).

Levite, Ariel E., Jentleson, Bruce W., and Berman, Larry (eds.), *Foreign Military Intervention: The Dynamics of Protracted Conflict* (New York: Columbia University Press, 1992).

Lewis, David M., *Sparta and Persia* (Leiden: E.J. Brill, 1977).

Liddell, Hart B.H., *The British Way in Warfare* (London: Faber, 1932).

—— *Strategy* (2nd revised edn.) (London: Meridian, 1991).

Luttwak, Edward N., *The Grand Strategy of the Roman Empire from the First Century A.D. to the Third* (Baltimore, MD: Johns Hopkins University Press, 1976).

—— *Strategy: The Logic of War and Peace* (Cambridge, MA:: The Belknap Press of Harvard University Press, 1987).

—— "Toward Post-Heroic Warfare", *Foreign Affairs* 74, 3 (May/June 1995), pp. 109–122.

Mahan, Alfred Thayer, *The Influence of Sea Power Upon History, 1660–1783* (London: Sampson Low, Marston, 1892).

—— *The Influence of Sea Power Upon the French Revolution and Empire, 1793–1812,* (2 vols.) (London: Sampson Low, Marston, 1893).

Mandelbaum, Michael, *The Fate of Nations,* (Cambridge: Cambridge University Press, 1988).

Mearsheimer, John J., *Conventional Deterrence* (Ithaca, NY: Cornell University Press, 1983).

—— *Liddell Hart and the Weight of History* (Ithaca, NY: Cornell University Press 1988).

—— *The Tragedy of Great Power Politics* (New York: W.W. Norton, 2001).

Meiggs, Russell, *The Athenian Empire* (Oxford: Clarendon Press, 1972).

Michell, Humphrey, *Sparta* (Cambridge: Cambridge University Press, 1952).

Nye, Joseph S., *Soft Power: The Means to Success in World Politics* (New York: Public Affairs, 2004).

Olmstead, A.T., *History of the Persian Empire* (Chicago, IL: The University of Chicago Press, 1948).

Organski, A.F.K. and Kugler, Jacek, *The War Ledger* (Chicago, IL: The University of Chicago Press, 1980).

Papasotiriou, Haralambos, *Byzantine Grand Strategy* (Ph.D. Diss., Stanford University, 1991).

—— *Byzantine Grand Strategy, 6th-11th century* (Athens: Poiotita, 2000) (text in Greek).

Paret, Peter (ed.), *Makers of Modern Strategy from Machiavelli to the Nuclear Age* (Princeton, NJ: Princeton University Press, 1986).

Platias, Athanassios, *High Politics in Small Countries* (Ph.D Diss., Cornell University, 1986).

—— "Thucydides On Grand Strategy: Periclean Grand Strategy During The Peloponnesian War", in *Thucydides: The Classical Theorist of International Relations, Études Helleniques/Hellenic Studies*, vol. 6, no. 2 (Autumn 1998), pp. 53–103.

Platias, Athanassios and Koliopoulos, Constantinos, "Thucydides on Grand Strategy II: Spartan Grand Strategy During the Peloponnesian War", *Études Helleniques/Hellenic Studies*, vol. 8, no. 1 (Spring 2000), pp. 23–70.

Platias, Athanassios G. and Koliopoulos, Constantinos, "Grand Strategies Clashing: Athenian and Spartan Strategies in Thucydides' "History of the Peloponnesian War"", *Comparative Strategy*, vol. 21, no. 5 (October-December 2002), pp. 377–399.

Posen, Barry, *The Sources of Military Doctrine* (Ithaca, NY: Cornell University Press, 1984).

Powell, Anton, *Athens and Sparta: Constructing Greek Political and Social History from 478 B.C.* (London: Routledge, 1988).

Quester, George, *Offense and Defense in the International System* (New York: Wiley, 1977).

Romilly, Jacqueline de, *Alcibiades* (Greek trans., 2nd edn.) (Athens: Asty, 1995).

Schelling, Thomas C., *The Strategy of Conflict* (Cambridge, MA: Harvard University Press, 1960).

—— *Arms and Influence* (New Haven, CT: Yale University Press, 1966).

Schwarz, Benjamin, "Strategic Interdependence: Learning to Behave like a Great Power", in Norman Levin (ed.), *Prisms and Policy: U.S. Security Strategy After the Cold War* (Santa Monica, CA: RAND, 1994), pp. 79–98.

Snyder, Glenn H., *Deterrence and Defense* (Princeton, NJ: Princeton University Press, 1961).

Starr, Chester G., *The Influence of Sea Power on Ancient History* (New York: Oxford University Press, 1995).

Ste. Croix, G.E.M. de, *The Origins of the Peloponnesian War* (London: Duckworth, 1972).

Strassler, Robert B. (ed.), The Landmark Thucydides: A Comprehensive Guide to the Peloponnesian War (New York: Free Press, 1996).

Strauss, Barry S. and Ober, Josiah, *The Anatomy of Error: Ancient Military Disasters and Their Lessons for Modern Strategists* (New York: St. Martin's Press, 1990).

Summers, Harry, *On Strategy II: A Critical Analysis of the Gulf War* (New York: Dell, 1992).

Sun Tzu, *The Art of War* (transl. by Samuel B. Griffith) (Oxford: Oxford University Press, 1963).

Taxiarchi, Despina A., "The Impact of Thucydides in Post War Realist Thinking and Its Critique", in *Thucydides: The Classical Theorist of International Relations, Études Helleniques/Hellenic Studies*, vol. 6, no. 2 (Autumn 1998), pp. 132–139.

Thucydides, *History of the Peloponnesian War* (trans. Rex Warner) (London: Penguin, 1972).

Van Evera, Stephen, *Causes of War: Power and the Roots of Conflict* (Ithaca, NY and London: Cornell University Press, 1999).

Vlahos, Angelos, *Commentary on Thucydides*, vol. I: Books I–IV (Athens: Estia, 1992) (text in Greek).

Walt, Stephen M., *The Origins of Alliances* (Ithaca, NY: Cornell University Press, 1987).

Waltz, Kenneth N., *Theory of International Politics* (Reading, MA: Addison-Wesley, 1979).

INDEX

Sun Tzu, xi, 1, 41, 138n, 155n
surprise, 18, 86, 99, 106, 114,
  133–135, 139n, 141n, 142n,
  162n, 169n, 172n, 181n
swaggering, 140n
Sweden/Swedes, 99
Syracuse/Syracusans, 65, 71, 94,
  111–113, 122, 124, 126, 129,
  130, 133, 134, 167n, 179n, 180n
Syria/Syrians, 85, 86, 116, 117

tactics/tactical level, 4, 10–12, 79,
  84, 109, 128, 140n-142n
Taiwan, 100
Taliban, 107, 108
Tanagra, 30, 150n
Tarentum, 113
technology, 11, 103, 104, 109, 119,
  142n, 172n, 175n, 177n, 178n
Tegea, 29, 123, 169n
terrain, 12, 109, 135
theatre strategy, 11
Thebes/Thebans, 29, 36, 56, 121,
  122, 134
Themistocles, 29
theory of victory, 6, 60, 68, 71, 82,
  139n, 159n
Thirty YearsbB.C.), 150n; (Sparta-
  Athens, 446/445 B.C.), 31, 39, 93
Thirty YearsbThrace, 69, 126, 152n
Threat, 7–9, 14, 15, 19, 32, 41, 43,
  48, 49, 52, 58, 62, 65–67, 71,
  75–77, 79, 80, 83–90, 93–101,
  124, 133, 148n, 152n, 156n,
  162n, 164n, 172n-174n, 176n
Thucydides, xi, xii, 1, 2, 21, 23, 26,
  32, 34–37, 40–42, 44, 55, 59, 60,
  69, 71–75, 77, 81, 82, 84, 85, 90,
  93–95, 101, 109, 110, 112, 114,
  116, 119, 121, 137n, 138n, 145n,
  147n-170n, 173n, 174n, 178n–
  180n, 182n
Tissaphernes, 63, 72, 122, 163n,
  167n

Total war, 103, 176n
Trans-Siberian railway, 114
Treaty of Epilycus, 72, 165n
Treaty of the Pyrenees, 97
Trireme, 44, 64, 105, 111, 112,
  157n
Trojan War, 166n
Tsushima Strait, 115
Turkey/Turks (see also Ottoman
  Empire/Ottomans), 5, 98, 161n
tyranny, 53, 73

ultimatum, 40, 66, 73
underestimation of the enemy, xi,
  110, 114, 115, 117, 182n
United States (see also America/
  Americans), 33, 36, 96–98,
  100–102, 104, 107–109, 164n,
  167n, 169n, 174n, 175n, 182n

Venezuela, 98
Verdun, 103
Vertical: dimension of strategy, 4, 5
Vietnam, 21, 51, 179n

Wagram, 17
Walls of Athens, 28, 46, 67, 74
Waltz, Kenneth, 33, 151n, 156n,
  160n
War of American Independence, 96,
  154n
Waterloo, 96
window: of opportunity, 78, 151n;
  of vulnerability, 172n

Xenelasia, 42, 57, 155n
Xenophon, 137n, 147n, 149n,
  167n, 168n, 170n,
Xerxes, 13, 143n

Yom Kippur War, 11,21
Yugoslavia/Yugoslavians (see also
  Serbia/Serbs), 105, 107, 178n